Published by

THE BIBLE FOR TODAY PRESS
900 Park Avenue
Collingswood, New Jersey 08108
U.S.A.

Phone: 856-854-4452
Orders: 1-800-John 10:9
e-mail: BFT@BibleForToday.org
website: www.BibleForToday.org
fax: 856-854-2464

March, 2002
BFT2955

Copyright, 2002
All Rights Reserved

ISBN # 978-1-732-17466-5

Acknowledgments

I wish to acknowledge the assistance of the following people:

- **The Congregation** of the **Bible For Today Baptist Church** (for whom these messages were prepared and to whom they were delivered) who listened attentively and encouraged their Pastor as he preached;
- **Yvonne Sanborn Waite**, my wife, who encouraged the publication of these sermons, read the manuscript, and gave helpful suggestions;
- **Dianne W. Cosby**, for typing these messages from the cassette tapes and putting them in computer format;
- **Pastor Richard N. Waite**, for editing the messages on the computer format, inserting the texts of various verses used and making them consistent;
- **Daniel S. Waite**, the Assistant to the Bible For Today Director, who guided the book through the printing process;
- **Barbara Egan**, our Bible For Today secretary who also read the manuscript and offered valuable comments.

Foreword

- **The Beginning.** This book is the **second** in a planned series of books based on expository preaching from various books of the Bible. It is an attempt to bring to the minds of the readers two things: (1) the **meaning** of the words in the verses and (2) the practical **application** of those words to the lives of both saved and lost people.
- **Preached Sermons.** These are messages that have been preached to our Bible For Today Baptist Church in Collingswood, New Jersey, broadcast over radio, and placed on our website **(www.BibleForToday.org)** for people all over the world to listen to should they wish. As the messages were originally preached, I took half a chapter each Sunday service, spending about forty-five minutes on each message. Much more could have been said concerning these six chapters in Galatians, but it is hoped that the seed thoughts will be developed further in the minds and hearts of those who read this book.
- **Other Verses.** In connection with both meaning and application there are many verses from other places in the Bible that have been quoted for further elaboration of Paul's discussion.
- **A Transcription.** It should be noted that this book is made up largely from the stenographic transcript of the tape recordings of the messages. These recordings are available in both audio and video formats. Though there has been some editing, the words are basically the same as the ones I used as I preached the sermons. This was the method Dr. H. A. Ironside used in his Bible exposition books.
- **The Audience.** The audience aimed at is the same as the audience that listened to the messages in the first place. These studies are not meant to be overly scholarly though there is some reference to various Greek words used by Paul. My aim is to help lay people to understand the Words of God. It is my hope that I can get as many as possible of my expositions in print so that my children, grandchildren, and children in the faith may be able to rejoice with me in the things the Lord has brought to my attention as I have preached from the verses in Galatians.

    Yours For God's Words,

D. A. Waite

DAW/w   Pastor D. A. Waite, Th.D., Ph.D.
Bible For Today Baptist Church

Table of Contents

Publisher's Data i

Acknowledgments iii

Foreword v

Table of Contents vi

Galatians Chapter One 1

Galatians Chapter Two 33

Galatians Chapter Three 63

Galatians Chapter Four 93

Galatians Chapter Five 123

Galatians Chapter Six 153

Index of Words and Phrases 181

About the Author 206

Order Blank Pages 207

Galatians Chapter One

Introductory Remarks

Galatians was written by Paul the apostle in about 60 A.D. on his third visit to Corinth. There are basically two errors that the Galatians were involved with. In this epistle, Paul straightens out both these errors.

The first error was a false teaching by the Judaizers. They were saying that people can be saved by keeping the Law of Moses. The Law of Moses was never made to save anybody. It was given to condemn all of us. This was the first error.

The second error was that once we are saved we are sanctified or perfected by the Law of Moses. In other words, after we are saved by faith in Christ, we must go to the Law of Moses, try to follow it, and be perfected by it.

These Judaizers came into the area of Galatia and were peddling this belief. For this reason, Paul wrote this letter to put an end to both of these heretical teachings.

Galatia was populated by the Gauls. We get the word "Gaul"atians from the word *Gaul*. The Gauls were heathen barbarians who came down in the Third Century B.C. and occupied the region of Galatia. Galatia was part of what we now call Turkey. These are the people to whom Paul was writing. The Galatians were being afflicted by these Judaizers who came from Jerusalem and taught the Galatians that even though they were saved by grace, they still had to live by the law.

Galatians 1:1

"Paul, an apostle, (not of men, neither by man, but by Jesus Christ, and God the Father, who raised him from the dead)"

"Paul, an apostle" Paul introduces himself as the author. The modernists and liberals around us say that Paul did not write this book, despite the fact that Paul is named as its author right here in the first verse. We believe the Bible. God has given to us the Scripture. Paul is not just an ordinary person; but, he is an apostle. The word, "Apostle," comes from the Greek word, APOSTELLO, which means *"a delegate, a messenger, one who is sent forth with orders."* [Greek words referred to in this book are in CAPITAL letters.] "APO" means *"from or forth."* "STELLO" means "TO SEND."

"(not of men, neither by man, but by Jesus Christ, and God the Father, who raised him from the dead)" Paul is an apostle *"not of men."* In Paul's day, some men were sent forth by themselves. Some men today are sent forth by themselves. God never called them into His ministry. Those who are in cults, and those who are unsaved were never called by God to be preachers or apostles. Some missionaries are the same way. They have not been sent forth by God. They are out on the highways and the byways of the world with the social gospel. They do all kinds of things which are socially acceptable, but Paul was not that kind of missionary. It was not a man who made Paul an apostle, but he was made an apostle by Jesus Christ and by God the Father Who raised Him from the dead. In this verse, we have a unity of the Father with the Son. God the Father and the Lord Jesus Christ are both united, co-eternal, and co-equal. They are part of the Trinity. The Liberals and the Modernists say that Jesus was merely a man and that he had nothing to do with the Father. This is not true according to this verse. Paul did not want to be an apostle. In fact he wanted to be a killer, as you know. When he went up to Damascus with letters from the Jewish leaders he was out for blood. He was out to imprison, to persecute, to prosecute, and to kill those who worshiped Christ. The Lord Jesus turned him around, made him an apostle, and sent him forth. The Lord Jesus Christ told Paul what to expect when he sent him forth as an apostle.

- **Acts 9:16**
  For **I will shew him how great things he must suffer** for my name's sake.

Paul's conversion is recorded in Acts 9, 22, and 26. Before his conversion, Paul was persecuting Christians. The Lord Jesus Christ asked Paul *"Why persecutest thou me?"* (Acts 9:4) Though Paul was persecuting Christians, he didn't think he was persecuting the Lord. Christians are related to the Lord Jesus Christ. When Paul persecuted Christians, it hurt the Lord Jesus Christ Who was in Glory. God turned Paul around. Paul was blinded at first. When he recovered form his blindness, he began to preach Christ. This led to his being severely persecuted himself.

That is Paul's background. He was the writer of the book of Galatians. He wanted the Galatians to know he was an apostle of Christ. He was going to show the Galatians some very powerful and strong words. First of all, he wanted to make it clear that it was the Lord Jesus Christ Who sent him and made him an apostle.

Galatians 1:2

"And all the brethren which are with me, unto the churches of Galatia"

"And all the brethren which are with me" Paul includes the brethren that were with him when he wrote. It is good that he included the Christians who are with him at Corinth when he wrote this letter. Paul says that his brethren who were with him were also writing this letter along with Paul.

"unto the churches of Galatia" By the reference to *"the churches of Galatia,"* we see that there was more than one church in that area. He was writing this letter to all the churches there. Today, some people believe that they must have a huge church. Such churches call themselves "mega churches." We have some "mega churches" in our country. We have some who are striving to build such "mega churches" in our area. In this verse we see that this letter was written to *"the churches of Galatia"* rather than only to one church. Sometimes when a church gets too large, it breaks off and starts other churches. Then when those other churches get too large, they start more churches also. That's the way to do it. Here we see *"churches,"*--a multiplicity of believers who loved the Lord Jesus Christ and were gathered in one place with one purpose. We see that the brethren were writing along with Paul to the churches of Galatia. As I said before, Galatia was located in what is now called the country of Turkey. Among various Bible teachers, there is a "southern Galatian theory" and a "northern Galatian theory" when discussing the exact location of Galatia. I won't go into that argument at this time. The map below shows where some believe Galatia was located.

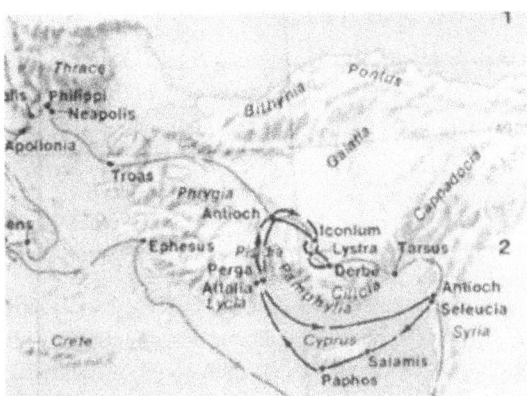

Galatians 1:3

"Grace be to you and peace from God the Father, and from our Lord Jesus Christ"

"Grace be to you" Paul's greeting to the churches of Galatia is *"grace."* That is an important word. That word is the Greek greeting, CHARIS. Paul also wanted to emphasize that these Galatians were out of line with regard to the teachings of grace. They were going after the law instead of grace. They were going for works to obtain salvation rather than God's grace through faith in Christ. Grace may be defined as *"unmerited, undeserved, and unearned favor from God."* **Grace is getting something we don't deserve.** We are completely lost people. Christ came to save lost people. If you realize you are lost, Christ came to save you. He died for you, and by His grace He will give to you, by faith in Him, eternal life. *"Grace be to you."* Paul starts out very kindly. He does not at first use a baseball bat to hit them over the head, but he will do this very soon in this letter. He is warming up. He starts out warmly and graciously as we should all start out in answering error. Even if we meet people who are "off the wall" and in error, we should be gracious.

"and peace from God the Father, and *from* our Lord Jesus Christ" Notice again, Paul is connecting the two Persons of the Trinity together, *"God the Father,"* and the *"Lord Jesus Christ."* In Verse 1 it was *"Jesus Christ, and God the Father."* The order is reversed here. It is now God the Father and then God the Son. They are united. The Holy Spirit is the third Member of the Trinity. Though there are three Persons, there is only one God. Each Person of the Trinity is of equal power and authority with the other two Persons.

It is only the Father and the Son who can give us *"peace."* I like the definition that we have used before for peace.

Peace

"Peace is the tranquil state of a soul assured of its salvation through Christ, and so fearing nothing from God and content with its earthly lot of whatsoever sort it is."

I have talked about the riot I had at my first church. I had just come out of the Chaplain Corps. The name of the church was Immanuel Baptist Church. I was preaching on the gift of peace, and then some of the members instigated what turned out to be a kind of riot. This was on October 29, 1961. In that sermon I used an illustration of peace as a little bird in a nest beneath Niagara

Falls with all the water rustling and all the thunderous noise all about. That little bird is still quiet and peaceful in his nest. That is what peace is. The Lord Jesus Christ can give us this kind of peace no matter what is around us. He can give us inward peace, and that is a great wonderful gift. Peace comes from God the Father and from God the Son when we trust the Lord Jesus Christ as our Saviour and Redeemer. Grace also comes from God the Father and from God the Son when we trust in the salvation He has provided.

Galatians 1:4

"Who gave himself for our sins, that he might deliver us from this present evil world, according to the will of God and our Father"

"Who gave himself for our sins" This *"who"* is a relative pronoun that goes back to *"our Lord Jesus Christ"* in verse 2, *"Who gave Himself for our sins."* The Lord Jesus Christ gave Himself in at least two ways.

First, He left Heaven's Glory to take upon Himself human form. He was perfect God, and, by the miracle of the Incarnation, He became perfect Man. He left the peace, glory and serenity of Heaven when He came into this wicked and sin-cursed world.

The second way that He *"gave Himself"* was at the Cross of Calvary. He *"gave Himself."* He suffered. He bled. He died. He was spat upon. He was cursed at and sworn at. On top of that, He took in His own body the sins of the entire world. We believe that He didn't only take the sins of the elect, or the ones who were chosen, but also the sins of the whole world. As John the Baptist exclaimed.

- **John 1:29**
  The next day John seeth Jesus coming unto him, and saith, **Behold the Lamb of God, which taketh away the sin of the world.**

"The sin of the world" includes the sins of every man, woman, and child in the entire human race that ever has been or will be born. It does not mean that everybody will be saved. It is not the sin question any longer. It is the Son question. What will the lost sinner do with the Lord Jesus Christ, the Saviour? Will he or she receive His salvation, or reject it? The sins have been paid for. If we have trusted Christ for our salvation and have been regenerated, our sins and our transgressions have been *"taken away,"* *"removed,"* and *"blotted out."*

- **Psalm 103:12**
  As far as the east is from the west, so far hath he removed our transgressions from us.

- **Isaiah 44:22**
  I have blotted out, as a thick cloud, thy transgressions, and, as a cloud, thy sins: return unto me; for I have redeemed thee.

The Lord Jesus Christ has taken away the sins of the world.

Christ has "given Himself for our sins." Some believe that He died **only** for the sins of the Jews. I do not believe this. Some believe it means that He died **only** for the sins of the elect. I do not believe this either. He did take away the sins of the believers. I do believe that. I believe He died for the sins of all the men, women, and children of all the nations and clans the world around.

He *"gave Himself for our sins."* Remember we said there were two words for the word *"for."* One word is "ANTI" which means *"in place of, or as a substitute for."* "HYPER" which is used here, means *"in the place of and also for the benefit of."* It has a positive connotation. Here are some verses that I would like to point out that speak of our Lord Jesus Christ's substitutionary atonement *"for us."*

- **Romans 5:8**
  But God commendeth his love toward us, in that, while we were yet sinners, **Christ died for us**.
- **Romans 8:32**
  He that spared not his own Son, but **delivered him up for us all**, how shall he not with him also freely give us all things?
- **1 Corinthians 5:7**
  Purge out therefore the old leaven, that ye may be a new lump, as ye are unleavened. For even **Christ our passover is sacrificed for us:**

Those last two words *"for us"* are left out of the Westcott and Hort corrupt Greek text. You do not find these vitally important words, *"for us,"* in the New International Version, or in the New American Standard Version, or in most other modern versions.

- **2 Corinthians 5:21**
  For **he hath made him *to be* sin for us**, who knew no sin; that we might be made the righteousness of God in him.
- **Galatians 3:13**
  Christ hath redeemed us from the curse of the law, **being made a curse for us**: for it is written, Cursed *is* every one that hangeth on a tree:

He was made a curse for us in our place. The cross was a cursed thing. They took the Lord Jesus down from the cross before the Passover began because it was a curse to be hung on a tree, especially over the Sabbath.

- **Deuteronomy 21:22-23**
  And if a man have committed a sin worthy of death, **and he be to be put to death, and thou hang him on a tree: His body shall not remain all night upon the tree**, but thou shalt in any wise bury him that day; (for he that is hanged is accursed of God;) that thy land be not defiled, which the LORD thy God giveth thee for an inheritance.
- **Ephesians 5:2**
  And walk in love, as Christ also hath loved us, **and hath given himself for us** an offering and a sacrifice to God for a sweetsmelling savour.
- **1 Thessalonians 5:10**
  Who died for us, that, whether we wake or sleep, we should live together with him.
- **Titus 2:14**
  Who gave himself for us, that he might redeem us from all iniquity, and purify unto himself a peculiar people, zealous of good works.
- **1 Peter 2:21**
  For even hereunto were ye called: because **Christ also suffered for us**, leaving us an example, that ye should follow his steps:
- **1 John 3:16**
  Hereby perceive we the love *of God*, because **he laid down his life for us**: and we ought to lay down *our* lives for the brethren.

"that he might deliver us from this present evil world"

What was the purpose for this? *"That He might deliver us from this present evil world according to the will of God and our Father."* The word, *"deliver,"* EXAIREO, means *"to lift up or to lift out."* If we are saved, Christ *"delivered us."* **Positionally**, He picked us up and lifted us right out of this wicked world. **Practically and realistically**, He wants to deliver us from its power on us while here on this earth. The Lord Jesus Christ does not want any of His own (all that believe and are saved) to be taken up and to be conquered by this wicked world. The world is all around us. Its filthiness is around us. Its swearing is around us. Its cursing is around us. The bad things on television are around us. We cannot keep completely away from the bad things that are around us. The purpose of Christ's death on our behalf, Who gave Himself for us, was that He may deliver us from this present evil world. We are in the world, as the Scripture says, but we are not of the world. All of the worldly things that the world enjoys, we should hate. Every sin that the world enjoys, if we are born-again believers, we should detest.

"according to the will of God and our Father" God's will is that the born-again Christians should be delivered.

Galatians 1:5

"To whom *be* glory for ever and ever. Amen." This goes back again to verse 3, *"our Lord Jesus Christ"* and to verse 4, *"the will of God the Father."* We must realize that God is all glorious. There is no sin in Him. There is no evil in Him. That is why He wants to take us to Heaven. First of all we must be saved. We must be cleansed by the blood of Christ. We must be justified in order for us to enter Heaven and to see the glory of God. We should ascribe glory to Him. Majesty, magnificence, and excellence belong to Him not only for a time but forever and ever. *"Glory"* has been defined as *"the glorious condition of blessedness into which is appointed and promised that true Christians should enter."* We will have glory. I love the gospel song entitled "Only Glory By And By." When the saved ones enter Heaven, we will see the glory of Christ. As Jesus told us in His high-priestly prayer.

- John 17:24
  Father, I will that they also, whom thou hast given me, be with me where I am; **that they may behold my glory, which thou hast given me**: for thou lovedst me before the foundation of the world.

The purpose of our salvation is that we may be with Christ and behold His glory and the glory of the Father. We will have new bodies, and we will be able to share that glory. John 14 speaks about this also.

- John 14:2
  In my Father's house are many mansions: if *it were* not *so,* I would have told you. I go to prepare a place for you.

Those of us who are saved will be in Christ's *"Father's house,"* beholding His glory. *"To whom be glory for ever and ever, Amen."*

Galatians 1:6

"I marvel that ye are so soon removed from him that called you into the grace of Christ unto another gospel"

"I marvel" With this verse, Paul begins to turn up the heat, to press the screws, to tighten things up. He is *"marveling."* He can't understand. He has been gracious up to this point. He has talked about grace, about peace, and about the sacrifice of our Lord Jesus Christ on the cross of Calvary that He might deliver us from this present evil world. He has ascribed glory to God the Father and glory to God the Son. Now he says he has begun to *"marvel."* I marvel right along with Paul how people who have received the Word of God, the pure Scripture, the pure grace, the pure gospel can be *"so soon removed"*

Galatians 1:6-7

by false teaching. Paul had laid down the foundation of this church on one of his missionary journeys. The word for "marvel," THAUMAZO, is in the present tense. It means *"to be wondered at, to be had in admiration."*

"that ye are so soon removed from him that called you into the grace of Christ" That word for "removed" is META-TITHEMI. META carries with it the force of change or *"to another place."* TITHEMI means *"to put or place."* This compound word means *"to put in another place, to transpose."* Brother Dick Carroll, an accomplished musician, knows how to "transpose" music. He can put the music up a key, or he can put it down a key. It is speaking of two things, one of which is to be put in place of the other. They had done exactly this. They had removed God's grace and had put law in its place.

"unto another gospel" It was Paul who had *"called"* them, that is, led them to Christ, and told them of the gospel. There are two Greek words for *"other."* One is ALLOS which means *"another of the same kind."* If we have a banana, and then we have another banana, that would be ALLOS or another of the same kind. This word is not ALLOS, but it is HETEROS which is *"another of a different kind."* I have one banana. I have one apple. The apple is "another," but it is *"another of a different kind."* This *"other"* gospel that the Galatians had was a removed "other." It had nothing to do with the true gospel. Paul had given them the gospel of Christ. He had preached Christ unto them. It's the salvation that God has provided by a Saviour, the Lord Jesus Christ. He is a sinless Saviour. He is both perfect God and perfect man. This is part of the gospel which means "good news." All of us are sinners and lost, but by grace and faith in Christ we can be saved and have eternal life.

This is what Paul preached, but the Galatians were removed to *"another"* gospel. As I mentioned before, there were two errors that Paul was trying to solve in this book of Galatians. The first one was the error of the Judaizers from Jerusalem who were saying that you have to be saved by keeping the law of Moses. That is *"another"* gospel. The second error was that you can be saved by faith in Christ, but you must be sanctified by keeping the law of Moses. That is *"another"* gospel also.

Galatians 1:7

"Which is not another; but there be some that trouble you, and would pervert the gospel of Christ"

"Which is not another; but there be some that trouble you" Paul is saying in this verse that the gospel they had adopted was not ALLOS or another of the same kind. Their gospel was not bananas and bananas, but bananas and apples mixed together. It would be the word,

HETEROS, which is an "other" of a separate and different kind. There are two different kinds of gospel here. One is the gospel of grace, and the other is the gospel of grace mixed with law, which is really not *"another"* of the same kind, but *"another"* of a different kind.

"But there be some that trouble you" Then Paul gives the reason: *"there be some that trouble you."* Whenever someone tells you that you can't be saved by grace through faith in the Lord Jesus Christ without works, that is troubling. Has anyone ever asked you if you were really born-again? This is a very important question. We must have the assurance that we are saved--born-again. We can be troubled if somebody upsets that assurance by telling us that we can't be saved through faith in Christ and tells us that we can't be saved through faith in Christ alone, but that we have to do something else.

The word used here for trouble is TARASSO. It means *"to agitate, trouble (a thing, by the movement of its parts to and fro."* That's troubling and disturbing, isn't it? Something is troubling when it is always moving. If you look at a basketball game or a tennis match, the players are moving all the time. That is troubling. Trouble also means *"to cause one inward commotion."* We cannot be inwardly disturbed or irritated. God wants us to have peace in our hearts and souls if we are saved. Trouble also means *"to take away his calmness of mind."* We cannot afford to take away our calmness of mind. If we're saved, the Lord has given us His peace which will keep us.

- **Philippians 4:7**
  And the **peace of God, which passeth all understanding,** shall keep your hearts and minds through Christ Jesus.

This troubling means *"to take away the calmness of the mind, to disturb someone's equanimity, his even handedness, his equal mindedness; to disturb, to disquiet, to make restless."* I get agitated myself when I think about all these definitions which mean to trouble someone. I do not want to be restless, do you? This word also means *"to render anxious or distressed; to perplex the mind of one by suggesting scruples or doubts."* God wants us to have peace of mind. He does not want us to be troubled. These people were troubling the Galatians, and Paul pointed out clearly the reason for this.

"and would pervert the gospel of Christ" The word for "pervert" is METASTREPHO. META implies something that is changed in some way. STREPHO means *"to turn."* The resultant meaning is *"to turn around"* the gospel of Christ. It is gospel perversion. That was what these false teachers were doing. Do we have any gospel perverters today? Yes, we do. We have many of them.

Galatians 1:8

"But though we, or an angel from heaven, preach any other gospel unto you than that which we have preached unto you, let him be accursed"

"But though we, or an angel from heaven" Today many are talking about angels. People are even on television talking about angels. Some say that an angel told them to do this or to do that. This is all false! They are not the real angels. After the September 11, 2001 terrorist crash into the World Trade Center in New York City, various religious leaders and others said these people became "angels." Angels are helpers for those who are saved by faith in Christ. They do not talk to us. They are standing by to help the believers. Many times angels keep the believers safe. Maybe some of you have experienced a near accident in your car. You cannot explain it, or I cannot explain it. I just feel as if the Lord had his hand on me and prevented a terrible accident. Hebrews 1:14 tells us what angels do.

- **Hebrews 1:14**
  Are they not all ministering spirits, **sent forth to minister for them** who shall be heirs of salvation?

This is the Biblical answer to what angels do. Paul says that even if an angel came from Heaven and preached another gospel, he should be accursed. This is indeed what happened in 1 Kings 13:18 where an angel was sent with another message. Remember, there were two prophets. One was a true prophet, and the other was a false prophet. The true prophet was sent by the Lord to pronounce evil upon the altar and to put a curse on the people. He was told by the Lord that after he delivered the message he was not to go back into the city. He was not to stay with anybody. God told him that directly. Then there was another prophet. He was a false prophet, and he persuaded the true prophet to violate the word of God. Here is how he did it in 1 Kings 13:18.

- **1 Kings 13:18**
  He said unto him, I *am* a prophet also as thou *art*; and **an angel spake unto me by the word of the LORD, saying**, Bring him back with thee into thine house, that he may eat bread and drink water. *But* **he lied** unto him.

He told the true prophet that he was a prophet also, and that an angel told him to take him back to his house to eat and drink. This is not what God had told the true prophet. This was a lie.

"preach any other gospel unto you than that which we have preached unto you, let him be accursed" We have some lying prophets today. Anyone who perverts and diverts the gospel of Christ is a lying prophet. Paul says that even if an angel says it, we are not to listen. We are to let him be accursed. That word accursed, ANATHEMA, means *"a man accursed, devoted to the direst of woes, a person or thing doomed to destruction."* He is Hell-bound. This is the most serious thing that could happen. Let him be accursed. Let him go into the pains and tortures of an eternal, everlasting lake of fire called Hell.

Let me suggest at least twelve false or *"other gospels"* that are current in the days in which we are living. I am sure that there are many more.

Twelve False Gospels

1. **There is the false gospel** that says we are saved by the law of Moses.

2. **There is the false gospel** that says we are saved by mixing law and grace.

3. **There is the false gospel** that says that we are saved by any good works.

4. **There is the false gospel** that says that we are saved by ordinances such as baptism, extreme unction, or any other ordinance.

5. **There is the false gospel** that says that we are saved only for a time and not eternally. Do not forget the truth that once we are born, we are born for the rest of our life. We cannot be unborn either in the physical or in the spiritual realm.

6. **There is the false gospel** that says only if we are the elect, and that the gospel is for the elect only, and not for the *"whosoever will"* (Revelation 22:17).

7. **There is the false gospel** that says that we are saved by the death of Christ but not by the shed blood of Christ in His death. This is the John MacArthur false gospel. He does not think that blood means blood. He says that blood is only a metonym or figure of speech for death. Part of this false gospel teaches that the blood of the Lord Jesus Christ was identical blood as that of any human being. It was in no way different blood. MacArthur teaches that it was "human blood."

8. **There is the false gospel** that says that we are saved by grace through saving heartfelt faith plus something else.

9. **There is the false gospel** that says that we are saved by Lordship salvation. That is another idea held by John MacArthur. Lordship salvation says that we have to make Christ our Lord before we become saved. How can a sinner

make Christ the Lord of his life? That would be salvation by works. You have to be saved first before you can make Jesus Christ Lord of your life. That is what the apostle Paul said **after** he was saved. *"Lord what wilt thou have me to do?"* (Acts 9:6)

10. **There is the false gospel** that says that we are saved by a non-Scriptural Christ calling Him a mere man or a mere human being.

11. **There is the false gospel** that says that we are saved by universalism. That means that everybody is saved without even believing in Christ. I heard Billy Graham say this exact thing. I have it on a tape recording. He was on the Robert Schuller telecast a few summers ago. He said whoever has not heard of Christ will be saved whether they are Hindus or Moslems or whoever they may be. Robert Schuller, that modernist unbeliever, said he was glad to hear Billy say that. Well, that is not the gospel that Billy Graham has been preaching in church after church all his life. What has happened to the man? That is *"another gospel."* That is a gospel that says we are universally saved even if we never believed in Christ. That is a false gospel.

12. **There is the false gospel** that says that we are saved if we deny Christ's Person or work. Those who preach a gospel that says Christ was not virgin-born are preaching *"another gospel."* Those who say Christ was not bodily raised from the grave are preaching a false gospel. Those who do not believe that Christ performed miracles are preaching a false gospel. The Person and the work of Christ must be the very essence of the gospel. It is the good news about Christ. That is the gospel of Christ.

- **Romans 1:16**
  For I am not ashamed of **the gospel of Christ**: for it is the power of God unto salvation to every one that believeth; to the Jew first, and also to the Greek.

You see it is the gospel of Christ which is important. If you take away His Deity or His true humanity, you have no gospel. You have no Good News. That is what is wrong with the Westcott and Hort false Greek text. In their text they leave out *"of Christ"* in Romans 1:16. They only say, *"I am not ashamed of the gospel."* What gospel? Gospel means "good news." Someone might have a new car, a new hat, or a new home. That may be good news, but it is not the Good News about Christ. It is not the gospel of Christ. This is very important.

The NIV takes *"of Christ"* out. The New American Standard takes *"of Christ"* out. These are false teachings in regard to the gospel. To have a false Christ, one who is not the Saviour exactly as the Bible teaches, is to have a false gospel.

Galatians 1:9

"As we said before, so say I now again, If any *man* preach any other gospel unto you than that ye have received, let him be accursed"

"As we said before, so say I now again" Paul repeats himself. That is good! Sometimes it is necessary to repeat yourself. Can they not read? Surely they can read. Can you not read? Surely you can read. When we read the Scriptures, we see that God has to repeat and repeat until finally some of it sinks in through our thick skulls. That is what Paul does here. He repeats that any who preach *"another"* gospel will be in the eternal fires of Hell.

"If any *man* preach any other gospel unto you than that ye have received, let him be accursed" Paul is very specific on this! You can see he has begun to hammer his readers with strong words. He is trying to straighten these Galatians out. We will see in these six chapters that he is just going to write on one theme. **That one theme is we are saved by grace through genuine faith plus nothing and minus nothing.** Works of the law cannot help! The law was given to condemn us. That is why the law of Moses was made. All that those ten commandments do is point an accusing finger at us. All ten of them show us that we are sinners, and we cannot be saved on our own. By grace, God sent His Son to fulfill the law because we cannot fulfill it. He fulfilled it for us. If we trust in Him, we are in Christ. We have fulfilled the law in Christ. This is a powerful thing.

Galatians 1:10

"For do I now persuade men, or God? or do I seek to please men? for if I yet pleased men, I should not be the servant of Christ"

"For do I now persuade men, or God?" To persuade, PEITHO, means *"to listen to, to obey, yield to, comply with."* We have preachers and Christians that seem to have as their whole goal to comply with whatever men may say. Do it if it feels good.

- Proverbs 1:10

My son, if sinners entice thee, **consent thou not.**

We have people all around who want us to be persuaded by men. They want us to buy narcotics and dope from them. They want to get us to do this because it is pleasurable.

"or do I seek to please men?" Do I yield to men or to God? Do I seek to please men? To please men, ARESKO, means *"to accommodate one's self to the opinions, desires, and interests of others."* Does this mean that we have to be mean, hostile, or bitter? No, I do not think that is the case. Can we not quietly say "no"? "No" means "no." Even if we say it softly, people sometimes feel that we are screaming it. Whether we say "no" loudly or softly, we should say "no." When we can please men without displeasing God, go ahead.

This is not what Paul is talking about. He is saying that we are not to please men to the exclusion of pleasing God. If you and I are in accord with the Word of God, we are pleasing God. I believe that you are here in church because you want to be here. There is not any person who forced you or coerced you to be here in this service. We praise God that you are here. If you are wanting the Lord's pleasure in your life, He wants you to do what he says. If while you are pleasing the Lord, you can also please one another, fine. That is not what Paul is saying here. Let us be kind to one another. Let us be helpful to one another; but not if we are not pleasing the Lord. Pleasing the Lord must take first place.

"for if I yet pleased men" If my main purpose was to please men, then I could not be a servant of Christ. We have people today such as modernists and liberals, neo-evangelicals, and even some Fundamentalists who seek to please men. They will not speak out against certain people or practices because they want to be friends with the men who hold to those doctrines even though they are false.

I think about our former president of Dallas Theological Seminary, Dr. John F. Walvoord. He was a former teacher of mine. Someone wrote him about Robert B. Thieme who has a heretical view about the blood of Christ and other doctrines. Dr. Walvoord wrote this person back and said that what Bob Thieme taught was false. He said that Thieme was saying that the blood of Christ is not necessary for salvation.

A few years ago, I wrote Dr. Walvoord myself. Though I am not quoting exactly, I wrote something along this line:

> Dr. Walvoord, here is a copy of the letter you wrote in regard to Bob Thieme's heresy of the blood of Christ. Here is what John MacArthur teaches on the blood of Christ. This is what you wrote on Bob Thieme. Now will you tell me what you think about John MacArthur.

Dr. Walvoord wrote me and told me what he thought, but asked me not to tell anybody. He was not consistent with what he had said about Bob Thieme. Dr. Walvoord is a godly man. He is a saved man. He was my teacher for five years. He is a good man, but he did not want to go on public record. He went on record about Bob Thieme who was a graduate of Dallas Theological Seminary also. Thieme graduated from seminary a year or two before I did. As of this writing I think he is still a Pastor in Houston, Texas. Apparently, John MacArthur is too important for Dr. Walvoord to come out publicly. MacArthur has many radio stations all over. He has a college, a seminary, and has written a commentary on the Bible.

Some men are political, and some men are not. Paul was not political. Dr. David Otis Fuller who wrote *Which Bible?* and *Counterfeit or Genuine?* was a godly man. He was a GARBC pastor in Grand Rapids, Michigan at the Wealthy Street Baptist Church for over fifty years. Dr. Fuller used to say this, *"There's nothing worse than a cheap church politician."* We have politicians everywhere. These politicians are not just in Washington. There are church politicians in many churches--even Fundamental churches--all around the world. I trust the Lord will keep us from politicians here in our church.

"I should not be the servant of Christ" Paul said that if his chief purpose were to please men, then he could not be a servant of Christ. That word for servant is DOULOS which means *"**a slave**, devoted to another to the disregard of one's own interests."* I have said it many times that I believe in Christian slavery. I believe every born-again Christian should be a bondslave of the Lord Jesus Christ! I am not talking about human slavery or the slaves of the South. I am talking about being a servant slave of the Lord Jesus Christ. I will say this until my dying breath. I repeat, I believe that everyone who is a born-again, blood-redeemed Christian should be enslaved to Jesus Christ his Master and Redeemer.

What do I mean by slavery? It means *"doing the will of another."* It means, as the Lord Jesus said in the Garden of Gethsemane, *"Not my will but Thine be done."* It is as Paul said at his conversion by the Lord Jesus Christ, *"Lord, what wilt thou have me to do?"* (Acts 9:6) Paul said that he was a servant of Christ. Who among us has taken three missionary journeys and after that has been transferred to a cruel Roman prison? Who among us has been shipwrecked nearly losing his life in the sea? Paul escaped by the skin of his teeth time and time again. Who but a servant and slave of the Lord Jesus Christ would do that? He was a missionary "par excellence" as they say. He was a missionary of the highest type. Paul was *"devoted to another to the disregard of his own interests."* He was *"doing the will of another, to the disregard of his own interest."* That is what DOULOS means. You and I have many interests. Are we who have been redeemed by faith in the Lord Jesus Christ going to put our interests first, or are we going to put Christ's interests first? The choice is up to us.

Galatians 1:11

"But I certify you, brethren, that the gospel which was preached of me is not after man" Paul is telling the Galatians that the gospel he preached was not *"after man."* In other words, man never told this gospel to him. This gospel is contrary to all of man's desires. Man says, "Do this and live." That is what all the religions of the world say, "Do this and live." The gospel of Christ says. "It is done. Just believe in the finished work of Christ and live." It is the difference between the word, **"do"** and the word, **"done."** It is the difference between the present tense and the past tense. The gospel of the Bible is contrary to all of man's existing religious beliefs.

Galatians 1:12

"For I neither received it of man, neither was I taught *it*, but by the revelation of Jesus Christ" You might wonder how Paul knew about the teachings about the Church as the body of Christ. Paul revealed this truth in the books of Ephesians and Colossians. He also revealed many new truths in the books of 1 Corinthians and in Romans. Peter did not have all these details. Paul knew these truths because the Lord Jesus Christ took him out in the Arabian desert for three years and taught him. That was a three-year seminary course taught by the Lord Jesus Himself. Paul learned all of this. Before he was saved, he had been taught at the feet of Gamaliel. He knew the books of Moses and the entire Old Testament backwards and forwards. But he did not know what Christ wanted him to preach and teach until the Lord Himself revealed it to him. He was taught by the Lord.

"but by the revelation of Jesus Christ" It was a special revelation from the Lord Jesus Christ which was the source of Paul's teaching. We have seen that the Judaizers had infected the churches of Galatia. These Judaizers were teaching that people must be saved by grace through faith in Christ, and after that they had to keep the law of Moses. Paul is making some headway. He is proving that he received his message from Christ and not from any man. He became very firm in his words when he said that if any man, or even an angel, preaches another gospel, let him be accursed. I would not want to wish the curse of Hell on anybody. Would you? Paul did. He was an apostle of Jesus Christ, and he could get away with it.

Galatians 1:13

"For ye have heard of my conversation in time past in the Jews' religion, how that beyond measure I persecuted the church of God, and wasted it:" What did Paul do before he met the Lord? Paul was zealous in his religious fervor and persecuted the churches beyond measure. The first mention of Paul is in Acts when he was called Saul.

- Acts 7:58

  And cast *him* out of the city, and stoned *him*: **and the witnesses laid down their clothes at a young man's feet, whose name was Saul.**

Paul was very happy that Stephen was being stoned, and he was a party to it. It is clear that Paul actively sought out Christians, whether men or women, and put them in prison.

- Acts 8:3

  As for Saul, **he made havock of the church**, entering into every house, and haling men and women **committed *them* to prison.**

Paul even went to the high priest to get papers giving him the authority to jail Christians.

- Acts 9:1-2

  And Saul, yet breathing out threatenings and **slaughter** against the disciples of the Lord, went unto the high priest, And **desired of him letters to Damascus** to the synagogues, that if he found any of this way, whether they were men or women, he might **bring them bound unto Jerusalem.**

He undoubtedly did slay some of the choice Christians of that day.

These Galatians in Asia Minor (now called Turkey) had heard of his behavior in the past. Our reputations get around. All of us have had a past. Paul had a past. I am glad that my past is past. Paul was glad his past was past. If we have had a bad past, we do not want to go back to it. We are glad that it is over. The sin and the wickedness we had before we were saved is something we do not want again.

That word persecuted, DIOKO, means *"to make to run or to flee, put to flight, or to drive away."* It means *"to be mistreated, suffer persecution on account of something."* He wasted, destroyed, and overthrew the churches of the Lord Jesus Christ.

Galatians 1:14

"And profited in the Jews' religion above many my equals in mine own nation, being more exceedingly zealous of the traditions of my fathers"

"And profited in the Jews' religion above many my equals in mine own nation" He profited (PROKOPTO) which means *"to go forward, advance, proceed or metaphorically promote."* He was advanced and promoted in his religious career. Some people are promoted and some people are not. This happens in the military also. For five years I was on active duty as a Chaplain in the U.S. Navy. I only received one promotion. I went from lieutenant junior grade to lieutenant senior grade. I went from one silver bar to two silver bars. The next promotion to lieutenant commander never came to pass. I believe the reason for this was that I faithfully preached the Word of God. The senior chaplains who were liberals and modernists did not like my preaching. They saw to it that I got bad "fitness reports" as they are called in the military. I was not advanced. After a few more years, I resigned my U. S. Naval Reserve Commission and left the military entirely. Promotion is not always possible. Sometimes the older generals are bypassed in order to promote the younger men who have these internationalist and false New Age ideas. Paul was promoted among many his *"equals."* That word, *"equals,"* SUNELIKIOTES, means *"one of the same age, an equal in age."* He was advanced and promoted above the people he grew up with who were his own age.

"being more exceedingly zealous of the traditions of my fathers" The word zealous, ZELOTES, means *"one burning with zeal."* A zeal is good if your zeal is for the right thing. We must be zealous for the Lord Jesus Christ! Paul was zealous for the traditions of the Jewish fathers. He would kill for it, and he did kill for it. He thought he was right. He thought he was doing God a service as he said. In Indonesia recently, twelve thousand refugees went to a Catholic monastery. As I am speaking, these refugees are being killed by soldiers. These soldiers are doing what they think is right. They are zealous, but they are zealous for a wrong thing. Paul was zealous for the traditions of his fathers. The word for *"traditions,"* PARADOSIS, is *"a giving over which is done by word of mouth or in writing."* It means

> *"the body of precepts, especially ritual, which in the opinion of the later Jews were orally delivered by Moses and orally transmitted in unbroken succession to subsequent generations, which precepts, both illustrating and expanding the written law, as they did were to be obeyed with equal reverence."*

They put the traditions of their Jewish fathers even above the Old Testament Words of God. That is what these traditions were. Paul was zealous for these traditions of the fathers, Abraham, Isaac, and Jacob. He was a Jew as he says in his own testimony. He mentions that he was *"an Hebrew of the Hebrews"* (Philippians 3:5).

Galatians 1:15

"But when it pleased God, who separated me from my mother's womb, and called *me* by his grace"

"But when it pleased God" Here is a vital difference. *"It pleased God"* to do something for the apostle Paul which was both amazing and miraculous. He was a killer, a murderer, and an imprisoner of Christians. God was pleased to do something to him, and for him, and with him. God is pleased to do the same for us. If we are saved by faith in Christ, we know that we are sinners saved only by grace without any works of our own. God wants to use us even as He wanted to use Paul.

"who separated me from my mother's womb" Paul realized that he was *"separated"* by God from his mother's womb. He was separated by God right from the beginning of his life. He was called by God's grace. He was not called from his mother's womb, but he was *"separated."* Now, does God know that people are going to trust Christ when they grow up? Yes, He does. Does He know if people are going to reject Christ and be bound for Hell? Yes, He knows that too. Even though Paul's early life was lived in a wicked and terrible manner, God saw that he was one day going to trust His Son as Lord and Saviour and be a great apostle. That is what this verse is teaching us.

"and called *me* by his grace" God's grace is the only thing that can call us out of darkness and into His marvelous light. Paul says God *"called me."* If we are born-again and saved Christians, we must be *"called"* by the Lord. Christians have to be sure of their calling. As the Scripture says we are to make our *"calling and election sure"* (2 Peter 1:10). We must be confident that we are saved. If you are not confident of that, you should make sure that you have been called of the Lord *"by His grace"* and through faith in His Son, the Lord Jesus Christ.

The same is true of preachers, missionaries, and pastors. I do not think that Matthias was *"called"* by the Lord. He was picked by the election of his peers. They had only two choices. Then they cast lots. The one who won the lots was chosen by that group to be the next apostle to take the place of Judas. The Lord Jesus did not tell these apostles to hold an election. On the contrary, He told them to tarry or wait in Jerusalem.

- Luke 24:49
  And, behold, I send the promise of my Father upon you: but **tarry ye in the city of Jerusalem, until ye be endued with power from on high.**

Instead of waiting, however, they held an election. We do that all the time in churches. I believe the one who was called by God's grace to take the place of the traitor, Judas, was the apostle Paul.

Preachers should be called. Unfortunately, many of them are not called. The modernistic liberals who are preachers, pastors, and teachers are not even saved and certainly have never been called by the Lord. Among the many Bible-believing pastors, some of them are not called by the Lord, but by their mothers. Their mothers wanted them to be preachers, and they just trained for the ministry. I think of a man out in California whose father is a pastor. Suddenly this man was about to be in an accident. As he was sliding down the street, he said, "God, if you save me from death in this accident, I'll be a preacher." I do not even know if this man was saved. His father was a preacher and now he is a preacher.

There is another man in this area who is a preacher. His father before him was a preacher. I do not know whether that man was ever called by the Lord. We do know definitely, however, that God did call Paul by His grace. It pleased God to do so. It pleases God to save any sinner. Does it not?

Galatians 1:16

"To reveal his Son in me, that I might preach him among the heathen; immediately I conferred not with flesh and blood"

"To reveal his Son in me, that I might preach him among the heathen" What was Paul called by God's grace to do? He was called to preach *"Him,"* Christ, *"among the heathen."* **The Lord Jesus Christ is the heart of the gospel.** This was his calling. God revealed to Paul the Lord Jesus Christ. Paul did not think the Lord Jesus Christ was the Messiah when he was killing Christians. He thought Christ was an imposter. But when God called Paul on his way to kill Christians, *"he fell to the earth"* (Acts 9:4). Paul was after blood on that one-hundred mile-journey to Damascus. But on his way, the Lord called him. He knocked him down and blinded him for several days. This is the reason why Christ revealed himself to Paul--to preach Christ among the heathen.

All we have to preach or should want to preach is Christ. Christ is the center of the gospel. He is the only One Who can save us. We should not preach magazines. We should not preach poetry. We should not preach comic books. We should not preach essays. We must preach Christ. That is what

Paul was called to do as an evangelist. He was not only gifted as an evangelist, but he built up the saints after they were saved. He stayed for three years in Ephesus building them up and teaching them the things of the Lord. He was commissioned to *"preach the gospel."*

- **1 Corinthians 9:16**
  For though I preach the gospel, I have nothing to glory of: for necessity is laid upon me; yea, **woe is unto me, if I preach not the gospel**!

By means of our national radio broadcasts we are preaching to people in the areas of Philadelphia, Maryland, Western Pennsylvania, Florida, and South Carolina. We are on one station in Northern Ireland. By means of our short-wave radio broadcasts we are preaching to people all over the world. By our Internet site **(www.BibleForToday.org)** under **"audio sermons,"** we are also preaching to people all over the world who are able to tune in on our site at any time day or night. In recent months, there were over 1,900 people per month who "downloaded" messages from our site. We preach to all kinds of lost, Hell-bound sinners whether they be Roman Catholic sinners or Protestant sinners or whoever they are. They all need to hear about the Lord Jesus Christ and be saved by faith in him. We also preach to saved people who need to be built up in the things of the Words of God. This is important. There are spiritually starving Christians in this country and all over the world.

"immediately I conferred not with flesh and blood" The normal thing for Paul to have done would be to ask different apostles and other Christian leaders what he should do next. Whenever a person feels that the Lord has called him into the ministry, he usually goes to school. He goes to a Bible institute or a seminary of some kind. By so doing, he does *"confer with flesh and blood."* This is not to say it is necessarily wrong. When he graduates from one of these schools and wants to get ordained, he might request several pastors to examine him concerning salvation, his call to the ministry and his doctrines. By so doing, this man *"confers with flesh and blood."* Again, this is not necessarily wrong.

Paul was a completely different person. He did not confer at all with flesh and blood. He did not confer with the apostles who went before him. He did not go up to Jerusalem and ask what he should do next. God revealed that unto him. Today we have a Bible that God has given to us. We can look in our Bibles to see what God wants us to do. In English, we must use the King James (Authorized) Bible and its underlying Hebrew and Greek texts to be sure we can see accurately all the will of God. Other versions might lead us astray in some of the details of God's will. To explain why I say this, I recommend my book, *Defending the King James Bible* (**BFT #1594-P**) available from The Bible For Today, 900 Park Avenue, Collingswood, New Jersey 08108.

As Christians, we do not need to *"confer with flesh and blood"* and ask what we need to do. We do not need to put our finger in the air to see which way the wind is blowing in order to see what to do. We can go to the Words of God. Paul immediately *"conferred not with flesh and blood."* Paul was indeed a rugged individualist.

Galatians 1:17

"Neither went I up to Jerusalem to them which were apostles before me; but I went into Arabia, and returned again unto Damascus" Paul was saved in Damascus which is the capital of Syria. He did not *"confer with flesh and blood"* and go back to Jerusalem. Instead, he went to be alone with the Lord in the Arabian desert. I am sure that the Lord Jesus Christ met and talked with him there. In fact, the next verse says, *"Then after three years I went up to Jerusalem."* After being in the desert, he returned to Damascus and then went up to Jerusalem. This shows his dependence on the Lord.

Between the Arabian desert and the Damascus visit, Paul took a three-year sabbatical, so to speak. During that time Paul did not talk to any of the apostles or anyone else. The Lord Jesus Christ revealed to Paul the gospel and the special ministry that He had for Paul. That is a miracle which had never been performed before. That is why Paul could write about the church being the body and Christ being the Head of the body in Ephesians and Colossians. He could write that because of the special revelation that Christ gave to him in the course of that three-year period in the desert. Sometimes we go to seminary or Bible school for several years, but in Paul's case the Lord Jesus Christ was his teacher. Christ told Paul exactly what to do and what to say. That is how he could write these books. God had to correct these Galatians who were being told to keep the Jewish law. God had to break them completely from that false teaching. The only way to do this was to get a special person like Paul. Paul was selected specially by God. He was trained specially by Christ. The Lord Jesus trained his apostles for three years. Judas was a traitor, and though unsaved was also trained by Jesus for three years. Paul was an apostle, and Christ trained him also for three years. I believe that the Lord Jesus Christ specially trained this man to be a preacher and teacher of the gospel.

Galatians 1:18

"Then after three years I went up to Jerusalem to see Peter, and abode with him fifteen days"

"Then after three years I went up to Jerusalem" After a wonderful three-year seminary graduate course taught by the Lord Jesus Christ, Paul *"went up"* to see Peter in Jerusalem. If you notice, Damascus is north of Jerusalem. Jerusalem is to the south of Damascus. You would think you would go **down** to Jerusalem and not **up**. But because Jerusalem is on a mountain, you never go **down** to Jerusalem. You always go **up** to Jerusalem. The mountain of Jerusalem, Mount Zion, is always **up**.

Notice that Paul went to see Peter. Peter was not the first Pope as the tradition of Rome teaches. If he were the first Pope, he broke all of the rules of the Roman Catholic Church by having a wife. Peter was married because the Bible talks about Peter's wife's mother.

- **Matthew 8:14**
  And when Jesus was come into Peter's house, he saw **his wife's mother** laid, and sick of a fever.

If Peter had a mother-in-law, then he also had a wife. He could not be the first Pope. Peter never gave any authority to himself. Paul went up to see Peter. When we get into chapter two, we are going to see Paul giving a little encouraging advice to Peter. Paul is going to reprimand Peter because Peter was wrong. Both Paul and Peter got their doctrine straight from the Lord Jesus Christ. Paul got his teaching after Peter received his missionary credentials. We will see later that there is going to be a major clash between Peter and Paul.

"to see Peter, and abode with him fifteen days" Nobody knows what Peter and Paul talked about. They had a private conference. We are not certain as to the details of it, and rightly so. I would imagine that Paul shared with Peter what Christ had taught him during the three years in the Arabian desert. He might have told him about the gospel of grace. He might have told him how people are not saved by keeping the law. He probably told him that people are not perfected by the keeping of the law after we are saved. Remember, these were the two errors that were being pushed upon the Galatians. The first error was that we are saved by keeping the law. The second error is that we are sanctified by keeping the law. We are sanctified, or set apart, after we are saved by the Holy Spirit of God. They probably went round and round about that. They talked together for fifteen days.

Galatians 1:19

"But other of the apostles saw I none, save James the Lord's brother"

"But other of the apostles saw I none, save James the Lord's brother" These were two of the Big Three, you might say. The ones who seemed to be in charge during the Lord's earthly ministry were Peter, James, and John. They were the three who went in when the Lord raised someone from the dead. They were also there at the Mount of Transfiguration. They saw Jesus transfigured and made whiter than snow, seeing His glory (Luke 9:28-32). So, Paul wanted to discuss these things first with Peter and then with

Galatians 1:19 — 25

James the Lord's brother. He wanted to discuss, I am sure, the gospel of God's grace and all of the things he had learned from the Lord Jesus Christ in the desert.

Perhaps James, the Lord's brother, was the writer of the book of James. We're not certain of this. We do know that there are **apparent** conflicts between the books of Paul and the book of James. In Romans, Paul said that we are saved by grace through faith alone. James said we are justified by works. The justification that James is talking about is before men. Before men, we are justified by works. Men cannot see our faith inside. Paul was talking about our justification before God. Before God, we are justified by faith plus nothing.

As Abraham believed God, it was counted unto him for righteousness. People could see that Abraham was a man of faith by what he did. His faith was seen by his sacrifice of his only son, Isaac. Remember, Isaac was born in a miraculous way. Sarah could not have any children. Then suddenly the Lord said she was going to have a child. When Isaac was born, God then told Abraham to take him up and offer him as a sacrifice on Mount Moriah. Faith played a part, but his faith also produced works. He obeyed God. You could see he was a man of faith. God had promised Abraham that in that son, Isaac, all the nations of the earth would be blessed. God promised that his descendants would be as numerous as the stars in the Heavens and as the sands of the sea. Abraham trusted that the Lord would do what he said. With faith he took Isaac up to slay him, believing, if necessary, God would raise him up to life.

- **Hebrews 11:19**
  Accounting that God *was* able to raise *him* up, even from the dead; from whence also he received him in a figure.

That is faith. God did not let Abraham go through with the sacrifice.

- **Genesis 22:12**
  And he said, **Lay not thine hand upon the lad**, neither do thou any thing unto him: **for now I know that thou fearest God**, seeing thou hast not withheld thy son, thine only *son* from me.

The faith of Abraham was also clearly seen when Abraham told his servants to stay behind on the mountain. Abraham told the servants that just he and Isaac were going up and the servants were to stay behind.

- **Genesis 22:5**
  And Abraham said unto his young men, Abide ye here with the ass; and **I and the lad will go yonder and worship, <u>and come again to you</u>**.

In the English, the meaning is not clear. Does *"come again"* mean that we will both go up and then I will come down by myself? Or does it mean we will both go up and we will both come down together? In the Hebrew it is very clear. It means we will both go up and we will both come back. That is faith, is it not?

Yes. James and Paul had a little bit of difference. I am sure they talked about some of these matters.

There is no conflict between the book of James and the book of Romans. Justification in the eyes of God is by faith alone. Justification in the eyes of men is by works and what we do. It is a sad thing when some believers who are saved by faith, born-again, and regenerated have works just like the world. That is indeed unfortunate. When the world looks at believers who are walking after the flesh and not after the spirit, they might say that we are just like they are. Such believers talk like those unsaved in the world. They dress like them. They live like them. They think like them. They argue like them. Everything is the same, and there is no difference. That is a sad thing. If we are saved by God's grace, there should be a straightforward difference between our walk and the walk of those unsaved in the world. Faith should produce good works. If faith does not produce good works, we wonder if there really is faith. That is what we are getting at. I am sure that Paul talked to James about this whole thing.

- **Ephesians 2:8-10**
  For **by grace are ye saved** through faith; and that not of yourselves: *it is* the gift of God: **Not of works**, lest any man should boast. For we are his workmanship, **created in Christ Jesus unto good works**, which God hath before ordained that we should walk in them.

We are not saved by good works, but we are *"ordained unto good works"* that we should walk in them. Genuine saving faith must precede the good works. In Romans, Paul talks about the faith. In the book of James, James talks about good works, as, in some way, being able to justify. They go together like love and marriage are supposed to. That is what the song says anyway. You do not want to get the cart before the horse. The horse is to pull the cart. The horse of faith is to pull the cart of works. Works follows, and faith precedes.

Galatians 1:20-21

"Now the things which I write unto you, behold, before God, I lie not. Afterwards I came into the regions of Syria and Cilicia" First Paul was in the desert for three years. Then he went to Damascus. After that, he went to Jerusalem for fifteen days. Then he went to the regions of Syria and Cilicia. Tarsus, Paul's hometown, is the capital of Cilicia. Remember, he was Saul of Tarsus. Perhaps he went back to his hometown to evangelize his mother, father, brothers, and sisters.

Galatians 1:22

"And was unknown by face unto the churches of Judea which were in Christ:" In other words, the churches of Judea, which are in the southern area, never laid eyes on Paul this whole time. We might call him a "loner." Paul was guided by the Holy Spirit of God. Is there anything wrong with being a loner? Some people say that it is a terrible disgrace to be a loner. They say you should be a part of various groups. There may be some truth in that. But on the other hand, if you and I are walking with Christ according to the Scriptures, is there anything wrong with walking alone? If others do not want to walk on the right path with us, then we ought to walk alone. Abraham walked alone. Daniel walked alone. Job walked alone. Many of the men of God in the Old Testament walked alone. Notice Jeremiah, the weeping prophet.

- **Jeremiah 15:17**
I sat not in the assembly of the mockers, nor rejoiced; <u>I sat alone because of thy hand</u>: for thou hast filled me with indignation.

The southern tribes of Judah and Benjamin refused to repent of their sins. Because of this, God sent them into Babylonian captivity. While there in Babylon, the prophet Jeremiah sat alone. He did not throw away the Words of God or forsake the Scriptures.

- **Jeremiah 20:9**
Then I said, I will not make mention of him, nor speak any more in his name. But *his word* was in mine heart as a burning fire shut up in my bones, and I was weary with forbearing, and **I could not *stay***.

He could not stop from preaching the Word of God. He said God's Words were the *"joy and rejoicing"* of his heart. (Jeremiah 15:16)

There is nothing wrong with being a loner. In a sense, we are loners in our **Bible For Today Baptist Church** in the sense that we set out alone. We set out in our home here at 900 Park Avenue, Collingswood, New Jersey. It is a well-built brick house. My mother-in-law, Gertrude Grace Sanborn, used to call it "Fort 900" for many reasons. It was built well, but also she knew that we stood on some principles. We continue to work on principle. We are loners, but we are not lonely. We have all of you people who are with us. We are together in this ministry.

- Ecclesiastes 4:9-10
  Two *are* better than one; because they have a good reward for their labour. **For if they fall, the one will lift up his fellow**: but woe to him *that is* alone when he falleth; for *he hath* not another to help him up.

It is good to have some counsel and help in our ministry. That is what people should do with one another. We should help each other if one of us gets off base. We should take one another aside and say. "Wait a minute. You have something on your tie." This is what one brother did to me recently. I was glad to know that and I soon removed the spot from my tie. I sometimes referred to the pianist as a piano player. One of the brethren said that he is not a "piano player," but he is a "pianist." Though these are small points, we can receive correction and instruction if we get off base in major points as well. There is nothing wrong if we are alone, if the Lord Jesus Christ is the One Who is with us. The Lord Jesus Christ was in prayer alone in Gethsemane. He was alone on the cross. There are some things in life that we have to do alone. If we have Jesus only, we are no longer alone. We are no longer lonely. He is our Friend and our Guide.

Galatians 1:23

"But they had heard only, That he which persecuted us in times past now preacheth the faith which once he destroyed"

What a wonderful thing that these Galatians can see how Paul has been changed. He had once persecuted them. They might have been thinking, *"In former times, Paul tracked us down, put us in prison, and sent us to our death. Now, Paul preaches to us the faith which he once destroyed."* I am different from Paul. I am preaching the faith of the Lord Jesus Christ. I never tried to destroy it. There are, however, some people who once destroyed the faith but later got saved and started preaching. Paul had a conversion that very few people have. It was like Paul was going north, and then God turned him around and made him go south. It was like Paul was going directly east, and then God turned him around and made him go west. He did the absolute opposite of what he had been doing. He was against Christ, and then he was strongly for Him. Paul had only one speed--full speed. I like that. You are either going to be all out for the devil in sin and wickedness which is wrong or one-hundred percent sold out to do God's bidding and God's will. That is what everyone of us ought to do

These Galatians had heard about Paul. Paul had a reputation. Now, he preached *"the faith."* Notice the words *"the faith."* It is not the personal faith that you have when you trust in Christ as Saviour, but it is *"the"* faith. With the

Galatians 1:23

Greek definite article before it, it refers to the body of Christian doctrine which is taught in the Bible. This is what Jude refers to.

- **Jude 1:3**
  Beloved, when I gave all diligence to write unto you of the common salvation, it was needful for me to write unto you, and exhort *you* **that ye should earnestly contend for the faith** which was once delivered unto the saints.

This is a reference to the body of Christian doctrine and the Scriptures for which we *"should earnestly contend."*

I picked up something from a church bulletin that someone gave me a while ago. I will not tell you the name of the church. I do not know who put this in the back of this bulletin, but it is not the gospel that Paul preached. It is supposedly the way of salvation.

♦ **The first thing** in this church bulletin for salvation was:
  "Are you sure of your relationship with God? You can be if you follow God's instructions on how to have a right relationship with him. Here's what to do. First, "admit that you have rebelled by not following God's perfect law."

I would put *"sinned"* in there instead of *"rebelled."* I think there are some people who are lost and bound for Hell who consciously have not "rebelled" against the Lord. They have just done what comes naturally. Some people in some churches do not like to use the word, *"sin."* I do not know the reason for this, but they do not like the vocabulary of the Bible.

- **Romans 3:23**
  For **all have sinned**, and come short of the glory of God;

This is the vocabulary of 1 John also.

- **1 John 1:9**
  If we **confess our sins**, he is faithful and just to **forgive us *our sins***, and to cleanse us from all unrighteousness.

This verse pertains to saved people, and not sinners. This verse is for believers.

♦ **The second thing** in this church bulletin about salvation was:
  "Believe that Jesus is God's only Son and that His death and resurrection is the only possible payment for your rebellion."

Notice that the quote from that church bulletin does not say God's *"only begotten Son."* The new versions take out *"only begotten Son."* This quote only talks about His death and resurrection. It says nothing about the blood of Christ shed for their sin. There is nothing mentioned that the Lord Jesus Christ died for them, but it says only that he died as *"the only possible payment for your rebellion."* It is weak there.

♦ **The third thing** in this church bulletin about salvation was:
"Ask Jesus to take the penalty for your rebellious actions (sin) so that you can be declared right with God."

You do not have to *"ask Jesus to take the penalty."* He did take the penalty for the sins of the world. Jesus has already done this.

- **John 1:29**
  The next day John seeth Jesus coming unto him, and saith, **Behold the Lamb of God, which taketh away the sin of the world.**

You do not have to *"ask Jesus to take the penalty for your rebellious actions."* This bulletin's way of salvation finally mentioned sin by means of an unquoted Scripture citation.

- **Romans 10:9**
  That **if thou shalt confess** with thy mouth the Lord Jesus, **and shalt believe in thine heart** that God hath raised him from the dead, thou shalt be saved.

- **John 1:12**
  But as many as **received him**, to them gave he power to become the sons of God, **even to them that believe on his name:**

♦ **The fourth thing** in this church bulletin for salvation was:
"Commit to place God first in your life by studying and obeying God's truth in the Bible. In order to have a right relationship with God, pray through the steps above and then commit yourself to grow in your Christian life by daily talking to God in prayer and reading the Bible. Share your decision with the pastor."

When someone comes to Christ as their Saviour, they do not *"place God first."* No, they place Christ first. Any Jew wants to place their God first. Any Muslim wants to place their "god" (Allah) first. Any modernist liberal wants to place their God first. In this context, "God" is an undefined Being, not necessarily the Bible's God. These groups do not even know who He is. You must accept the Lord Jesus Christ as your Saviour. *"He must increase, and I must decrease."* (John 3:30) You are not talking about some mushy word, *"God,"* where you do not know if it is the God of the Muslims, or the God of the Hindus, or the God of the Jews, or the God of the Bible.

I think these four points above are a very ineffective way of *"preaching"* the gospel. Paul was not preaching a mushy four points. Paul's gospel was something like this:

> *"Everyone, man, woman, boy or girl all over the world is lost. If they don't get saved, they will end up in conscious suffering in Hell for all eternity. These individuals are in sin, and God considers them to be sinners. God loved them as sinners. He sent his only begotten Son, the Lord Jesus Christ, to Calvary's cross to suffer, to bleed, and to die in their place in behalf of their sins. They must personally receive the Lord Jesus Christ as their Saviour by genuine heart-felt repentant faith plus nothing and minus nothing. Then and only then can God declare them righteous before Him."*

That is the gospel of the Lord Jesus Christ. That is something to believe. Christ loved you and wants to be your Saviour. After you have been saved, you should live for Christ.

The presentation of the gospel in that bulletin seems to me to be off base. It has the modern words and the modern flare. There is nothing about being "born-again" like the Lord Jesus said. There is nothing about being saved. The church that printed that bulletin is not a liberal church. They claim to be Fundamental, but are probably neo-evangelical. They do not use the terms that the Bible uses. They seem to be ashamed of the terms. I am not ashamed of any of the terms that the Bible uses. The Bible uses the term *"saved."* It talks about being *"born-again."* I do not think that these four little points on the back of that bulletin are going to save any sinners. Paul preached *"the faith which he once destroyed"* because Christ saved him and called him. Paul's life was dramatically changed.

Galatians 1:24

"And they glorified God in me" When they saw that Paul was now straight where he used to be crooked, they glorified God. The word, *"glorify,"* DOXAZO, means *"to cause the dignity and worth of some person or thing to become manifest and acknowledged."* Certainly we can glorify God in all that we do. Being saved and talking about God's dignity and worth glorifies God. My wife had a booklet which had a poem *"Are All The Children In."* You can read it on the next page. It tells a powerful story.

Are All The Children In?

I think ofttimes as the night draws nigh
Of an old house on the hill,
Of a yard all wide and blossom-starred
Where the children played at will.
And when the night at last came down
Hushing the merry din,
Mother would look around and ask,
"Are all the children in?"
'Tis many, and many a year since then,
And the old house on the hill
No longer echoes to childish feet
And the yard is still, so still.
But I see it all, as the shadows creep
And though many the years have been
Since then, I can still hear my mother ask,
"Are all the children in?"
I wonder if when the shadows fall
On our last short, earthly day,
When we say good-bye to the world outside ,
All tired with our childish play,
When we step out into that other Land
Where mother so long has been,
Will we hear her ask, just as of old,
"Are all the children in?"

By Florence Jones Hadley

We have many unsaved people all around this world. Are all of these people in? Are we doing our best to lead them to the Lord? That is the challenge the Lord would leave with us today.

Galatians Chapter Two

Galatians 2:1

"Then fourteen years after I went up again to Jerusalem with Barnabas, and took Titus with *me* also"
This *"fourteen years"* period is a reference to the time of the Jerusalem Council as mentioned in Acts 15:36-40. Paul had his first missionary journey and then returned to Jerusalem. There was a difference of opinion between Paul and Barnabas. Because of that, Paul did not take Barnabas with him on his second missionary journey. Paul wanted to take Silas, and Barnabas wanted to take John Mark. Christians today have differences also and can't work together.

- Acts 15:36-40
  And some days after **Paul said unto Barnabas, Let us go again and visit our brethren** in every city where we have preached the word of the Lord, *and see* how they do. And **Barnabas determined to take with them John, whose surname was Mark.** But **Paul thought not good** to take him with them, who departed from them from Pamphylia, and went not with them to the work. And **the contention was so sharp between them, that they departed asunder** one from the other: and so **Barnabas took Mark**, and sailed unto Cyprus; And **Paul chose Silas**, and departed, being recommended by the brethren unto the grace of God."

We see in Acts 12:25 that John Mark was originally with Paul and Barnabas on his first missionary journey. God called out Paul and Barnabas to the mission to which He had called them. God sent them forth as missionaries. John Mark went with them on this first missionary journey, but half way along the line John Mark went home (Acts 13:13). I guess he got home sick. He was not the stalwart missionary that Paul wanted to have with him on his second missionary journey. He said, in effect, *"No, I am not going to take him. Barnabas, if you want to take him, go right ahead."* So the difference of opinion was great between these two missionaries. It was decided that Paul would take Silas and go on his way. Barnabas took John Mark. We never hear much more about John Mark throughout the book of Acts. In 2 Timothy 4:11 Paul mentioned that Mark was then *"profitable . . . for the ministry."* Mark later wrote the Gospel that bears his name.

The Jerusalem Council in Acts 15 decided what would take place after Jews and Gentiles became Christians. After a person is saved and becomes a Christian, he or she is no longer considered by God to be a Jew or a Gentile. God considers them to be only "Christians." This Jerusalem Council decided that there were only four things they were to bring over from the law of Moses. They were not to bring over the ceremonial sacrifices like the Day of Passover and the Day of Atonement. **Christians who were formerly either Jews or Gentiles were not to follow any of the Jewish ceremonial requirements**. Circumcision (though it might be done for other reasons) was not to be practiced by Christians as a special part of the Jewish religion.

Only four things in Acts 15:29 for Christians

- **First**, they were to abstain from meats offered to idols. They were not to worship idols. That is definite.

- **Second**, they were not to eat blood. That is why the Jewish have Kosher killing where they slit the throat of animals and drain their blood.

- **Third**, they were not to eat anything strangled because when you strangle something, the blood is still in it. That is why you should not just wring the neck of the animal (such as a chicken) when you prepare your food. You need to slit the neck and drain the blood from the animal for it to be kosher.

- **Fourth**, they needed to abstain from fornication. Fornication is usually sexual relations before marriage, but in some contexts, it includes also these acts on the part of those who are married.

These four things were the only things that were to be brought over from the law of Moses. Fourteen years after the Lord Jesus had instructed him in the desert, Paul went up to Jerusalem and took part in the Jerusalem Council with Peter, James, and John who were the leaders in the early church. It is important to see that Paul brought Titus with him on his first missionary journey. Titus was later to become the pastor of the church at Crete, an island in the Mediterranean Sea. Paul wrote an entire book in the New Testament to Pastor

Titus, teaching him necessary truths concerning his personal and pastoral ministry on that isolated island. It must have been a privilege to have been taught by Paul the apostle. That is why it is important for us to know God's Word, to study God's Word, and to be taught by God through the ministries of the prophets of the Old Testament and the apostles of the New Testament.

Galatians 2:2

"And I went up by revelation, and communicated unto them that gospel which I preach among the Gentiles, but privately to them which were of reputation, lest by any means I should run, or had run, in vain."

"And I went up by revelation, and communicated unto them that gospel which I preach among the Gentiles, but privately to them which were of reputation" When Paul went to the Jerusalem Council recorded in Acts 15, he gave a report on the gospel that he was preaching. He had been preaching the gospel privately for fourteen years. This gospel was revealed to Paul by the Lord Jesus Christ Himself. He did not want to make any mistakes. While Paul had been preaching this gospel to the Gentiles, Peter, James, and John had been preaching to the Jews. There should be no contradiction, and there was no contradiction.

What was the gospel that Paul preached? Part of his gospel had to do with Christ as God's Lamb Who took away the sin of the world.

- **John 1:29**
  The next day John seeth Jesus coming unto him, and saith, **Behold the Lamb of God, which taketh away the sin of the world.**

The Lamb of God was the Lord Jesus Christ, God the Son, Who was sent by God the Father. The Lord Jesus Christ was perfect God and perfect Man. He was the Substitute for the sins of the entire world by shedding His blood in his death on the cross of Calvary. That is part of Paul's gospel. There are further parts of this gospel that included Christ's burial and bodily resurrection.

- **1 Corinthians 15:14**
  ¹ Moreover, brethren, I declare unto you the gospel which I preached unto you, which also ye have received, and wherein ye stand; ² By which also ye are saved, if ye keep in memory what I preached unto you, unless ye have believed in vain. ³ For I delivered unto you first of all that which I also received, how that **Christ died for our sins** according to the Scriptures; ⁴ And that **he was buried**, and that **he rose again the third day** according to the Scriptures:

There are still other parts of Paul's gospel that concern grace, faith, and works.
- **Ephesians 2:8-10**
  For **by grace** are ye saved **through faith**; and that not of yourselves: *it is* **the gift of God**: **Not of works**, lest any man should boast. For we are his workmanship, **created in Christ Jesus unto good works**, which God hath before ordained that we should walk in them.

Included in *"salvation"* is *"godly sorrow"* that *"worketh repentance"* (2 Corinthians 7:10). This speech must be properly and Scripturally understood also. With proper and genuine faith in the Lord Jesus Christ for salvation, there must be a proper repentance of sin and a desire to *"walk in newness of life"* (Romans 6:4). God warns that *"the devils also **believe** and tremble"* (James 2:19) and yet are not saved. Their *"belief"* is not a proper and genuine belief. There is no repentance and willingness to change their direction.

- **2 Corinthians 7:10**
  For **godly sorrow worketh repentance to salvation** not to be repented of: but the sorrow of the world worketh death.

Though there are many other things that Paul preached which might be included in Paul's *"gospel,"* these are some of the most important parts. Those of us who are saved through genuine faith in Christ are saved not by what we do (our works) but are saved by trusting in what Christ has done for us on the cross of Calvary as He died for our sins. That makes us saved. That is the gospel that Paul preached.

Notice Paul said *"that gospel which I preach."* That word *"preach,"* KERUSSO, means *"to proclaim after the manner of a herald always with the suggestion of formality, gravity and an authority which must be listened to and obeyed."* A herald is one whom the king sent forth with a message that he was to proclaim to the king's subjects. Paul was a herald for the Lord Jesus Christ. A herald does not alter the message. A herald does not change the king's decree. A herald simply declares the message. Those of us who preach the gospel cannot change the Words of God. We cannot change the gospel. We are to be heralds. That is all we are. We must *"proclaim after the manner of a herald."* A herald spoke with *"formality, gravity, and authority."* He spoke in a manner which *"must be listened to and obeyed."* That is the force of this word. Paul was a preacher of the gospel of the truth unto the Gentiles.

"lest by any means I should run, or had run, in vain"
Paul did not want to be *"running"* in vain. That word for *"run,"* TRECHO, means *"to spend one's strength in performing or attaining something."* Paul did not want to be expending all of his strength in vain. That word for *"in vain,"* KENOS, is used *"metaphorically, of endeavors, labors, acts, which result in nothing, vain, fruitless, without effect."* In other words this could mean

"spinning your wheels." If you have ever been stuck in a snow bank, you know what it is like to spin and spin your wheels and yet go nowhere. That is what Paul did not want to have happen to him. Paul communicated to the apostles what he had received directly from the Lord Jesus Christ so that his labors would not result in fruitlessness and ineffectiveness. Have you ever felt that way? Have you ever felt like you were spinning your wheels? Have you ever had a day like that where you did not know what you accomplished? That is what Paul did not want to have happen. He did not want to run his race *"in vain."* God does not want us to live our lives after we are saved by His grace with no purpose. Our purpose should be to serve and glorify our Saviour.

Galatians 2:3

"But neither Titus, who was with me, being a Greek, was compelled to be circumcised" This is kind of strange wording. He uses the word *"neither"* and then the word *"compelled."* What it means is that Titus was not under any obligation to be circumcised because he was a Greek and not a Jew. In spite of that, the Judaizers compelled Titus to be circumcised. That was a terrible thing. Titus, who later became a pastor on the island of Crete, was compelled to be circumcised even though he was not a Jew. He was forced to be circumcised and to take part in the Mosaic law. This aggravated Paul, and it should have aggravated him. It is my understanding that some male babies today are circumcised for various reasons, health being one. There has been a recent argument by some in the medical field that says that we should not circumcise male children. This was done here as part of the Jewish law, and Paul was against it completely.

Galatians 2:4

"And that because of false brethren unawares brought in, who came in privily to spy out our liberty which we have in Christ Jesus, that they might bring us into bondage"

"And that because of false brethren unawares brought in" These *"false brethren"* were the reason that Titus was forced into complying with the law of Moses. There is nothing worse than a *"false"* brother. It is one thing if there is an unsaved person teaching. They are lost. You are not as likely to listen to them. But when they call themselves *"brethren,"* and say that they believe the Bible, we have to be extra careful when they teach false doctrine and/or heresy.

There are two words that need some definitions: (1) **"apostasy"** and (2) **"heresy."**

Apostasy is departing from the faith and having no connection with it. It means that the one holding to it is lost.

Heresy, on the other hand, is holding to some of the faith but departing from some of it in a certain area or areas. Heresy is much more difficult to detect.

Apostasy is out and out denial of the Lord Jesus Christ's miracles, His deity, His bodily resurrection, and all these fundamentals of the faith.

Heresy, however, is something that is taught by *"false brethren."* They are saved, but they depart from the faith in some points. This is a serious thing, and it is more difficult to discern.

John MacArthur is an example of a leading Christian speaker with a wide international following and a popular ministry who teaches a very serious heresy about the blood of the Lord Jesus Christ. He teaches that the blood of Christ is not necessary for salvation because he does not believe the word, *blood,* really means blood. For him **and his followers**, blood is a metonym or figure of speech for death, but Christ's blood does not mean blood. He says that we are not saved by the blood of Christ but by the death of Christ. He simply equates the two and says blood means death. A further part of this heretical teaching is that he claims that Christ's blood was merely "human blood" which is no different in any way from the blood of every other human being that ever was born. That is a heretical teaching, even though John MacArthur is a professing Christian. False brethren are difficult to detect.

A second illustration of a heresy among professing Christians concerns the death of the Lord Jesus Christ. I believe that it is a heresy to teach that the Lord Jesus Christ died **only** for the sins of the "elect" rather than for the sins of the entire human race. The Lord Jesus did die for the sins of the elect, but He also died for the sins of every sinner of the whole world who has ever been born. Their question is did He shed His blood needlessly? No, He shed His blood for the forgiveness of the sins of all the world.

Does that mean I am teaching Universalism? Does that mean I am teaching that if Christ died for all, then all are saved? No, I am not teaching that. The Bible does not teach this. The Bible says that eternal life is a gift, but we must accept that gift. We must receive that gift. Christ died for the sins of the whole world, but we must accept that free gift. If we do not receive His gift by faith in Christ, we are lost and will end up in the everlasting fire of Hell. I believe this is one of the teachings of *"false brethren."*

"who came in privily to spy out our liberty which we have in Christ Jesus" Paul said these false brethren came in secretly and with stealth so that the church was unaware that they were there. This is what God warns us about in Acts.

- Acts 20:29
  For I know this, that **after my departing shall grievous wolves enter in among you,** not sparing the flock.

We have to be very careful of those who profess faith in Christ but are *"false brethren."* We must stand by the teachings of the Scriptures. I do not want to teach anything false from this pulpit or from anywhere else. These *"false brethren"* of Paul's day were called Judaizers because they wanted to bring the Christians into the Jewish faith again. They wanted to bring them right back under the bondage of the law of Moses.

"that they might bring us into bondage:" Notice that these *"false brethren"* wanted to bring the Galatian Christians into *"bondage."* The word, *"bondage,"* KATADOULOO, is a compound containing the word "slave" (DOULOO) in it. It means *"to bring into bondage, enslave."* They wanted to bring the Christians into the slavery of the law of Moses. That is what the law was. It was a slave master. The law could never save a soul. All the law could do was to point out the fact that we are sinners, lost, and bound for Hell. That is all the law could do. None of us could keep the law. The Lord Jesus kept the law, and when we trust Christ as our Saviour we are free from the law. He is the One who has kept every single part of God's righteous standard. These Judaizers wanted to bring these Christians back into bondage. Many things bring us back into bondage. Doing the will of another is what bondage is. Bad habits bring a person into bondage. Pornography brings a person into bondage. Drugs bring a person into bondage. Christ can break this bondage, and only Christ can break any bondage.

I just heard this week from a lady in Canada who asked if I could recommend a candidate to be a preacher for her church. She said her previous pastor left because he was a pornographer. His father before him was a pornographer. I told this woman that I would rather not recommend someone to go into this furnace of fire and possibly have him to be burned up in that little church in Canada as he faced the results of these former problems.

It is a sad thing indeed. These Judaizers wanted to bring these Christians into the bondage of the law. If Paul had not written this little book of Galatians, we would not have the tools to correct such a situation.

Galatians 2:5

"To whom we gave place by subjection, no, not for an hour; that the truth of the gospel might continue with you:"

"To whom we gave place by subjection, no, not for an hour:" Paul said he did not submit to the Judaizers' teaching for one second. He would not let the Judaizers bring them back under the bondage of the law of Moses. These Judaizers demanded that Gentile Christians should be circumcised. But Paul would have none of it. We must take our stand today as well on matters of a similar nature.

There are people who say that water baptism saves you. This is the teaching of Rome. This is the teaching of some modernists. They say that water baptism gives that baby regeneration. The Church of Christ teaches falsely that if you have not been baptized by immersion, you are lost. I believe this is a false and unscriptural teaching.

"that the truth of the gospel might continue with you"

Paul wanted the *"truth of the gospel,"* clean, plain, and true, to *"continue."* That is what we want to do in the world in which we live. The *"truth of the gospel"* is what sets us free from the bondage of the law.

- **John 8:32**

  And ye shall know the truth, and **the truth shall make you free**.

The truth is that the law of Moses is not for the Christian. The law of Moses is bondage. When we know the truth of the Word of God, we will be set free.

- **John 8:36**

  If the Son therefore shall make you free, **ye shall be free indeed**.

Jesus sets us *"free indeed"* from sin. The Lord Jesus can make us free from sin's bondages of all kinds whether it be pornography, hard drugs, alcohol, tobacco, prostitution, homosexuality, gambling, cursing, or even the law of Moses. Nobody but the Lord Jesus can set us free. We who are saved were once in the bondage of the Devil,

- **2 Timothy 2:26**

  And *that* they may recover themselves out of **the snare of the devil, who are taken captive by him at his will**.

We do not have to do anything to be in Satan's bondage. We are in bondage from birth. We are *"in the snare of the devil"* from our birth.

The Lord Jesus Christ told even the religious Pharisees that they had the *"devil"* as their father.

- **John 8:44**

  Ye are of *your* father the devil, and the lusts of your father ye will do. He was a murderer from the beginning, and abode not in the truth, because there is no truth in him. When he speaketh a lie, he speaketh of his own: for he is a liar, and the father of it.

One example of the false teaching of Bishop Westcott and Professor Hort was their belief in the universal *"fatherhood of God."* The quotations are found in my book, *The Theological Heresies of Westcott and Hort* (**BFT #595**). They believed that all people are the children of God because they are under the fatherhood of God. No, there are two fatherhoods. Before we are saved, we are

Galatians 2:5-6   **41**

under the fatherhood of Satan. We are under the bondage of the Devil. When we are saved through faith in Christ, we no longer have to serve Satan. We no longer have to serve our flesh. The Lord Jesus Christ is our Saviour. He can set us free from anything that would bring us into bondage. The *"truth of the gospel"* should stay with us permanently and continue.

Galatians 2:6

"But of these who seemed to be somewhat, (whatsoever they were, it maketh no matter to me: God accepteth no man's person:) for they who seemed *to be somewhat* in conference added nothing to me:"

"But of these who seemed to be somewhat" Many people today *"seem to be somewhat."* That is, they think they are more important than they are. The question is what does God think about us.

"(whatsoever they were, it maketh no matter to me" The ones spoken of here were, perhaps, the leaders of the church. Paul's gospel was straight. It was directly from the Lord Jesus Christ and sanctioned by Him. Peter, James, John, and the other leaders of that church added nothing to the gospel. They all agreed that this was exactly what Paul should preach. Paul was not bashful or afraid in the presence of the authorities in the church because his authority was from Christ. He got his message directly from Heaven.

"God accepteth no man's person:) for they who seemed *to be somewhat* in conference added nothing to me" If you and I know the truths of the Bible, we should not let any leader in authority, or even a *"conference"* of many leaders, lead us astray from those Biblical truths. We should stand by the Scripture.

- Acts 10:34
  Then Peter opened *his* mouth, and said, Of a truth I perceive that **God is no respecter of persons**:

God considers each saved believer in the same way. He does not treat one person in one way and another person in a different way. He does not accept any man's *"person."*

- Romans 2:11
  For there is **no respect of persons with God**.
- Ephesians 6:9
  And, ye masters, do the same things unto them, forbearing threatening: knowing that your Master also is in Heaven; **neither is there respect of persons with him**.

God does not care who you or I are. You and I are on an equal footing. The greatest sinner in the world or the littlest sinner in the world are both equal in

the eyes of God. They are both sinners and are bound for Hell. The biggest saint and the littlest saint are on the same footing in the eyes of God. We are all saved through the grace of Christ. There is no difference. There are many verses on this teaching.
- **Colossians 3:25**
  But he that doeth wrong shall receive for the wrong which he hath done: and **there is no respect of persons.**
- **James 2:1**
  My brethren, have not the faith of our Lord Jesus Christ, the Lord of glory, **with respect of persons.**
- **James 2:9**
  But if ye have respect to persons, ye commit sin, and are convinced of the law as transgressors.
- **1 Peter 1:17**
  And if ye call on the Father, **who without respect of persons judgeth** according to every man's work, pass the time of your sojourning *here* in fear:
- **Jude 16**
  These are murmurers, complainers, walking after their own lusts; and their mouth speaketh great swelling *words*, **having men's persons in admiration because of advantage.**

Many respect persons *"because of advantage."* They say, in effect,
"If you wash my hand, I will wash yours. If you scratch my back, I will scratch your back. What can I do for you, and what can you do for me. If you can do something for me, I will bow down and respect your person."
Each saved Christian is needed by the Lord for His ministry and work.

Galatians 2:7

"But contrariwise, when they saw that the gospel of the uncircumcision was committed unto me, as *the gospel of the circumcision was* unto Peter" These Galatian Christians saw that God had given to Paul the truth of the gospel to the Gentiles. He was sent to the Gentiles with a message, and he delivered that message faithfully. They also saw that the *"gospel of the circumcision"* was committed unto Peter. They were glad for that. They did not add anything more to it. They could see that this was a fact.

Galatians 2:8

"(For he that wrought effectually in Peter to the apostleship of the circumcision, the same was mighty in me toward the Gentiles:)"

"For he that wrought effectually in Peter to the apostleship of the circumcision" The One Who *"wrought effectually"* in Peter and Paul was the Lord Jesus Christ and the Holy Spirit of God. You and I can accomplish nothing for God by our flesh. It is only the Holy Spirit of God Who enables us to do what we need to do for the Lord. It must be by means of the Spirit of God if we are to witness effectually for Christ. It must be by means of the Spirit of God if we are to pray effectually. It must be by means of the Spirit of God if we are to preach effectually about the things of the Lord. It must be by means of the Spirit of God if we are to overcome the things of this flesh.

If you are born-again, you have the Spirit of God indwelling your body.

- 1 Corinthians 6:19-20
  What? know ye not that **your body is the temple of the Holy Ghost *which is* in you,** which ye have of God, and ye are not your own? For ye are bought with a price: therefore **glorify God in your body, and in your spirit, which are God's.**

The Holy Spirit is the One Who can effectually work in your life and in your body. There are many different kinds of fleshly sins. Even though we are saved, we still have our old flesh. When we are saved, the flesh is not eliminated though some churches erroneously teach "sinless perfection" or "entire sanctification" with the total elimination of the sin nature. If you are married, ask your spouse if you still have your flesh. If you are a son or a daughter, ask your parent if you still have your flesh. If you are a mom or a dad, ask your children if you still have your flesh. You have plenty of flesh. The Person who overcomes the things of the flesh is God the Holy Spirit Who lives inside your body if you are born-again. If you are not born-again you have the evil spirit from Satan. It is called *"the spirit that now worketh in the children of disobedience"* (Ephesians 2:2). .

"the same was mighty in me toward the Gentiles" The same power of God the Holy Spirit was *"mighty"* in Paul in his ministry to the Gentiles. This is the power of God. Even today, you can sense the power of God (or its lack) as a preacher preaches or as a Sunday School teacher teaches or as you witness. Paul was effective not because he was educated, not because he was brought up at the feet of Gamaliel, not because he knew the law of Moses, not because he knew the entire Old Testament backwards and forwards, not even because he met Jesus Christ personally on the road to Damascus and had a personal conversion. He was effective because God's Holy Spirit inside of his body and spirit effectually worked in him. If the Holy Spirit of God effectually works in you and in me, we are going to be successful and mighty also in the ministry that God has for us.

In our **Bible For Today Baptist Church**, we are not Pentecostal. We are not charismatics. We are Baptists. But we do not minimize the power of the Holy Spirit of God in the bodies of Christians. The Holy Spirit of God must be empowering us if we are going to have any power at all with the Lord. That does not mean we speak in tongues or have these special sign gifts. We do not believe these gifts are with us today. We believe those were sign gifts that were given at the foundation of the church. When the Bible was completed, those sign gifts left. But we still believe that the Spirit of God must empower Christians in their ministry for the Lord Jesus Christ. If we have been redeemed, we do not belong to ourselves anymore.

- **1 Corinthians 6:19-20**
  What? know ye not that **your body is the temple of the Holy Ghost** *which is* in you, which ye have of God, and **ye are not your own**? For ye are bought with a price: therefore glorify God in your body, and in your spirit, which are God's.

Christ bought the Christians with the price of His own shed blood on Calvary. Because of this, He owns you lock, stock, and barrel. He owns your body, and he owns your spirit. That is what Christians need to hear, believe, understand, and practice. Some Christians say they believe this, but many of them do not seem to practice it today. They do not live like God really owns them. They do not believe Christ owns them. They do not act like they are bought with a price. They do not live like they believe that they should glorify Christ in their body. They want their body to do what they want it to do. They say, in effect, *"I'll go where I want to go, I'll do what I want to do, I'll eat what I want to eat, I'll drink what I want to drink."*

Let me tell it to you straight, if you will not misunderstand me. This ownership is very much like a form of Divine and very loving "slavery." We were on the slave market of sin, in servitude and bondage to the devil. In loving kindness and grace, God bought us off that slave market of sin by the payment of the price of the blood of His only begotten Son, the Lord Jesus Christ. By this purchase, God now owns us. We have become His life-long "slaves." We are to serve Him for the rest of our lives without regard to our own wishes, plans, and purposes. We must be desirous of doing His will rather than our own. Do not misunderstand me, I am NOT talking about human "slavery." I do not believe in that. How many Christians do you know who live in this sold-out manner, serving willingly the Lord Jesus Christ? I wish there were many more than there are in the world today.

It is the Spirit of God Who effectually worked in Peter and in Paul. Why do you think that Paul was willing to go on his three missionary journeys? He was on his second missionary journey as he is writing this book of Galatians. He went all over that part of the world on all three of his missionary journeys. On his fourth journey he went to Rome at the government's expense. He did not have to pay a dime. The whole crew almost died on that ship to Rome because of a terrible storm. Why do you suppose he continued? Just one or two of those things which opposed Paul would have dropped most of us to our feet. We might say, *"I'm not going on another missionary journey. I'm not going to preach. I'm not going to lead another soul to Christ. I'm just going to quit."* Paul did not say this. Why? Because the Holy Spirit of God lived in Paul's body. He was bought with a price, and he was Christ's humble servant-slave. The Lord was able to be glorified by Paul's dedication to Him.

Galatians 2:9

"And when James, Cephas, and John, who seemed to be pillars, perceived the grace that was given unto me, they gave to me and Barnabas the right hands of fellowship; that we *should go* unto the heathen, and they unto the circumcision." Here are the big three apostles probably at the historical Jerusalem Council mentioned in Acts 15. In this Council, James was evidently the spokesman. Cephas, another name for Peter, was there, as well as the apostle John. These seasoned apostles could see the power of God in Paul's life. They heard about the churches that he had established on his first missionary journey. The *"right hands of fellowship"* means that Paul and Barnabas were accepted by the rest of the apostles. When people join a church, usually they have extended to them the *"right hand of fellowship."* This is a Biblical usage. Paul was commissioned to go to the heathen Gentiles. Peter, James, and John were going to minister to the Jews.

Notice the first part of verse nine. It says *"who seemed to be pillars."* Pillars are leaders. Are you a pillar? Many churches have their pillars. Some pastors are pilloried (held up to scorn) by the pillars. Pillars are important. If you have a building that is held up by pillars, what happens when the pillars fall? Part of the roof falls. Sometimes there are several pillars holding up a room. What happens when those pillars fall? The ceiling falls. I hope that each one in this room are pillars that will support a building of the Lord Jesus Christ so that it will not collapse.

The story of Samson shows us how pillars support a building. It was Samson who, because of his love for silly women, lost his power with God. A woman will cause a man to loose his power with God. A man will cause a woman to loose her power with God. In this case this woman coaxed Samson into telling her the source of his strength. She coaxed him into telling her that he was a Nazarite. He could not cut his hair. Not that his strength was in his hair, but he was told not to cut his hair. When his hair was cut, his power was cut. The Spirit of God left him. They put out his eyes and used him like an animal to grind grain. Finally, they had a big feast and made sport of Samson. They all laughed at him because he was blind.

Samson asked a little lad to take him over to the pillars of the building. There were thousands of wicked Philistines who were enemies of God in this building. Samson was shown the pillars. He prayed to the Lord once more to return his strength. He realized he was a sinner. He realized he was wrong in his connection to these wicked women.

- **Judges 16:30**
  And Samson said, **Let me die with the Philistines**. And he bowed himself with all his might; and the house fell upon the lords, and upon all the people that were therein.

A pillar is an important thing. I hope that each of us in our homes and communities are *"pillars"* of our Lord Jesus Christ. We must be pillars and supporters of the truth.

- **1 Timothy 3:15**
  But if I tarry long, that thou mayest know how thou oughtest to behave thyself in the house of God, which is the church of the living God, **the pillar and ground of the truth**.

That is what we have here a local church. As such, it is one of the *"pillars and ground of the truth." "James, Cephas, and John"* were all pillars of the church.

Galatians 2:10

"Only *they would* that we should remember the poor; the same which I also was forward to do."

I believe this is referring to the believing Christians who were *"poor"* rather than the poor of the world generally. The Scriptures do not teach a "social gospel" popular with the modernistic and new-evangelical world that teaches we should feed the world, house the world, clothe the world, and give jobs to the world. The believers' responsibility is to their own families and to those in the family of God.

- **Romans 15:26**
  For it hath pleased them of Macedonia and Achaia to make a certain **contribution for the <u>poor saints</u> which are at Jerusalem**.

We are members of a family. We are responsible for those who are not able to do things. I believe that we should first take care of the poor and the needy who are of the household of faith. That is the first line of attack.

There is nothing wrong with feeding. There is nothing wrong with clothing. There is nothing wrong with housing. We are all sitting here well fed, housed, and clothed. I am not against that. But feeding the world is not the prime ministry of the local church. The ministry that the Lord Jesus Christ has given the churches does not include feeding, clothing, and housing the poor of this world. We would run out of money, first of all. There are billions without food, clothing, and housing. The second thing we would run out of is personnel. How many born-again believers do we have to take care of all of this? When the Lord Jesus sent out His twelve he told them to take no bread or money.

- **Mark 6:8**
 And commanded them that they should **take nothing** for *their* journey, save a staff only; **no scrip, no bread, no money** in *their* purse:

He did not commission them to feed the world. He said that the disciples should be fed by those to whom they were ministering. He did not command them to house the world or find jobs for the world.

If there are some believers who are members of our believing body and are in trouble or poor or need our help, then we should help them all we can. If we can individually help other people in the world in exceptional cases, that is all right. But first of all we must help fellow believers. We should first provide for our own family of faith.

- **1 Timothy 5:8**
 But if any provide not for his own, and specially for those of his own house, **he hath denied the faith**, and is worse than an infidel.

He has denied the faith. He provides not for the things of his own house. We have a household of faith made up of born-again Christian believers. If anyone needs helps, we should seek to provide such help.

That is one of the wonderful things that we have in our missionary ministry to Liberia, West Africa. Twenty-five per cent of all that comes into our church goes to home and foreign missions. At present, we support five foreign and four home missionaries. Pastor St. Solomon Joah is our missionary in Liberia. As of now, he has a broadcast on three radio stations. He helps those believers who are in need. The people of Liberia lack sufficient rice and other food. They are not only poor in body, but also they are poor in Spirit. They do not have the gospel. Pastor Joah preaches the gospel. He is preaching the gospel of the grace of God all over Liberia.

The gospel is making inroads in the apostasy and unbelief in his country. Mrs. Waite and I have been over in his church for Bible conferences twice in Liberia and once in Sierra Leone. It was bad enough then, believe me. They did not have much of anything then, but now they have even less. He praises God for you folks who have helped him. The Lord has allowed our local church to assist Pastor Joah over in Liberia. He preaches the same as I preach. He is a separatist, Fundamentalist Baptist preacher. He uses the King James Bible. He defends the truth of the Word of God. As I said before, Mrs. Waite and I have been with him in Africa three times for a Bible conferences. I know what he teaches and what he believes. He has about two hundred in his local church. He keeps leading them to the Lord and bringing them into the church. By supporting Pastor Joah we are ministering to the poor believers in West Africa.

Galatians 2:11

"But when Peter was come to Antioch, I withstood him to the face, because he was to be blamed."

"But when Peter was come to Antioch" Wait a minute. Here, Paul is rebuking the supposed first pope of Rome, Peter. He was not the first Pope of Rome as the Roman Catholics are teaching. In this passage, the apostle Paul is rebuking the apostle Peter.

"I withstood him to the face, because he was to be blamed" There are people who say that we should never rebuke or criticize a Christian for any reason. Just let them do what they want to do. Never publicly expose them. Here in the book of Galatians, Paul did just that very thing. He did it because Peter was wrong and was to be blamed. Notice he named names. That is another thing that many people do not like. They do not like us to name names. When people are doing wrong things and when doctrinal errors are there, the Bible teaches that we are to name names and expose them.

- Ephesians 5:11
  And <u>have no fellowship with the unfruitful works of darkness, but rather reprove them</u>.

How can a person know what we are talking about if we simply say some preacher or some man or some evangelist that believes the heathen can be saved without ever hearing the gospel or believing in Jesus Christ. If I just said that, nobody would know to whom I was referring. If I named the name of Billy Graham who said that recently on the Robert Schuller television show, everybody would know exactly whom I meant. We must steer clear of some of the heresies of Billy Graham. He started out one way, and he is ending up quite another way. When he said that the heathen can be saved without even hearing of Christ, Robert Schuller said, *"Oh, I am so glad to hear you say that, Billy."* Paul publicly rebuked Peter. He named names. How about John MacArthur who says that the blood of Christ cannot save us? He says the blood of Christ cannot cleanse us. He says that Christ had human blood just like ours. He says that "blood" is merely a metonym for "death" and doesn't really mean "blood" at all.

Galatians 2:11

- **1 John 1:7**
  But if we walk in the light, as he is in the light, we have fellowship one with another, and <u>the blood of Jesus Christ his Son cleanseth us from all sin.</u>

  Paul named the name of Peter and withstood him. There was a clash between these two Christian leaders. Paul was not mean to Peter. I do not like to be mean to anybody. I try to be as gracious as I can be, but I attempt to be very clear in these matters. This is what the Bible expects Christians and especially Pastors to do. Those who never name anybody would not be like Paul. Paul came to Antioch in Syria north of Jerusalem. That is where Paul and Barnabas were called to be missionaries. In that place, Paul had a face-to-face confrontation with Peter. Notice, it was a face-to-face confrontation. When some people rebuke others, they do not want a face-to-face confrontation. The Bible is clear, even with pastors-bishops-elders and other leaders.

- **1 Timothy 5:19-20**
  Against an elder receive not an accusation, but before two or three witnesses. **<u>Them that sin rebuke before all, that others also may fear</u>**.

  There is another thing about rebuking fellow believers and leaders to consider. Some people believe that before you can say anything about anybody, you have to write them or call them first. If that were the case, we would have to call the heretic Harry Emerson Fosdick or some of the other modernists. When people publicly--either on radio, television, or in books--say or print things that are false, that is public. Now, it is different if someone has a personal sin that is private where nobody knows about it. It has never been publicized. It has never been on the radio. It has never been on television. If you and I know about it, we are not to publicize it until first we go to that individual and try to win him or her back to the right way. That is what the Scripture says we are to do. If it is a public thing and everybody knows about it, then we can expose it publicly.

  As quoted above in 1 Timothy 5:10, Paul talks about, *"them that sin."* That means the pastors, bishops or elders. Timothy was to *"rebuke before all, that others also may fear."* That is a command. Paul did this in his writing, and it stands as a benchmark in the New Testament to show us two things about leaders.

  (1) One--that leaders do make mistakes.
  (2) Two--that when they do make mistakes, those who have the Biblical position, have all the facts, and are led of the Holy Spirit should rebuke them and straighten them out, if possible, as Paul did to Peter.

Galatians 2:12

"For before that certain came from James, he did eat with the Gentiles: but when they were come, he withdrew and separated himself, fearing them which were of the circumcision"

"For before that certain came from James, he did eat with the Gentiles: but when they were come, he withdrew and separated himself" This is an explanation of verse eleven. Here is the reason why Paul rebuked Peter to his face. Here is the reason that Peter was to be blamed. Peter regularly ate with the Gentiles. He saw no problem with that. But when James, who was a Jewish leader, came for a visit, Peter stopped eating with these same Gentiles.

My question is this? Do you and I act the same no matter who is around? Or do we have special actions for special people? This is what Peter did. He played up to the Gentiles. Part of the Jewish law was that the Jews were not to associate with the Gentiles. Peter was being all things to all men and eating with the Gentiles. Now, if that were right, should he not be the same when the Jews came from Jerusalem? Should he not keep on eating with the Gentiles?

"fearing them which were of the circumcision" Peter separated himself because he feared those of the circumcision. He feared what they would say about him. Peter was wrong. He should not have segregated the Gentiles and the Jews. If they were saved, they were Christians. In Christ there is neither Jew nor Gentile.

- Galatians 3:28
  There is neither Jew nor Greek, there is neither bond nor free, there is neither male nor female: for ye are all one in Christ Jesus.

If we are saved, we are neither Jews nor Gentiles. That may have been our background, but we are members of the body of Christ. Now we are Christians. That is a whole different classification. Is there a double standard? Are we hypocrites? That is an important question that we should ask ourselves.

Separation is Scriptural. We are to separate from evil. We are to separate from false doctrine if it is done in a proper way and for the proper reason. Peter separated himself from those Gentiles because he knew that those Judaizers would point the finger at him, and blame him for associating with these terrible, wicked Gentiles. So, he separated himself for the wrong reasons.

We can fear no man if we are following the Lord Jesus Christ and his Word.

- **Proverbs 25:25**
  The fear of man bringeth a snare: but whoso putteth his trust in the LORD shall be safe.

We are to fear no man. We are only to fear our Saviour, the Lord Jesus Christ. That was the reason that Paul rebuked Peter and withstood him to the face. Paul went right up to him and said, *"Peter, you're wrong."* This is not easy, but it is what we have to do when the occasion demands it.

Galatians 2:13
"And the other Jews dissembled likewise with him; insomuch that Barnabas also was carried away with their dissimulation"

"And the other Jews dissembled likewise with him" Here *"other Jews dissembled."* The force of that word is that these Jews were acting hypocritically. They acted in a hypocritical manner. Peter was a leader. When leaders fall, many of the non-leaders fall with them. When the leader is crooked, some followers might also be crooked. Some followers stay straight no matter what the leader does. That is what they ought to do. Some of these Jews dissembled and were hypocritical like Peter was.

"insomuch that Barnabas also was carried away with their dissimulation" Barnabas who had been under the ministry of Paul for many years was commissioned from the church of Antioch in Acts chapter 13.
- **Acts 13:2**
  As they ministered to the Lord, and fasted, the Holy Ghost said, **Separate me Barnabas and Saul for the work** whereunto I have called them.

These men are close associates. When you get a leader who is leading people astray, he might get other leaders, who ought to know better, to go astray. When Paul writes to the Galatian Christians, he had to set it straight. To set it straight he even had to rebuke both Peter and Barnabas because they were wrong. They were hypocrites, and Paul was going to set them straight. In doing this, I am sure Paul was not popular. But that was not his main goal in life. His main goal in life was to please the Lord Jesus Christ Who had saved him, and called him to be His apostle.

Galatians 2:14

"But when I saw that they walked not uprightly according to the truth of the gospel, I said unto Peter before *them* all, If thou, being a Jew, livest after the manner of Gentiles, and not as do the Jews, why compellest thou the Gentiles to live as do the Jews?"

"But when I saw that they walked not uprightly according to the truth of the gospel" He saw that they were not walking uprightly. That is a beautiful Greek word, ORTHOPODEO. It means literally, "straight foot." We get the word "orthopedic" from that, like orthopedic shoes. They did not walk in a straight line or on a straight course. They were walking in a curved path. They were off the path. We need to measure everything according to God's truth of the gospel. The Lord Jesus Christ saved us by His grace through faith. We are not saved by works of the law. That would not be walking *"uprightly according to the truth of the gospel."*

"I said unto Peter before *them* all, If thou, being a Jew, livest after the manner of Gentiles, and not as do the Jews, why compellest thou the Gentiles to live as do the Jews?" Peter was walking like the Gentiles walked, but when the Judaizers came, he stopped walking that way. Peter changed and went back to walking with the Jews while they were around. By these actions, Peter was numbered with the other Judaizers who were disturbing the Gentile Christians. They were saying to the Gentile Christians that once you are saved by faith in Christ, you must keep the law and the ordinances and be circumcised. He said that they must do all of the Jewish laws. Paul said, in effect, *"Why are you telling these Gentiles they must live like Jews when you are walking with the Gentiles? You are doing wrong."*

What if we had to live under the law of Moses? Most of us here in the audience are Gentiles by birth. If we are born-again, we are now Christians. Just think what we would have to do if we had to live by the Law of Moses. I counted up one day in my Bible the number of obligatory sacrifices the Jews had to offer each year. They numbered over 1,297. In addition to this number there would be sacrifices for every sin and trespass each individual committed. If we who are saved had to do this, it would be a burdensome thing. If the Christian churches would have started out on the wrong foot back in the first century, that would all be upon us today. Paul wanted to set this straight. That is why he wrote the book of Galatians. That is why he openly rebuked and withstood Peter.

There are times and places when you have to stand up for the Lord Jesus Christ. Here in the book of Galatians was a time when Paul had to stand up full measure against Peter who had been a Christian long before Paul. Peter had walked with Christ for three-and-a-half years. He was also the apostle who had denied Christ three times. Paul stood up against Peter because of the truth of the gospel. He stood for a proper cause. Praise God that he did!

Galatians 2:15

"We who are Jews by nature, and not sinners of the Gentiles," Paul says that Peter and he were Jews *"by nature,"* that is, by birth. The Gentiles were just sinners before they came to Christ. Our forefathers were idol worshipers. They worshiped Satan and everything else. We have some Gentiles here in this United States of America who are still as lost as they can be. The Jews insulted the Gentiles and called them dogs. The Jews thought that they were superior to everybody else. An Orthodox Jew is said to spit when they talk about the Christian faith.

Galatians 2:16

"Knowing that a man is not justified by the works of the law, but by the faith of Jesus Christ, even we have believed in Jesus Christ, that we might be justified by the faith of Christ, and not by the works of the law: for by the works of the law shall no flesh be justified."

"Knowing that a man is not justified by the works of the law" Even the Jews of the Old Testament knew that they could never be justified by the works of the law. That word, *"justified,"* means *"to be declared absolutely righteous in the eyes of God."* We are not righteous because of what we do. We are not made righteous by keeping the works of the law. We have to trust the Lord Jesus Christ as our personal Saviour and be born-again by faith in Him. He who fulfilled all the law of Moses on our behalf can justify us. We believe by faith and are justified or made righteous. We can be "in Christ." If we are in Christ, we do not do the works of the law. The books are clean because of what Jesus Christ did for us. Every time we sin here on earth, the books are dirty. If we are saved by faith in Christ, we have a clean page in Heaven. There is no way that we can keep this page clean except by the blood of Jesus Christ which cleanses us from all sin.

- 1 John 1:7
  But if we walk in the light, as he is in the light, we have fellowship one with another, and **the blood of Jesus Christ his Son cleanseth us from all sin.**

Even though we are sinners down here, the Lord makes us white. We cannot say that Christians do not sin. That is contrary to Scripture.

- **1 John 1:10**
  If we say that we have not sinned, we make him a liar, and his word is not in us.

There are some people who teach sinless perfection. Just ask their spouse if they are perfect. Just ask their son or daughter if they are perfect. We are declared righteous by faith in Christ but this is not necessarily practical righteousness. It gives us a righteous standing and justification in the courts of Heaven. We who are saved should seek to live righteously here on earth in order to match our perfect standing with the Lord in Heaven.

"but by the faith of Jesus Christ, even we have believed in Jesus Christ" It says that we are saved *"by the faith of Jesus Christ."* There are two kinds of genitives in the Greek language. There is an objective genitive and a subjective genitive. I can explain it this way. When you say a person has a *"love of golf"* or a *"love of sports"* or a *"love of swimming,"* you are saying that this person has a love **for** golf, sports, and swimming. It does not mean that golf, sports, or swimming loves him. 2 Corinthians 5:14 says *"the love of Christ constraineth us."* Notice that word *"of."* It is the objective genitive. It is my love **for** Christ. If it were taken as a subjective genitive, then it would mean the love of Christ for us. Here it is the objective genitive. It is my faith **in** Christ that justifies me. My faith toward Christ saves me from my sin.

There are some people who are confused by this genitive. I have had people phone about this. They believe that everybody who is saved is saved by Jesus Christ's faith. That would mean that the Lord Jesus Christ would have to have faith for everybody that is saved. This is a strange doctrine. I think this is connected with hyper-Calvinism where only the elect are saved. So Christ's faith saves the elect. I tell these people that this verse is talking about faith **in** Christ. It is the objective genitive which means faith toward Christ, not Christ's faith to us. It further says *"even we have believed in Jesus Christ,"* so obviously that is an objective genitive. It is our faith in Christ that saves us.

"that we might be justified by the faith of Christ, and not by the works of the law: for by the works of the law shall no flesh be justified" That is the faith of Scripture. This is what people who want to work for their salvation do not believe. They believe that to have God give you eternal life by your faith in Christ is foolish. They say they do not want any part of that. All of the world's religions say that we have to work to go to Heaven. They say that is the only way to get to Heaven. My friend, that is the only way you can't get to Heaven.

Galatians 2:17

"But if, while we seek to be justified by Christ, we ourselves also are found sinners, *is* therefore Christ the minister of sin? God forbid."

"But if, while we seek to be justified by Christ, we ourselves also are found sinners, *is* therefore Christ the minister of sin?" We all sin. Even we sin who have been declared righteous by Christ's dying on the cross for those sins. Even while we are seeking to be justified and declared righteous by faith in Christ we are found to sin. We ourselves *"are found sinners"* here on this earth, and we are often not righteous in day-to-day practice even though we have been declared righteous by the court of Heaven and on the books of Heaven. Is *"Christ the minister of sin?"* Did we get those sins because Christ is the minister of our sin, and He made us sin? No, Paul says *"God forbid."* We are not perfected. There is not one single person in the whole world who is absolutely sinless except the Lord Jesus Christ.

"God forbid" Some have used that phrase, *"God Forbid,"* as an example of dynamic equivalency in the King James Bible. They criticize the King James for that. Let me be honest about it. This phrase is found twenty-four times in the King James Bible. That was an expression in 1611 which was clearly understood. It is used nine times in the Old Testament and fifteen times in the New Testament. The phrase in the New Testament is ME GENOITO. ME means *"not."* GENOITO is the optative form of a verb similar to our verb, *"to be."* It means literally, *"May it not be"* or *"may it never be"* or *"may it never once even begin to be"* or *"may it not be thought possible."* That is the force of ME GENOITO. The King James translators used this expression from their day, "God forbid." In other words, *"may it never come to pass, may God forbid it."* This is what they are saying. Technically, since the word, *"God,"* does not occur here, they say this is dynamic equivalency.

What should be pointed out, however, is that the King James Bible translators did not use dynamic equivalency as one of their major principles in translation, unlike most of the modern versions.

Dynamic Equivalency

Dynamic equivalency does three things: (1) it adds to the Hebrew or Greek words, (2) it subtracts from the Hebrew or Greek words, and (3) it changes the Hebrew or Greek words in some other way.

As a matter of principle, you will find this occurring very few times in the King James Bible.

In the New King James Version I found over two thousand examples of this dynamic equivalency. In the New American Standard Version I found by actual count over four thousand examples of dynamic equivalency. In the New International Version I stopped counting after I found over six thousand six hundred and fifty-three examples of dynamic equivalency. I took two years and eight months on this project, a little each day. My computer (an old TRS 80 Radio Shack model) was filling up, so I stopped counting at that number. I did not want to spend the rest of my life on the NIV finding thousands upon thousands of additional examples of dynamic equivalency. What I am saying is that the King James Bible may have a few, but very few, examples of dynamic equivalency because that was not their primary purpose. This is one instance that the critics point to when alleging that "all translations use dynamic equivalency." Let's get honest about it. How often is "dynamic equivalency" used in our King James Bible? Very, very seldom. The King James translators were accurate. They translated what they found in their Hebrew and Greek texts.

Getting back to the text, is Christ responsible for sin? *"God forbid."* The Lord Jesus Christ never causes us to sin. If you are saved and blame the Lord Jesus Christ for your sins, you are wrong. This is not true. The Lord Jesus would never cause us to sin. He died for our sins. He died in our place so that we would be free from the power of our sinful natures. In fact, he is our *"advocate,"* or lawyer to get us out of trouble when we do sin.

- 1 John 2:1
  My little children, these things write I unto you, that ye sin not. And if any man sin, **we have an advocate with the Father**, Jesus Christ the righteous:

Galatians 2:18

"For if I build again the things which I destroyed, I make myself a transgressor." Can you imagine building again something you despised and destroyed? For instance, you take our three-story home. Suppose you did not like it because you did not think that it was useful to you. You decide that you want a rancher. So you bulldoze this house and destroy it because you don't like it. You are discarding it. You would surely not build again a three-story house just like the one you destroyed, would you? That would be a foolish thing to do.

Paul is talking about the fact that he has forsaken the law of Moses. So, he does not want anything to do with that again. The law of Moses will not save us or sanctify us. It will not do anything for us at all. Now that we have been saved by grace through faith, we must not go back under the Jewish law. If I did this, I would be a *"transgressor."* I would be building again that which I destroyed.

People often fall back into the old life. When they are saved and born-again, Christ delivers them from that old life. Then things come up in their life and they might say, *"I'm going to go back into the world."* That is what Peter did when he went back to fishing after Christ's crucifixion. That is not what we should do. We should not build again the things which we destroyed.

- **2 Peter 2:2**
  But it is happened unto them according to the true proverb, **The dog *is* turned to his own vomit again**; and the **sow that was washed to her wallowing** in the mire.

That is not what we should want to do. Paul does not want us to build back up that which we have destroyed. We are in Christ through faith, and we must not want to go back to the works of the law. Otherwise, we are going to be a *"transgressor"* of that law because it is impossible to keep it.

Galatians 2:19

"For I through the law am dead to the law, that I might live unto God." The Lord Jesus Christ fulfilled the law's requirement. He fulfilled every single provision of the law's requirements. Paul says he is *"dead to the law."* Can a dead man obey the law of speed? Can a dead man eat? No, he cannot do a thing. In Paul's day, there were some Jewish Christians who had been saved by the blood of Christ, but still acted like Jews. They wanted to put Christians who were saved back under the entire law or at least some parts of the law.

Even today there are some Jewish Christians who want to get others to follow parts of the Mosaic law. I know of a Jewish man who is a missionary to the Jews who wants the Gentiles to stop eating pork. I have two thoughts about this.

(1) First: I know it is forbidden under the law of Moses. Is this man trying to get the Gentiles back under any part of the law of Moses? If he is, that is wrong.

(2) Second: if you do not want to eat pork, that is fine. I do not eat pork or any other red meat because I have had cancer. Various research has suggested that, in my condition, it would be better for me to avoid red meat. What you do is your own business, but this Jewish missionary is trying to get people back under the law of Moses. We should not be under any part of that law. We should live unto God.

Galatians 2:20

"I am crucified with Christ: nevertheless I live; yet not I, but Christ liveth in me: and the life which I now live in the flesh I live by the faith of the Son of God, who loved me, and gave himself for me."

"I am crucified with Christ" This is a tremendous verse. Many believers do not understand what that is all about. To be crucified with the Lord Jesus Christ is hard to understand. First of all, He died almost two thousand years ago on the cross of Calvary. How can we be crucified with Christ now? How could Paul say that he has been crucified with Christ? Even in Paul's day, thirty years or so had passed since Christ had been crucified. If we are saved, God considers that everything the Lord Jesus Christ did, we have done in Him. We were crucified with Him. We were buried with Him. We were raised with Him. We ascended with Him. We are seated at the right hand of the throne of God with Him. Everything that Christ did, we who are *"in Christ"* did with Him. The Bible teaches this clearly. If we were not with Christ in all these things, we are not a part of Him and are not saved.

" nevertheless I live" How can a dead man live? The Lord Jesus was crucified. He died a physical death although some of the modernists and liberals do not say He died. They say He just swooned, and the cold recesses of the tomb revived Him. They say that He got out of the tomb because He never died. No, this is not right. The Lord Jesus Christ did die. One of the Roman soldiers thrust a spear into His side, and water and blood came out. He died for our sins. He was dead. How can one who was crucified live? Is that not contradictory? He is living right now because of His bodily resurrection.

"yet not I, but Christ liveth in me" Then Paul explained it. Many times in our Christian theology, we teach that God the Holy Spirit indwells the born-again individual. That is true. Usually we think of God the Holy Spirit indwelling the Christians. However, in the book of John it talks about both God the Father and the Lord Jesus Christ wanting to make Their abode in us.

- **John 14:23**
  Jesus answered and said unto him, If a man love me, he will keep my words: and **my Father will love him, and we will come unto him, and make our abode with him**.

This verse shows that God the Father and God the Son are abiding within the saved believing Christians.

- **1 Corinthians 6:19-20**
  What? **know ye not that your body is the temple of the Holy Ghost which is in you**, which ye have of God, and ye are not your own?

Here God the Holy Spirit is abiding with these saved Christians. In other words, all three Persons of the Trinity indwell the born-again believers. Paul says that *"Christ liveth in me."* That is the indwelling of the Person of the Lord Jesus Christ. Is not the Lord Jesus omnipresent, that is, everywhere present? Christ is indwelling the believers just like the Holy Spirit indwells the believers. The *"yet not I"* wording reminds me of a story that is told of one of the early church fathers. Before he was saved, he was a wicked Hell-bound, and Hell-deserving sinner. He would frequent dens of iniquity, drinking places, houses of prostitution, and other places where the sinners gathered. One day he was walking down the street and one of the prostitutes saw him and waved at him, wanting him to be with her like before. She called his name and said, *"Hi there, sweetheart, it is I."* The regenerated man replied, *"Yes, but it is **not I**,"* and walked away from her! That is the difference that Christ can make in your life. Yes, all of the redeemed ones can say with Paul, *"Christ liveth in me."* He has different plans for us once we have been saved by His grace through faith in Him.

"and the life which I now live in the flesh I live by the faith of the Son of God" If we who are born-again by the Spirit of God would just let the Lord Jesus Christ live out through us, what a radiance we would have! What an impact we would have in this wicked world! They would see us and read us like a letter.

- **2 Corinthians 3:2**
  Ye are our epistle written in our hearts, known and read of all men:

We are living *"epistles"* or letters, *"known and read"* by all men. The world does not see Christ. He has gone to Heaven. They don't even see the Bible. They don't read the Bible, but they "read" saved Christians just like a letter. May they see Christ living in us and the *"fruit of the Spirit"* rather than wickedness and the works of the flesh.

- **Galatians 5:22-23**
  But **the fruit of the Spirit is love, joy, peace, longsuffering, gentleness, goodness, faith, meekness, temperance**: against such there is no law.

"who loved me, and gave himself for me" At certain seasons, many people give gifts. Christ did not give a tangible, objective gift like money or cars. He gave Himself. He gave Himself for me and for you and for everyone who has ever been born or ever will be born. This is "unlimited atonement." As I have said before, there are two Greek prepositions translated *"for"* in English. (1) ANTI means, *"in place of, or instead of, or as a substitute for."* (2) The other is HUPER which means *"in the place of, or instead of, or as a substitute for"* but also *"as a benefit for."* It carries with it a positive benefit which ANTI does not imply. HUPER is the word which is used here. Let me mention twelve verses which use this word so you can see the beneficial effect as well as the substitutional effect.

- **Romans 5:8**
  But God commendeth his love toward us, in that, while we were yet sinners, Christ died **for us**.
- **Romans 8:32**
  He that spared not his own Son, but delivered him up **for us** all, how shall he not with him also freely give us all things?
- **1 Corinthians 5:7**
  Purge out therefore the old leaven, that ye may be a new lump, as ye are unleavened. For even Christ our passover is sacrificed **for us**:
- **2 Corinthians 5:21**
  For he hath made him *to be* sin **for us**, who knew no sin; that we might be made the righteousness of God in him.
- **Galatians 3:13**
  Christ hath redeemed us from the curse of the law, being made a curse **for us**: for it is written, Cursed *is* every one that hangeth on a tree:
- **Ephesians 5:2**
  And walk in love, as Christ also hath loved us, and hath given himself **for us** an offering and a sacrifice to God for a sweetsmelling savour.
- **1 Thessalonians 5:10**
  Who died **for us**, that, whether we wake or sleep, we should live together with him.
- **Titus 2:14**
  Who gave himself **for us**, that he might redeem us from all iniquity, and purify unto himself a peculiar people, zealous of good works.
- **Hebrews 9:12**
  Neither by the blood of goats and calves, but by his own blood he entered in once into the holy place, having obtained eternal redemption ***for us***.

Galatians 2:20-21

- **1 Peter 2:21**
  For even hereunto were ye called: because Christ also suffered **for us**, leaving us an example, that ye should follow his steps:
- **1 Peter 4:1**
  Forasmuch then as Christ hath suffered **for us** in the flesh, arm yourselves likewise with the same mind: for he that hath suffered in the flesh hath ceased from sin;
- **1 John 3:16**
  Hereby perceive we the love *of God*, because he laid down his life **for us**: and we ought to lay down *our* lives for the brethren.

From the above verses you can see the substitutionary death of the Lord Jesus Christ for the benefit of those who trust Him truly. What a gift that Christ died **for us**!

Galatians 2:21

"I do not frustrate the grace of God: for if righteousness *come* by the law, then Christ is dead in vain."

"I do not frustrate the grace of God" If we could receive righteousness by keeping the law, then why did the Lord Jesus Christ have to come into this world? Why did he have to suffer, and bleed, and die on the cross of Calvary? If this were true, then he died in vain. He died for nothing. We would not need Him. Many people believe this way. They say we do not need Christ. We do not need to be a Christian. We can just get righteousness and forgiveness on our own. They are saying, in effect, *"I can forgive myself. I am my own forgiver."*

How can a sinner forgive a sinner? It is only the Lord Jesus Christ Who can forgive us because He is sinless. He died for us. That word, *"frustrate,"* ATHETEO, means *"to do away with, to set aside, to discard."* We do not set aside the grace of God. That is what you do when you take Christ out of the picture. Peter was wrong in trying to mix the law of Moses with the grace and faith in Christ.

"for if righteousness *come* by the law, then Christ is dead in vain" The law of Moses could not bring *"righteousness."* The book of Hebrews makes this plain.

- **Hebrews 7:19**
  For **the law made nothing perfect**, but the bringing in of a better hope did; by the which we draw nigh unto God.

If the law could have brought perfection, then truly *"Christ is dead in vain."* Have you ever done anything in vain? The Scripture talks about another use of the phrase, *"in vain."*

- **Exodus 20:7**
  Thou shalt not take the name of the LORD thy God in vain; for the LORD will not hold him guiltless that taketh his name **in vain**.

As I said before, sometimes it seems like we just spin our wheels. We put our car on an icy street, and we cannot move one way or the other. Our wheels are moving wonderfully. They are just going and going and going. But our car is not moving at all. Paul did not want to conduct his ministry *"in vain,"* nor did he want people to believe that Christ died *"in vain."* The way some Christians act, it seems like they are acting as though He died in vain. The Lord Jesus must be at the center and at the circumference of our faith. Otherwise, it would seem that He would have died *"in vain."*

Praise the Lord for this man, Paul, who stood up even against the important apostle Peter. He did not have to do it. Nobody who rebukes another Christian leader wants to do it. Nobody wishes they have to do it. These people who divide on the Bible version issue say that we are divisive because we stand for our King James Bible. I say on our radio broadcasts, both daily and weekly, to those other Fundamentalists who use the false Westcott and Hort Greek New Testament text and versions based upon it,

"If you would like to join us, come on over and we will have unity. No problem! Come on over. We are not going to join you because you are wrong on the Bible version issue. But if you want to join us, let us have unity again like we always did before these new versions came."

I am all for unity. I love it. It is wonderful, but unity at the expense of truth, never. As someone has wisely stated: *"Better to be divided by TRUTH than to be united by ERROR."*

Dear Paul stood up against Peter for a right cause. If you could get righteousness by the law of Moses, then Christ would have died in vain. He did not die in vain. He died for every sinner who was ever born. I am glad that He died for you and for me. Aren't you?

Galatians Chapter Three

Galatians 3:1

"O foolish Galatians, who hath bewitched you, that ye should not obey the truth, before whose eyes Jesus Christ hath been evidently set forth, crucified among you?"

"O foolish Galatians, who hath bewitched you" Do you like to be called a fool? I am sure the Galatians did not like to be called foolish, but Paul calls them *"foolish."* These Galatians were absolutely without any understanding. The Galatians were barbarians who lived in what is present-day Turkey. The apostle Paul calls them foolish. He wonders who had charmed them just like a witch.

"that ye should not obey the truth" It was a terrible thing that they were not obeying the truth. The truth is that salvation is by faith in the Lord Jesus Christ plus nothing and minus nothing. It is faith in the Lord Jesus Christ's finished work on the cross of Calvary that brings salvation from sin. It is faith in Christ's dying for our sin, shedding His precious blood for us. It is faith that Jesus was buried and that He was raised bodily from the grave.

"before whose eyes Jesus Christ hath been evidently set forth, crucified among you" Notice those words. The Galatian Christians were relying on the law of Moses to save and to sanctify them. It seems like they were trying to crucify the Lord Jesus Christ again. In the Roman Catholic mass the Lord Jesus Christ is said to be crucified over and over again. In other words, they are making a sham of the crucifixion of Christ. Remember a verse in the preceding chapter.

- Galatians 2:21
    I do not frustrate the grace of God: **for if righteousness come by the law, then Christ is dead in vain**.

Jesus Christ would not have had to come if we could be saved by the law.

Galatians 3:2

"This only would I learn of you, Received ye the Spirit by the works of the law, or by the hearing of faith?"

"This only would I learn of you, Received ye the Spirit"
These Galatians are saved believers. God saved them from heathenism, from idolatry, and from all sorts of false worship and beliefs. Paul asked them if they had received the Spirit of God, and they had.

- **Romans 8:9**
  But ye are not in the flesh, but in the Spirit, if so be that the Spirit of God dwell in you. **Now if any man have not the Spirit of Christ, he is none of his**.

Every Christian has the Holy Spirit of God indwelling him. If you have never been born-again, the Holy Spirit does not indwell you. We who are Christians are not our own. We are *"bought with a price,"* the price of the precious blood of Christ.

- **1 Corinthians 6:19-20**
  What? know ye not that your body is the temple of the Holy Ghost which is in you, which ye have of God, and **ye are not your own? For ye are bought with a price**: therefore glorify God in your body, and in your spirit, which are God's.

"by the works of the law, or by the hearing of faith?"
The question is did you receive the Spirit by the works of the law? Did I receive the Spirit by the works of the law? No, nothing I could do could possibly merit the receiving of the Holy Spirit of God. I received the Holy Spirit only by faith when I truly trusted in Christ as my Saviour. Only when I accepted Him and received Him as my Saviour, then and only then, did the Holy Spirit indwell my body. He indwells your body if you are born-again. You did not receive the Holy Spirit by works. You received Him by the hearing of faith.

- **Romans 10:13**
  For whosoever shall call upon the name of the Lord shall be saved.

That is how we have the Holy Spirit of God indwelling us. It is a wonderful gift.

Galatians 3:3

"Are ye so foolish? having begun in the Spirit, are ye now made perfect by the flesh?" Here again he calls them *"foolish."* If I were to say that to this audience, you would probably all get up and leave. We do not like to be called fools. Paul then asks them if it makes any sense to begin your salvation by the Spirit and not continue to be perfected

Galatians 3:3

or matured by the Spirit. Our works from our flesh did not save us, and our works from our flesh will not mature us. We are not made mature and full-grown by the works of the flesh.

I would like to quote some thirteen verses on what our flesh is. If we really understand these verses, we are not going to have any confidence in our flesh. We will not believe it possible to fulfill the law of Moses by our flesh.

- **John 3:6**
  That which is born of the flesh is flesh; and that which is born of the Spirit is spirit.

You cannot change the flesh. You can put it in the undertaker's casket. You can powder it. You can comb its hair, but flesh is still flesh. It is not going to change. We are not going to change our flesh until the Lord Jesus gives us new resurrected bodies.

- **John 6:63**
  It is the spirit that quickeneth; **the flesh profiteth nothing**: the words that I speak unto you, *they* are spirit, and *they* are life.

- **Romans 3:20**
  Therefore **by the deeds of the law there shall no flesh be justified in his sight**: for by the law *is* the knowledge of sin.

- **Romans 7:18**
  For I know that in me (that is, in my flesh,) dwelleth no good thing: for to will is present with me; but *how* to perform that which is good I find not.

If no good thing dwells in our flesh, how can we fulfill the law of God? It is impossible. It must be by the Spirit of God.

- **Romans 8:3-4**
  For what the law could not do, in that it was weak through the flesh, God sending his own Son in the likeness of sinful flesh, and for sin, condemned sin in the flesh: That the righteousness of the law might be fulfilled in us, who walk not after the flesh, but after the Spirit.

Dr. Lewis Sperry Chafer, my teacher at Dallas Theological Seminary for his last four years of life and the founder of that school, used to illustrate that. When you put a fork in an over-cooked roast and try to lift it out of the roasting pan, the whole thing falls. Is there anything wrong with the fork? No. The fork is solid, but it is *"weak through the flesh."* The flesh just falls right down. The law of God is perfect, but we cannot keep it. It is weak through our flesh and is impossible to keep.

- **Romans 13:14**
  But put ye on the Lord Jesus Christ, and **make not provision for the flesh**, to *fulfil* the lusts *thereof*.

- 1 Corinthians 1:29
  That **no flesh should glory in his presence**.
- Galatians 2:16
  Knowing that a man is not justified by the works of the law, but by the faith of Jesus Christ, even we have believed in Jesus Christ, that we might be justified by the faith of Christ, and not by the works of the law: **for by the works of the law shall no flesh be justified.**
- Galatians 5:16
  This I say then, Walk in the Spirit, and **ye shall not fulfil the lust of the flesh.**
- Galatians 5:19
  Now the works of the flesh are manifest, which are *these*; Adultery, fornication, uncleanness, lasciviousness,
- Galatians 6:8
  For he that soweth to his flesh shall of the flesh reap corruption; but he that soweth to the Spirit shall of the Spirit reap life everlasting.
- Philippians 3:3
  For we are the circumcision, which worship God in the spirit, and rejoice in Christ Jesus, and **have no confidence in the flesh.**
- 1 John 2:16
  For all that *is* in the world, **the lust of the flesh**, and the lust of the eyes, and the pride of life, is not of the Father, but is of the world.

In Romans 3:2 Paul wrote, *"received ye the Spirit by the works of the law or by the hearing of faith."* Then in verse three he asked, *"are ye so foolish? having been in the Spirit, are ye now made perfect by the flesh?"* It is impossible to be made perfect in the flesh. There is no such thing!

Galatians 3:4

"Have ye suffered so many things in vain? If *it be* yet in vain." These Christians were suffering for their faith in Christ. They were being persecuted. If they had to be saved by the works of the law, then why were they suffering so? They were suffering at the hands of the Judaizers. These Judaizers were people who were Jews who came to Christ for His salvation, but they wanted all of the Gentiles to be under the law of Moses. They should have stayed with the Spirit of God, and not with the works of the flesh.

Galatians 3:5

"He therefore that ministereth to you the Spirit, and worketh miracles among you, doeth he it by the works of the law, or by the hearing of faith?" Paul is the one who is speaking here. He is ministering to these Galatian Christians the Spirit of God. He was working miracles by faith, not by *"the works of the law."* Apostolic miracles were for the apostolic times. I believe the Scriptures teach that apostolic miracles have ceased. I believe that the miracles have stopped since the Bible has been completed and we have all of the revelation of God.

- **1 Corinthians 13:8**
  Charity never faileth: but **whether there be prophecies, they shall fail; whether there be tongues, they shall cease; whether there be knowledge, it shall vanish away**.

In fact, the next two verses tell us when these special sign gifts will *"fail," "cease,"* and *"vanish away."*

- **1 Corinthians 13:9-10**
  For we know in part, and we prophesy in part. But **when that which is perfect is come, then that which is in part shall be done away.**

I believe *"that which is perfect"* refers to the perfection and completion of the New Testament books which occurred in about 90 or 100 A.D.

In fact, we were reading today in the gospel of Matthew how the Lord Jesus sent out the twelve apostles. Notice what He commanded them.

- **Matthew 10:8**
  Heal the sick, cleanse the lepers, raise the dead, cast out devils: freely ye have received, freely give.

The Lord Jesus said that this was a gift that God gave to these apostles. They cleansed the lepers. They healed the sick. They made the blind to see. They even raised the dead. Those tremendous miracles were in the apostolic times. When John the Baptist asked Jesus, *"Art thou he that should come? or look we for another?"* (Luke 7:19), Jesus made this reply.

- **Luke 7:22**
  Then Jesus answering said unto them, Go your way, and tell John what things ye have seen and heard; how that **the blind see, the lame walk, the lepers are cleansed, the deaf hear, the dead are raised**, to the poor the gospel is preached.

There were miracles in the apostolic times, but when the Bible was completed, the sign miracles from God ceased. There was no longer a need for them because God's Word had been perfected or completed. It is fully here.

Galatians 3:6

"Even as Abraham believed God, and it was accounted to him for righteousness." *"Abraham believed God."* This is an illustration of what happened to Abraham. God said that he was going to make of Abraham a large nation with millions and millions of people. God told Abraham that if he were able to count the stars of the sky, that is how large his family would be.

- **Genesis 15:5**
  And he brought him forth abroad, and said, **Look now toward Heaven, and tell the stars, if thou be able to number them: and he said unto him, So shall thy seed be.**

At that time Abraham had no children. He had no son, but he still believed that God would multiply his seed in accordance with His promise.

- **Genesis 15:6**
  And **he believed in the LORD; and he counted it to him for righteousness**.

Later on, Abraham had a son he named Ishmael. He was the wrong one because he was the bondwoman's son, not the son of promise. Finally, miraculously, Abraham had a son by Sarah whom he named Isaac. He was the son of promise.

"Abraham believed God." In Genesis chapter twenty-two, Abraham did what God told him to do. God saw his genuine faith because of his works. Abraham believed God. That word for "believe" in Hebrew is the word, AMAN. This is the word from which we get our English word, *"amen."* It means *"I believe, I am trusting, or I have confidence."* Abraham said *"amen"* to God. He had faith and confidence in God.

How can faith be transferred into righteousness? It is only God that can do it. We cannot do it. I cannot transfer your faith into righteousness, but God can. That is His miracle. If you are here right now and are genuinely believing in the Lord Jesus Christ, you are saved by the grace of God through faith. You are regenerated by the Holy Spirit of God. God says that faith is counted or reckoned for righteousness. In God's books and in the court of Heaven, we have a righteous standing before God. That is how God reckons our personal faith in Christ.

That word for "accounted" is a good word. It is LOGIZOMAI in the Greek language. It means *"to reckon, to count, to compute, to calculate, to take into account."* In a metaphorical sense it means *"to pass to one's account or to impute."* The word deals with reality. If I LOGIZOMAI or "reckon" that my bank book has $25.00 in it, then it has $25.00 in it. It is a fact. I reckon it is a fact. Otherwise I am deceiving myself. This word refers to facts and not suppositions. I know that I have $25.00.

A reckoning of righteousness by faith is not that we are absolutely righteous in our flesh. God wants us to aim at that. That is our goal. If you aim at nothing, you will hit it every time. He wants us to aim at perfect righteousness. On the books of Heaven, God has declared us righteous if we have accepted Christ as our Saviour. That is our standing before God. Our state is how we are living before the world right here and now. We have to face our state living day by day. As God said, *"Be ye Holy; for I am Holy"* (1 Peter 1:16). Not that we will ever attain it in our mortal bodies, but we have to aim at it. We have been reckoned and accounted on the books of Heaven by faith as being absolutely righteous. That is why we can go to Heaven when the Lord Jesus comes for us in the rapture or when we die to go home with the Lord. That is why we can go to Heaven. We go to Heaven because we have been justified by the blood of Christ through faith in Him. We are saved and set apart by faith.

Galatians 3:7

"Know ye therefore that they which are of faith, the same are the children of Abraham." We are not Jews or Israel. There are some Covenant Theologians all over the world that teach that the Christians are now Israel. They believe that there are no more unfulfilled promises for national Israel. We do not agree with that. There are promises for national Israel which will be fulfilled during the Millennial reign of the Lord Jesus Christ.

We are in the same childhood relationship with Abraham because Abraham was a child of faith and we are children of faith if we are saved. We, if we have trusted Christ by faith, are children of Abraham. We are not, however, Jews. Abraham lived before there were any Jews. He was before the ten tribes which became the Jews or the Israelites. The tribe of Judah is where the word *"Jew"* is derived. Abraham also preceded the law of Moses by four hundred and thirty years. We are the children of Abraham if we are believing in Christ by faith in the Lord Jesus Christ.

Galatians 3:8

"And the Scripture, foreseeing that God would justify the heathen through faith, preached before the gospel unto Abraham, *saying*, In thee shall all nations be blessed."

"And the Scripture, foreseeing that God would justify the heathen" God can *"foresee"* anything. He can foresee you and me. He can foresee whatever we do and wherever we go. You may say that it is a sovereign choice on my part. That is true, but God can foresee what we do. He knows exactly what choice we are going to make. You try to figure that out? I cannot figure it out. If you play chess on the computer, that computer can just about figure out what move you are going to make next. It can beat you usually unless you're a real expert. God foresees even before we make the choice. I do not even know what I am going to do next. I do not know what words are going to come out of my mouth, but God knows and foresees. He foresaw right down through the corridors of time that *"God would justify the heathen."* That is us. How wonderful this is.

"through faith, preached before the gospel unto Abraham, *saying*, In thee shall all nations be blessed" Just think, the *"gospel"* was preached to Abraham. This is the gospel about the Lord Jesus Christ. We do not often think about that. We think the gospel was only preached after the Lord Jesus Christ's death. The gospel was preached to Abraham about the Seed that would come. That Seed was Christ. He preached the gospel to Abraham saying, *"in thee shall all the nations be blessed."* (Genesis 12:3)

This is referred to again when speaking of the events in Genesis 22:1-19. If God told you to offer your son or daughter on an unfamiliar mountain, would you do it? The faith of Abraham was that even if he offered his only son on Mount Moriah, God would raise him up again if need be.

- **Hebrews 11:17-19**
  <u>**By faith Abraham, when he was tried, offered up Isaac**</u>: and he that had received the promises offered up his only begotten son, Of whom it was said, That in Isaac shall thy seed be called: <u>**Accounting that God was able to raise him up, even from the dead; from whence also he received him in a figure.**</u>

The faith of Abraham was there. It took Abraham, Isaac, and Abraham's servants three days to travel to this mount. How many young men would obey their father? We have disobedience everywhere we turn. Children slap, kick, and curse their mothers and fathers. I was a teacher for nineteen years in the Philadelphia public school system. I could tell from parents' night how the various children treated their parents.

Abraham said *"I and the lad will go yonder and worship, and <u>**come**</u> again to you."* (Genesis 22:5) In the English we do not know if Abraham and Isaac would come back again or just Abraham. You have to look at the Hebrew underneath that English. In the Hebrew it says, *"I and the lad will go. And we* [both of us] *will come again."* How can that be? It took a tremendous, gigantic, and colossal faith for Abraham to believe that. God told him to sacrifice his son. He was to slay him as a burnt offering. Abraham believed that

Isaac would be raised from the dead. He believed that he would get off that altar and then walk away with him back to those two young men who were waiting at the foot of the mountain. Picture that.

There was no offering. Isaac did not know that he was the going to be the sacrificial lamb. This is a picture of Calvary. The Lord Jesus Christ was the *"Lamb of God which taketh away the sin of the world."* (John 1:29) Abraham said, *"God will provide himself a lamb for a burnt" offering."* (Genesis 22:8) Talk about faith. God was going to *"provide Himself a lamb."* There are two ways to look at this phrase. God will do the providing of the lamb, or God will provide Himself to be the lamb. The Lord Jesus was the Lamb Himself.

Galatians 3:9

"So then they which be of faith are blessed with faithful Abraham." Isaac was not a fool. He was a young man of about nineteen. Would your teenager be bound and allow himself to be put on an altar? Isaac knew what was coming. He saw his father's knife. He saw the fire. Isaac was obedient, and the Lord Jesus Christ was obedient in going to the cross of Calvary for your sins and for my sins.

This was a picture of Calvary. When Bill Gothard told this story in a seminar I attended, he did not mention Calvary. He drew on the chalk board a picture of Abraham offering Isaac. The only thing he says about this Genesis 22 story is that it is an example of the obedience of sons to their fathers. He did not refer to Christ and Calvary's cross. He did not give a sense of what that picture means in type form.

In the book of James, we see that faith plus works is made perfect. All of us can see Abraham's works in what he did. He obeyed God. God could see his faith. He wanted to write this whole story so that we could see Abraham's faith by his works. James talks about what people see and what God sees.

Abraham called that place Jehovah-jireh. (Genesis 22:14) That is a Hebrew word that means *"the Lord will see to it or the Lord will provide."* That is exactly what the Lord did. He provided a ram for Abraham and the *"Lamb of God"* for our salvation.

- **Genesis 22:18**
  And **in thy seed shall all the nations of the earth be blessed**; because thou hast obeyed my voice.

Galatians 3:8 refers to this very verse here. Genesis 22:18 is foreseeing that the heathen will be saved in Abraham's *"seed,"* which is Christ.

Later on we will see that this seed is Jesus Christ. That is the gospel. In Christ all the nations will be blessed. Those who are trusting the Lord Jesus Christ by faith are blessed. Are you trusting the Lord Jesus Christ by faith? I do not know your hearts, but the Lord does. If you are trusting Christ and have faith in the Lord Jesus, God says you are blessed. You do not have to have a lot of money. You do not have to have a large home. You do not have to have many good friends or relatives. You do not have to have a big car. God says you are blessed if you have genuine faith in His Son. If you are saved, God has blessed you. Ephesians 1:3 says we are blessed *"with all spiritual blessings in heavenly places in Christ."* I think He has also given us some spiritual blessings here on earth as well.

Galatians 3:10

"For as many as are of the works of the law are under the curse: for it is written, Cursed *is* every one that continueth not in all things which are written in the book of the law to do them." There are two verses to remember here. One of them is the verse that is quoted.

- **Jeremiah 11:3**
  And say thou unto them, Thus saith the LORD God of Israel; **Cursed *be* the man that obeyeth not the words of this covenant,**

There is another verse as well.

- **James 2:10**
  For **whosoever shall keep the whole law, and yet offend in one *point*, he is guilty of all.**

This verse makes it clear that those that are under the law are obligated to keep every part of that law. They have to believe and follow everything, or they will stay accursed. How can everyone keep the whole law of Moses? How can you even keep the first five books of Moses? How about just the first book of Genesis? We cannot do it. If we cannot do it, then we are under the curse and we are bound for Hell. If it were not for our faith in Christ, we would still be cursed. We are not trying to keep the law. The Lord Jesus kept the whole law of Moses on our behalf that His righteousness might be passed upon us by faith in Christ.

Notice that phrase, *"it is written."* That is a perfect tense in Greek. Every time you see this phrase, *"it is written,"* it represents the perfect tense in Greek. The phrase, *"it is written,"* occurs sixty-three times in the New Testament. Just the word, *"written,"* which is also in the perfect tense occurs one hundred and forty-one times. There are three things that the perfect tense shows.

(1) First, it shows that the action is a past event.

(2) Second, it shows that the action is carried over to the present time and that it is true also in present time.

(3) Third, it shows that the action is also true in the future time.

What does *"it is written"* mean? It comes from the word, GRAPHO.

GRAPHO means *"to write, with reference to the form of the letters."* We are talking about the preservation of the Hebrew Words of God in the Old Testament and the Greek Words of God in the New Testament. This verb, "to write," refers to the form of the letters. It means *"to delineate [or form] letters on a tablet, parchment, paper, or other material."* It also means *"to express in written characters, to commit to writing (things not to be forgotten), write down, record."* It usually refers to those things which stand written in the sacred books of the Old Testament.

When Paul quotes from the Old Testament saying *"it is written"* in the perfect tense, he is saying to these Galatians, that these words stood written in the past when Moses wrote down the letters in the Hebrew language. Since it is in the perfect tense, he is also saying that these words still stand written today. He is also saying that these words will be preserved and will stand in written form into the future. So it stands true to this very day. It will stand true till the Lord Jesus returns. It is written, it stands written, and it is preserved. This is a proof for verbal preservation of the Hebrew and Greek Words of the Bible.

That is why I believe that God Who promised to preserve His words in every syllable and in every letter of His Hebrew and Greek Words has kept His promise. I believe that God always keeps His promises. There are some Fundamentalist leaders rising up all over this country saying that God has not preserved His Words of Hebrew and His Words of Greek . There is a "coalition" of major Fundamental schools who take this position. They are led by Bob Jones University, Detroit Baptist Seminary, Central Baptist Seminary, and Calvary Baptist Seminary. They teach that God has simply preserved His "Word" in general. They say that He has simply preserved "the meaning, the message, the thoughts, the concepts, or the ideas" but not the "Words." They say we have errors in the Hebrew words which we have in our present Hebrew manuscripts. I do not agree with this. They say we have errors in our Greek manuscripts.

I do not agree with them. I believe that God Who has promised to preserve His Words has kept that promise. When Paul says, and when Jesus says, and when all of the other writers say *"it is written,"* God is trying to get through to all Fundamentalists, neo-evangelicals, modernists, liberals, apostates, Roman Catholics, and everyone else that He has kept His promise to preserve His Words. I believe that God has preserved His Words in the Masoretic Hebrew Text and the Textus Receptus Greek Text underlying the King James Bible. Here He has kept His Words as He has promised.

Galatians 3:11

"**But that no man is justified by the law in the sight of God, *it is* evident: for, The just shall live by faith."** This phrase is repeated four times in the Bible.
- Habakkuk 2:4
  Behold, his soul *which* is lifted up is not upright in him: but **the just** shall live by his faith.

I believe the emphasis here is on *"the just."*
- Romans 1:17
  For therein is the righteousness of God revealed from faith to faith: as it is written, **The just shall live** by faith.

I believe the emphasis here is on *"shall live."*
- Hebrews 10:38
  Now **the just shall live by faith**: but if *any man* draw back, my soul shall have no pleasure in him.

I believe the emphasis here is on *"by faith."*

By faith and not by works, we can live. That Greek word, "*live*," ZAO, means *"to have true life and worthy of the name."* There are a lot of unsaved people running around this world who are living, but they are not living a life *"worthy of the name."* If we are in Christ, we can live a life worth living.

Galatians 3:12

"**And the law is not of faith: but, The man that doeth them shall live in them."** This is true. Law is not of faith. If you are "doing" the law and if you live and practice the law, you are not living by faith. You are living by what you "do." That is an obvious thing. He is trying to teach these things to the Galatian Christians.

Galatians 3:13

"**Christ hath redeemed us from the curse of the law, being made a curse for us: for it is written, Cursed *is* every one that hangeth on a tree"**

"**Christ hath redeemed us from the curse of the law, being made a curse for us"** Notice that Christ has *"redeemed us."* If we try to be saved by keeping the law, we are under the curse because we could not keep it all. He has redeemed us. That word redeemed, EXAGORAZO, means *"to buy on the open market."* AGORA is the Greek word for a market place. EXAGORAZO is *"to redeem by payment of a price to recover from the power of another, to ransom, buy off."* People are held for ransom all

over the world. The kidnappers want to get money. Christ has redeemed us from the slave market of sin. We were in our sin and under the curse because of Adam, Eve, and Satan. If we're saved, Christ has bought us with His own precious blood. He has redeemed us by paying a price to set us free.
- **Colossians 1:13**
Who hath **delivered us from the power of darkness**, and hath translated *us* into the kingdom of his dear Son:

That is what the Lord Jesus has done for us who are saved.

"for it is written" There is that perfect tense once again, *"it is written."* It has been written in the past; it stands written in the present, and it will stand written into the future. The Words of God have been preserved. This is Bible preservation of the Words of the Hebrew and the Words of the Greek. This is the "preservation" spoken of in Scripture.
- **Psalm 12:6-7**
The <u>words</u> of the LORD are pure words: as silver tried in a furnace of earth, purified seven times. **Thou shalt keep them**, O LORD, **thou shalt <u>preserve</u> them** from this generation for ever.

"Cursed *is* every one that hangeth on a tree" Paul is quoting from Deuteronomy.
- **Deuteronomy 21:22-23**
And if a man have committed a sin worthy of death, and he be to be put to death, and thou hang him on a tree: His body shall not remain all night upon the tree, but thou shalt in any wise bury him that day; **(for he that is hanged *is* accursed of God**;) that thy land be not defiled, which the LORD thy God giveth thee *for* an inheritance.

That is why the Jews had to get the dead bodies down from the cross before the sun went down and the special Sabbath Feast Day began. It was a curse to be hanged on a tree. The Lord Jesus was *"made a curse for us."* He took upon His body all the sins of all the world, including the sins of all the men, women, and children of the world. If He had not been made a curse for us, we would have to be made a curse for ourselves and go to an eternal lake of fire called Hell. He took in His own body on the cross the Hell, the damnation, the trouble, and the terrible judgment that was due to every one of us. He took the curse for us. Praise God for Him who was *"made a curse for us."* We are grateful to God that by faith in Christ we can be saved. We do not have to keep those hundreds of laws of Moses. We can be blessed with faithful Abraham. May we, by faith, continue to live our lives so that they will be pleasing to Him.

Galatians 3:14

"That the blessing of Abraham might come on the Gentiles through Jesus Christ; that we might receive the promise of the Spirit through faith."

"That the blessing of Abraham might come on the Gentiles through Jesus Christ" In verse fourteen we see the result of His bearing our sins in His own body. The Lord Jesus was made a curse that we might receive the *"blessing of Abraham."* Notice, it is the blessing of Abraham *"through Jesus Christ."* Remember in verse eight, it said that God before had preached the gospel unto Abraham. He told Abraham about the Lord Jesus Christ. He told Abraham that the world would be blessed through His seed. The Lord Jesus Christ was Abraham's seed, not seeds plural. Jesus was that Seed which would come to redeem all mankind. I am sure God told Abraham that Christ would die on the cross of Calvary to redeem all of mankind from their sins.

"that we might receive the promise of the Spirit through faith" Paul wrote the book of Galatians to correct two errors. First, the Galatians thought they could be saved by keeping the law of Moses. Second, they thought they could be sanctified by keeping the law of Moses. Both of these ideas were in error. We are saved by God's grace through faith in His Son, the Lord Jesus Christ. We are sanctified or set apart by God's Holy Spirit. This was a blessing received by us Gentiles through God's promise to Abraham. This is the blessing that God has promised us through Christ that we could be saved through Abraham's faith and through Abraham's coming Seed.

Galatians 3:15

"Brethren, I speak after the manner of men; Though *it be* but a man's covenant, yet *if it be* confirmed, no man disannulleth, or addeth thereto."

"Brethren, I speak after the manner of men; Though *it be* but a man's covenant" A covenant is an agreement or an accord. It is something you agree to like marriage. People break marriages all the time. It is a sad thing. Marriage is a covenant that is signed, sealed, and delivered by two different people. Today, unfortunately, as soon as many couples get married, they seem to be ready to break up. It is a sad thing. In the Naval Chaplain Corps, I stopped marrying people who were in the Navy or the Marine Corps for this reason. The Scriptures warn us of this condition.

- **2 Timothy 3:3**
  Without natural affection, **trucebreakers**, false accusers, incontinent, fierce, despisers of those that are good

"*Trucebreakers*" or those who do not keep their promises are a sign of the last time.

"yet *if it be* confirmed, no man disannulleth, or addeth thereto" In a contract, you sign a written agreement saying this is what will happen. Unless you disannul that written agreement by an amendment, it must stand. It used to be that a man or a woman's word was their bond. It took just a word. This is no longer the case. Now, even when it is written down in black and white, people sometimes do not keep their agreements. The principle of a covenant or an agreement is that it should stand and not be disannulled or added to at all.

One of the leaders of Communism in Russia, gave his view of "treaties." He said that *"Treaties are like pie crusts--made to be broken."* That was his idea about promises. That is what they do in the Communist world. As I am speaking, on the floors of Congress, they are debating the so-called test-ban treaty. We are saying that we agree never to test anything again. Communist Russia, China, and Cuba can agree to this on paper, but then they will break it. I am glad, at least right now, that the Senate and the House are against this test-ban treaty. I am not for killing people by atomic weapons. Do not get me wrong. We have to be ready when the liars, cut-throats, and Communists come after us. It is still a Communist world, no matter how they announce that Communism is dead. The same people are running the show. If you have a different proprietor in a store and he is running the store the same way as it always has been run, then it is the same store. It does not matter if a different person is running the store if the store is run the same way. It is the same store. It is the same way with the Communist world. The same actors are in the saddle.

The idea is inspection. With this test-ban treaty, the men who have read the fine print say that this treaty is not sufficient because we cannot inspect and see if they are not testing nuclear weapons. The United States will keep its agreement if they sign it. That is just the way we are, but they will not keep their agreement. That is a deplorable situation.

Galatians 3:16

"Now to Abraham and his seed were the promises made. He saith not, And to seeds, as of many; but as of one, And to thy seed, which is Christ."

"Now to Abraham and his seed were the promises made" Here is the New Testament interpretation of the Old Testament verse. That is a wonderful thing when the Holy Spirit of God interprets the Old Testament by the New Testament truth.

- **Genesis 22:18**
  And **in thy seed shall all the nations of the earth be blessed**; because thou hast obeyed my voice.

The Lord Jesus Christ was the promised *"Seed"* to Abraham in this verse. Jesus said that Abraham saw Jesus' day. It is wonderful that Abraham rejoiced to see the day of Jesus.

- **John 8:56-58**
  Your father **Abraham rejoiced to see my day: and he saw it, and was glad.** Then said the Jews unto him, Thou art not yet fifty years old, and hast thou seen Abraham? Jesus said unto them, Verily, verily, I say unto you, **Before Abraham was, I am.**

Jesus is the eternal Son of God, and was before Abraham. God promised this to Abraham. He knew ahead of time about the Seed, Jesus Christ, Who had come to redeem all mankind by the shedding of His blood on the cross of Calvary as a sacrifice for sin.

"He saith not, And to seeds, as of many; but as of one, And to thy seed, which is Christ" Paul makes a point on the basis of a singular word versus a plural word. That is a difference on one letter. That is one of the good things about our King James Bible. There is a strict accuracy with which they translate singular and plurals. This is not so with the New International Version. This is not so with the New King James Version. This is not so with the New American Standard Version. None of these versions are as accurate as they should be about singulars and plurals. If they want to make it singular and the Hebrew or Greek has it plural, they do what they want to do. If the Greek or Hebrew has it plural and they want to make it singular, they do it. They are not properly translating the Words of God. What if, in their error, they translated this word *"seeds"* instead of *"seed"*? That would take away the proper interpretation and meaning. This specific interpretation gives us the methodology of translation of the Bible, whether it is in Spanish, French, German, or whatever the language. We must take heed to singular and plurals.

We must not simply put what we want to put. The King James Bible has translated this correctly.

Galatians 3:17

"And this I say, *that* the covenant, that was confirmed before of God in Christ, the law, which was four hundred and thirty years after, cannot disannul, that it should make the promise of none effect."

"And this I say, *that* the covenant, that was confirmed before of God in Christ, the law, which was four hundred and thirty years after" Here is the picture. These Galatian barbarians had to get it straight as to the law and grace. The Bible says the covenant which was made by God to Abraham was confirmed. That is a perfect tense. The perfect tense in the Greek language is something that has been done in the past, is true and continued into the present, and will still be true and continue into the future. This covenant made by God to Abraham continues right on into eternity. That promise concerns the Lord Jesus Christ. It was never abrogated, never set aside, never added to, never disannulled. When God gave Moses the law in Exodus chapter twenty, it was four hundred and thirty years after Abraham was given this promise concerning the Lord Jesus Christ as the *"Seed."*

"cannot disannul, that it should make the promise of none effect." The law cannot disannul this promise. That is what God says. That word to disannul, AKUROO, means *"to render void, deprive of force or authority."* You cannot deprive the promise given to Abraham concerning Jesus Christ's death. That word for make of *"none effect,"* KATARGEO, means *"to render idle or inoperative, inactivate, to cause a person or thing to have no further efficiency, to cause to cease, do away with, abolish, put an end to, annul."* It is not abolished. The Lord Jesus Christ in His death, burial, and resurrection will never be changed or altered one bit. His finished work continues right on into the future. The law of Moses cannot alter it. Anything after the law of Moses cannot alter it. Anything before the law of Moses cannot alter it.

Galatians 3:18

"For if the inheritance *be* of the law, *it is* no more of promise: but God gave *it* to Abraham by promise." God promised Abraham there would be a *"Seed,"* namely the Lord Jesus Christ. The inheritance was not of the law. What inheritance? It is the inheritance of Heaven, the inheritance of grace, the inheritance of eternal life. You cannot be saved by the law of Moses even though these Judaizers were saying this. You cannot be sanctified or made holy by the law of Moses even though they were also saying this. You cannot do it that way. If the inheritance of eternal life is by the law, then it cannot be of promise. God gave it to Abraham by promise, and God keeps His promises. He never fails to keep His promises.

That is one of the reasons why I have talked about the preservation of the Hebrew and the Greek Words of the Old and New Testament. That is the thing I push forward every time I talk about our King James Bible and the Greek and Hebrew texts which underlie that Bible. God promised to preserve His words. The Lord Jesus promised that His Words would be preserved.

- **Matthew 24:35**
  Heaven and earth shall pass away, **but my words shall not pass away.**

The Lord Jesus is here speaking about the writing of the entire New Testament.

- **John 16:13**
  Howbeit when he, the **Spirit of truth**, is come, **he will guide you into all truth**: for he shall not speak of [or from] himself; but whatsoever he shall hear, *that* shall he speak: and he will shew you things to come.

- **John 14:26**
  But the Comforter, *which is* the **Holy Ghost**, whom the Father will send in my name, **he shall teach you all things, and bring all things to your remembrance, whatsoever I have said unto you.**

The Lord Jesus is the Author of all the words of the New Testament. The Holy Spirit merely took the Lord Jesus' Words and then communicated them to the writers of the New Testament. If that is true of the New Testament, why is it not true of the Old Testament by analogy? The Lord Jesus is the Word, the Revelator, and the One Who reveals. He was the Author of all the Hebrew Words as well. When the Lord Jesus said that *"my words shall not pass away,"* I believe it. This means the preservation of all of the Words and even letters of both the Hebrew Old Testament and the Greek New Testament. I believe, by faith and study since 1971, we have those preserved Words and letters in the Hebrew and Greek texts which underlie the King James Bible.

There are men who say that we cannot believe it. They say that the Words have passed away. There are even Fundamentalists who are saying this, such as men from Bob Jones University, Detroit Baptist Seminary, Central Baptist Seminary and Calvary Baptist Seminary. Dan Wallace from the neo-evangelical Dallas Theological Seminary said, *"The Bible never promises to preserve his words."* I believe the Lord Jesus Christ has promised that.

- **Matthew 5:17-18**
  Think not that I am come to destroy the law, or the prophets: I am not come to destroy, but to fulfil. For verily I say unto you, **Till Heaven and earth pass, one jot or one tittle shall in no wise pass from the law**, till all be fulfilled.

The *"jot"* is the smallest letter of the Hebrew alphabet. It is just like an apostrophe. The *"tittle"* is the smallest distinguishing feature between two Hebrew letters. Not one part of a letter shall fail. The Lord Jesus believed in Bible preservation of letters and even parts of letters. He promised it, and I know He keeps His promises. He gave it to Abraham by promise, and He gave it to us by promise.

He has preserved His Hebrew and Greek Words. I believe He has preserved His Words in the Traditional Masoretic Hebrew Text which underlies our King James Bible and the Textus Receptus Greek text which underlies our King James Bible. Some of these Bible-believing leaders disagree with me on this. I do not care. I cannot prove it to anyone who is not willing to accept it. These are the promises of God.

He promised to preserve His Words. By the way, while I am on the subject of His **"Words"** versus the **"Word"** of God, let me talk about a book written from a Fundamentalist viewpoint, *From the Mind of God to the Mind of Man*. These men say that God has only preserved His "Word" but not His "Words." They say that only the "Word" of God is preserved. By this they mean only the "message, thoughts, concepts, and ideas" but not the very "Words" of the Hebrew and Greek Texts. To us in former days, the "Word" of God was identical in meaning to the "Words" of God. But this new brand of "Fundamentalists," as they still call themselves, are coming up with something that is different. They have a new wrinkle in this matter. They do not say the "Words" of God are preserved but just the "Word" of God. They hold up the King James Bible and the Textus Receptus Greek and say that both of these are the "Word" of God. They hold up the New American Standard Version and say that is also the "Word" of God, and, by extension for them, so is the Westcott and Hort Greek Text on which the NASV is based.

Wait a minute. In the Greek New Testament Text, the New American Standard Version differs from the Greek text of the King James Bible in at least five thousand six hundred and four places. It drops out two thousand eight hundred and eighty-six Greek words. It has three hundred and fifty-six doctrinal errors. How can they say both are the "Word" of God unless they redefine terms? That is what they are doing. When they say it is the "Word" of God, they just mean the message of God, the thoughts of God, the ideas of God, or the concepts of God. Their Greek Text has dropped out or changed many words. What good is a message, thought, idea, or concept without the words? We have to have the very "Words" that are preserved. What if we did not have the "Words"?

- **John 3:16**
  For God so loved the world, that he gave his only begotten Son, that whosoever believeth in him should not perish, but have everlasting life.

Every Word of that verse is important. God promised to preserve His Words, and He keeps His promises. I am glad that we have a promise-keeping God, a God who cannot lie.

Galatians 3:19

"Wherefore then *serveth* the law? It was added because of transgressions, till the seed should come to whom the promise was made; *and it was* ordained by angels in the hand of a mediator."

"Wherefore then *serveth* the law? It was added because of transgressions" What was the purpose of the law? It was added because of transgressions. That word for *"transgressions,"* PARABASIS, is from the prefix PARA *"from, by, besides"* and from the root word, BAINO, which means *"a stepping, walking."* Thus it means *"to step over."* It is *"the breach of a definite ratified law."* Metaphorically it means

"to create transgressions, i.e. that sins might take on the character of transgressions, and thereby the consciousness of sin be intensified and the desire for redemption be aroused."

God gave the law so that He could show that we have been guilty of violating His law. It was given so that transgressions could be seen clearly. If there were no laws against speeding, could you ever be arrested for speeding? No! There has to be a law first. If you break the law, then you are guilty. That is why the law of Moses was revealed so that God could point out, *"Thou shalt not kill. Thou shalt not steal."* and all the other laws. If we did not have a law that said we could not shoot someone, then nobody could hold us guilty for this. Am I right? There has to be a law saying we cannot do something. Then and only then can we really "violate" that law. Then we are held guilty for our action. The law of Moses was brought into effect so that transgression could be shown to be real.

"till the seed should come to whom the promise was made; *and it was* ordained by angels in the hand of a mediator" That Seed was the Lord Jesus Christ as it said in earlier verses. Angels were there in the giving of the law.

- **Deuteronomy 33:2**
  And he said, The LORD came from Sinai, and rose up from Seir unto them; he shined forth from mount Paran, and **he came with ten thousands of saints**: from his right hand went a fiery law for them.

"*Saints*" or "holy ones" might be a reference to angels. When God gave the law of Moses, angelic beings apparently were there.

- **Act 7:53**
  Who have **received the law by the disposition of angels**, and have not kept *it*.

This also mentions angelic involvement in the giving of the law. The Scripture in Exodus 19 does not specifically mention angels. There was thunder. There was lightening, and the whole mount of Sinai was smoking. That is why the people did not want to get near that mountain. God said that if they touched the mount, they would die. It was *"ordained by angels, in the hand of a mediator."* That *"mediator"* was Moses.

- **John 1:17**
  For **the law was given by Moses**, but grace and truth came by Jesus Christ.

Galatians 3:20

"Now a mediator is not *a mediator* of one, but God is one." A mediator is one who intervenes between two. That is what this word, MESITES, means. It is *"one who intervenes between two, either to make or restore peace and friendship, or form a compact, or for ratifying a covenant."* He is an arbitrator. Jesus Christ is the only mediator between God and man.

- **1 Timothy 2:5**
  For *there is* one God, and **one mediator between God and men, the man Christ Jesus**;

Jesus is that one Mediator, not the woman, Mary. The Roman Catholic Church has announced her as both the mediatrix, the feminine of mediator, as well as virtually a co-redemptrix. According to Rome, Mary mediates between us and God. They say that we can pray to Mary, and she will take care of things. They say that any mother would get something for the people from her son. No, it is not Mary, the saints, the pope, the rabbi, the preacher. It is not anyone, but the Lord Jesus Christ who is our Mediator.

- **Hebrews 8:6**
  But now hath he obtained a more excellent ministry, **by how much also he is the mediator of a better covenant**, which was established upon better promises.

- **Hebrews 9:15**
  And for this cause **he is the mediator of the new testament**, that by means of death, for the redemption of the transgressions *that were* under the first testament, they which are called might receive the promise of eternal inheritance.
- **Hebrews 12:24**
  And to **Jesus the mediator of the new covenant**, and to the blood of sprinkling, that speaketh better things than *that of* Abel.

I am glad we have a Mediator at the Father's right hand Who intercedes for us saved people when we sin.

- **1 John 2:1**
  My little children, these things write I unto you, that ye sin not. And if any man sin, **we have an advocate with the Father, Jesus Christ** the righteous:

God does not want any believer to sin, but if we do, we have an Advocate, the Lord Jesus Christ. An advocate is similar to a mediator.

Paul talked about a covenant in verses fifteen and seventeen. God made a covenant with Abraham in Genesis 15:1-18. He divided five different animals. This was the custom when you *"cut a covenant"* in Abraham's time. When you made a covenant, you divided into two parts the pieces of an animal. Those who made the covenant walked between these divided pieces. That signified a bond that would never be broken. That is the way they made a covenant.

In the case of the Abrahamic covenant, it was different. If you study covenants and dispensations in the Old Testament, there are two kinds of covenants. There are covenants that are conditional. If we do not keep a conditional covenant, then the covenant is broken. There are also unconditional covenants. In an unconditional covenant, it does not matter what we may do. God said it, and He is going to fulfill it. That is what the Abrahamic covenant was. It is an unconditional covenant. Here is what God did.

- **Genesis 15:12**
  And when the sun was going down, **a deep sleep fell upon Abram**; and, lo, an horror of great darkness fell upon him.

He put Abraham to sleep. Abraham did not walk between those pieces with the Lord. The Lord did it Himself. Abraham was sleeping.

- **Genesis 15:17**
  And it came to pass, that, when the sun went down, and it was dark, **behold a smoking furnace, and a burning lamp that passed between those pieces.**

That is the unconditional nature of the Abrahamic covenant which has a promise to all of us who are in Christ. That promise is that in Him, the Seed of Abraham, all the nations of the earth would be blessed. They are blessed in Christ if they trust Him. Obviously if they do not accept Jesus as Saviour, they cannot be blessed. By faith in Christ, we can receive the promise that was made to Abraham.

Galatians 3:21

"Is **the law then against the promises of God? God forbid: for if there had been a law given which could have given life, verily righteousness should have been by the law."** We saw this in Galatians 2:21. If we could get righteousness by keeping the law, why did Jesus have to come, bleed, suffer, and die for the sins of the world. The law could not give life. No law of any kind could produce life. There is no way at all that any work can give us righteousness.

Galatians 3:22

"But the Scripture hath concluded all under sin, that the promise by faith of Jesus Christ might be given to them that believe." These Scriptures conclude that every man, woman, boy, or girl have sinned.
- Romans 3:23
  For all have sinned, and come short of the glory of God;
- Romans 7:14
  For we know that the law is spiritual: but **I am carnal, sold under sin**.

The Scriptures have concluded this. That is a good word. Concluded, SUGKLEIO, means *"to shut up together, enclose, to shut up on all sides, to enclose like a shoal of fishes in a net, shut up completely."* We are lost and bound for Hell. It reminds me of the auction in Mountain Grove, Missouri when my wife and I were visiting her sister, Beverly. All of the steers were ready to be sold for slaughter. They were packed in like sardines. They could hardly move. When we approached them, they would back up a little bit. That was all they could do. God has concluded, like the fish in a net or the steers on auction, that all of us are under sin. That word sin, HAMARTIA, means *"to miss the mark, to miss or wander from the path of uprightness and honor, to wander from the law of God."* Everyone of us are all concluded under sin either in thought, word, or deed.

Galatians 3:23

"But before faith came, we were kept under the law, shut up unto the faith which should afterwards be revealed." Again that word, *"kept,"* is used. It is from PHROUREO. It means *"to guard, protect by military guard, either to prevent hostile invasion, or to keep the inhabitants of a besieged city from flight."* People were kept under the law and bound so that they could not leave or get out. They were just bound by the law of Moses and shut up without any possibility of righteousness. I am glad that the Lord Jesus Christ has come. We now have ability to have faith and trust in Him. If that is our condition, He has forgiven us of all our sins and has cleansed us from all unrighteousness. We are no longer trapped in this law of Moses which we could not keep. All the law does is to remind us that we have no hope as long as we are obligated to keep the whole law. Thanks be to God that faith in Jesus Christ has been revealed to us.

Galatians 3:24

"Wherefore the law was our schoolmaster *to bring us unto Christ, that we might be justified by faith."* *"Schoolmaster"* is an interesting term. It comes from two Greek words, PAIS, which is *"child,"* and AGO which means *"to lead."* It is literally *"a child leader or a leader of children."* Technically this word is used for

> *"a tutor i.e. a guardian and guide of boys. Among the Greeks and the Romans the name was applied to trustworthy slaves who were charged with the duty of supervising the life and morals of boys belonging to the better class. The boys were not allowed to so much as to step out of the house without them before arriving at the age of manhood."*

The child was guarded and was not to leave the house for fear he would be harmed in some way. The law was our schoolmaster.

This schoolmaster was a terrible thing. It would keep us down. It reminds me of a friend's oldest son. She said that her son shut her in her house. She said that her son put her on the second floor because the doctor said that she was doing too much. This son was being a *"schoolmaster."* The law of Moses was a *"schoolmaster"* until the Lord Jesus came.

Remember what that word, *"justified,"* means. It is *"when God declares you to be just and perfectly righteous."* This does not mean that we are just in the sense that we are perfect here on earth. It means that we have been pronounced just and righteous on the books of Heaven. That is made possible only by genuine faith in the Lord Jesus Christ. That is not by the works of the law of Moses. It is a wonderful thing to be justified by faith.

Galatians 3:25

"But after that faith is come, we are no longer under a schoolmaster." We no longer have to have this tutor. We do not need this guardian to watch and keep us. We no longer have to have the law of Moses. There were three divisions of the law of Moses: (1) the commandments or moral law; (2) the ordinances or ceremonial law, and (3) the judgments, or civil law. We are not bound by any part of that law.

Some Christians today want to place us under the *"ten commandments."* We keep the nine of the ten that are repeated in the New Testament. As Christians we do not keep, *"Remember the Sabbath day, to keep it holy."* (Exodus 20:8) We do not worship on the seventh day of the week. We worship the Lord Jesus on the first day of the week. I realize there are some Seventh Day Baptists and some Seventh Day Adventists who worship on Saturday, but they are wrong in doing this.

I know that some Christians refer to Sunday as the Sabbath. In fact, I called a man who was a lawyer and asked him a question. Then he said, *"I hope you have a good Sabbath."* He is a saved man, but he has put himself under part of the law of Moses. I did not say anything or argue with him. I said, *"thank you"* and hung up. Some Christians are still Sabbath-keeping people. The laws of the Sabbath are found in the Old Testament, but they are not repeated for Christians to follow in the New Testament. The disciples worshiped on the first day of the week. They worshiped when the Lord Jesus arose from the dead. It was a new beginning. They were not under the law. Sunday worship has nothing to do with the law of Moses. We are free.

A pastor asked me for a name of a good man who ministered to the Jewish Christians. I gave him the name of a man. This pastor said he did not want this man because he wanted all of the Gentiles to abstain from eating pork. He wanted people to do this, not because of health reasons, but because it was part of the law of Moses. This pastor was afraid that this Jewish convert was going to try to get the Gentiles to keep other parts of the law as well. Many of the "Jews for Jesus" who are Messianic Jews also try to get Christians to keep the law.

God says that there are three kinds of people.
- **1 Corinthians 10:32**
  Give none offence, neither to the **Jews**, nor to the **Gentiles**, nor to **the church** of God:

You are either a Jew, a Gentile, or a member of the church of God, that is, a Bible-believing born-again Christian. If you are a real and pure Jew, you are not saved. If you are a real and pure Gentile, you are not saved. If you are of Jewish background or Gentile background and are saved, then you are a member of *"the church of God."* You are a Christian and neither a Jew nor a Gentile. Your salvation just wipes away your former relationships. One of our ladies has a Jewish mother which makes her a Jew, but she is now saved and worshiping with us because she has become a Christian and is no longer considered to be a Jew. I was born with a Gentile background, but I am now saved. I am no longer considered a Gentile because I am a Christian.

Many of these "Jews for Jesus" or Messianic Jews wish to segregate themselves together rather than to join with other Christians who were formerly "Gentiles." They do not mix together. They keep various feast days. That is not what we ought to do. I believe that is false.

We are not under the school master. Christ has redeemed us from the law, lock, stock, and barrel. That is New Testament Christianity. The Roman Catholic Church is still under the law. They have their priests in robes just like the Old Testament priests. They have the sacrifice of the mass just like the Old Testament priests. Harold Camping of Family Radio is under some of the law. He believes that all the promises of Israel are fulfilled in the church. He does not believe in a national Israel only a spiritual Israel. He believes we are still under some parts of the Mosaic law. I am glad to be free. *"After that faith is come, we are no longer under a schoolmaster."* That is what the Bible says. I did not say it. I believe it because the Bible says it.

Galatians 3:26

"For ye are all the children of God by faith in Christ Jesus." When I was in the University of Michigan, I used to work in the Michigan Union Cafeteria. I witnessed to different ones who were waiters like I was. I usually gave them this verse. There was one man who was fine when I gave him the first half of this verse, *"for ye are all the children of God."* But his countenance fell and his teeth almost dropped out when I finished the verse *"by faith in Christ Jesus."* You have to have the last part of that verse, or the first part is not true.

The modernists and the liberals say that we are all the children of God whether or not we have faith in Christ Jesus. They believe in the universal fatherhood of God and the universal brotherhood of man. Westcott and Hort believed this too. Some Fundamentalists say that Westcott and Hort were wonderful Christians and have them in Heaven when they were in fact modernist apostates. The liberals today say that we are all the children of God. They believe there is so much good in the worst of us and so much bad in the best of us. They believe that we have a spark of the divine. If we are not saved and do not have the Spirit of God indwelling us, we do not have any spark of the divine. We only have the sin nature. But we can have a new nature when we come to Christ by genuine faith.

He does not say that some of you are more children than others. I realize that in different ways some of us are more childish than others. We are all children of God if we are born-again and are on an even playing field. It is not the clergy and the laity. It is not the preacher and the people. It is not the priests and various other things. We are all the children of God. We come to Him as His children on an even basis. I hope and pray that everyone of us continues to grow stronger and stronger and become more and more mature. I hope we *grow in grace, and in the knowledge of our Lord and Saviour Jesus Christ.* (2 Peter 3:18) That is what He wants us to do.

Galatians 3:27

"For as many of you as have been baptized into Christ have put on Christ." I believe this *"baptizing into Christ"* is the baptism of the Holy Spirit. This is not the water baptism that is required by those of us who are believers. The Lord Jesus said

- **Matthew 28:19**
  Go ye therefore, and teach all nations, **baptizing them** in the name of the Father, and of the Son, and of the Holy Ghost:

This is part of our two ordinances, the Lord's supper and baptism. We believe this is talking about the baptism of the Holy Spirit as mentioned in 1 Corinthians.

- **1 Corinthians 12:13**
  For by one Spirit are we all baptized into one body, whether *we be* Jews or Gentiles, whether *we be* bond or free; and have been all made to drink into one Spirit.

Seven ministries of the Holy Spirit

To the Lost
1. The convicting of sin, and
2. The restraining of sin.

To the Christian
1. The baptism of the Holy Spirit,
2. The indwelling of the Holy Spirit,
3. The regenerating of the Holy Spirit, and
4. The sealing of the Holy Spirit. Those four are never to be repeated. As soon as we come to Christ by genuine faith, we partake of these four ministries of the Holy Spirit. The fifth one,

> 5. The filling of the Holy Spirit, can be repeated over and over again as we need to be filled and controlled by the Holy Spirit for service.

The first four of these ministries to the Christian are instantaneous and are not related to feelings. The fifth one can be experienced over and over.

Baptism of the Holy Spirit is not speaking in tongues. I know that some of you are formerly from the tongues and the charismatic movement. This is not the baptism of the Holy Spirit that charismatics are speaking about. They say that it is speaking of tongues. The filling of the Spirit is not the baptism of the Holy Spirit.

- **1 Corinthians 12:13**
  For **by one Spirit are we all baptized into one body,** whether *we be* Jews or Gentiles, whether *we be* bond or free; and have been all made to drink into one Spirit.

> **The Baptism of the Holy Spirit**
> The baptism of the Holy Spirit does two things for us. It joins us to two kinds of persons. (1) It joins us to Christ our Head, and (2) it joins us to fellow- believers.

When we are saved, we have put on the Lord Jesus Christ, just as one puts on a piece of clothing.

Galatians 3:28

"There is neither Jew nor Greek, there is neither bond nor free, there is neither male nor female: for ye are all one in Christ Jesus." When Paul wrote this, there were slaves all over the Roman Empire. *"In Christ Jesus"* we are neither bond nor free. There is no distinction. *"There is neither male nor female."* This is *"in Christ Jesus."* In the here and now, there are males, and there are females. Definitely males and females are different and separate, but if we're saved, we are all one in Christ Jesus. The feminists, the women's liberationists, and the lesbians like Virginia Mollenkott and others misinterpret this verse. They say that here and now there is no male or female. Therefore, we can have female with female sex and male with male sex. This is horrendous. It gives reasonableness for the homosexual life style. The homosexuals use this verse to say that their life style is acceptable. This verse is saying that *"in Christ Jesus"* there is neither Jew nor Greek. This is referring to the spiritual realm when we are saved. We are

Christians. There is the exegesis. There is the difference. There is the interpretation. *"In Christ Jesus"* we are one. There is unity. The Lord Jesus does not look down upon us because we are a Jew or Gentile, bond or free, male or female. We are one in Christ Jesus.

Jesus was asked if there was marriage in Heaven. This was His answer.

- **Matthew 22:30**
  For in the resurrection **they neither marry, nor are given in marriage, but are as the angels of God in Heaven**.

He said they are like the angels of God. There is no gender with the angels. There will not be marriage or giving in marriage in Heaven. We who are saved will have our glorified bodies just like Christ. Will we all have male bodies meaning there are no more female bodies in Heaven? I do not know if this is the way it will be or not. The Lord Jesus Christ was a male. But according to the lesbian Virginia Mollenkott Jesus was not a male. In her book *Women, Men, and the Bible*, she wrote that Jesus was not a male but was androgynous. In the Greek the ANDRO part of this word is male and the GYNOUS part is female. Thus it means male/female. This is foolish. The Lord Jesus was a male. There is no getting around it. These homosexuals and lesbians are misusing this verse that says we are one in Christ. Right here in this world, there are Jews. There are Gentiles. There are males. There are females. There are bond. There are free. But in Christ, all those who are saved are *"one."* In the spiritual realm all of these things have passed away.

Galatians 3:29

"And if ye *be* Christ's, then are ye Abraham's seed, and heirs according to the promise." Notice, if we are saved and are Christians, we are *"Abraham's seed."* Remember, *"Now to Abraham and his seed were the promises made. He saith not, And to seeds, as of many; but as of one, And to thy seed, which is Christ"* (Galatians 3:16). That Seed was Christ. That is if you are saved, if you are redeemed, if you are regenerated by the Holy Spirit then you are heirs according to the promise. That is the status that we have. We are heirs.

There are some Christians that think that believers are spiritual Israel. They think that we are Abraham's seed in the sense of being spiritual Jews. They think that all of the promises of Israel are fulfilled in the church. We do not believe that at all. There is still a future for national Israel. Mr. Harold Camping, on his radio program, teaches that there is no more future for national Israel. He believes that the church is now Israel. No, this is not what this verse means.

Remember, "Israel" did not come into being until Abraham's grandson. Remember Abraham had a son, Isaac. Isaac had a son, Jacob. God changed his name to "Israel" (Genesis 32:28). Jacob had twelve sons who later were called the twelve tribes of Israel. There was no Israel in Abraham's time. We are not "Christian Jews." There is still a future for national Israel. God has promised one day to make them the head and not the tail.

That does not mean we always have to agree with national Israel. They are in unbelief right now. I do not agree with their giving atomic secrets to other countries that ought not to have them and on other matters. We are not Israelites. God will keep His promise. One day in the millennial reign of Christ, Israel will be the nation of glory on this earth. It will be the nation of headship and the nation of promise. Other nations will come and worship in Jerusalem, and the Lord Jesus will reign from sea to sea and from shore to shore. We are Abraham's seed, and we are heirs according to promise. In Romans 8:17 it says we are *"heirs of God, and joint-heirs with Christ."* Everything that Christ has is ours. He is the Son of God and God the Son. He owns the cattle on a thousand hills, and everything He owns belongs to the believers as well.

Galatians
Chapter Four

Galatians 4:1

"Now I say, *That* the heir, as long as he is a child, differeth nothing from a servant, though he be lord of all." This illustrates the relationship between the law of Moses and the grace of God which is in Christ, the promised Seed. Here is a child who is the heir. Even though this child is a small little infant, he will one day own all that was formerly his father's. His father is going to give him everything in his inheritance. As long as he is a child, he does not own anything. He is just a baby. That is what the law was. It was just a baby. It is certainly a good thing to be an heir if we have inheritance from our parents. But when we are children, we do not receive that inheritance. In some states, we have to be at least twenty-one years of age before we can receive a formal inheritance, unless there are other provisions made.

There is a problem with squandering an inheritance when we get it. I think of a young man who got an inheritance when he reached a legal age. As soon as he got his inheritance, he bought a car and went out and, within a short time, wrecked it. That whole inheritance was almost burned up in one accident. The laws are very clear. You cannot give an inheritance to a baby. They can get it, but they cannot receive the full benefits until they reach a certain age. As long as the heir is not at the age of maturity, he is just like a servant. He says, "Yes sir and no sir" and sweeps up around the house even though he is the lord of the house. He is no different from a servant. That is what Paul is teaching here.

Galatians 4:2

"But is under tutors and governors until the time appointed of the father." The *"tutor"* was a servant one who cared for the tutelage of children. He cared for the child whether the father was dead or the father is alive. This is a picture of the law of Moses. The *"governor"* was the manager of the household duties. He superintended whatever was in the house. The management of the house was entrusted to him. He cared for the expenditures and receipts of the house. This governor took care of children who were not yet of age *"until the time appointed of the father."*

There was a set time when the Lord Jesus Christ would appear. That set time was at the incarnation of our Saviour. Until that set time this child (Israel) was under the governor. In previous verses I talked about the schoolmaster. The law was our schoolmaster to lead us to Christ. The Jews were under that law as a schoolmaster until the Lord Jesus Christ would come.

Galatians 4:3

"Even so we, when we were children, were in bondage under the elements of the world." Remember, Paul was writing to the Jews who were saved. Many feel that the area of Galatia was in the area known today as Turkey. They were barbarians before they were converted to Christ. Until Christ came into our lives, we were all under bondage. If we are not saved, we are still under that bondage. There are a number of verses on bondage.

- **2 Timothy 2:26**
  And *that* they may recover themselves **out of the snare of the devil, who are taken captive** by him at his will.
  That is exactly what the devil has done to everyone of us if we are unsaved.
- **Romans 8:15**
  For **ye have not received the spirit of bondage** again to fear; but ye have received the Spirit of adoption, whereby we cry, Abba, Father.
- **Galatians 2:4**
  And that because of false brethren unawares brought in, who came in privily to spy out our liberty which we have in Christ Jesus, **that they might bring us into bondage**:
- **Galatians 4:9**
  But now, after that ye have known God, or rather are known of God, how turn ye again to the weak and beggarly elements, **whereunto ye desire again to be in bondage**?
- **Galatians 5:1**
  Stand fast therefore in the liberty wherewith Christ hath made us free, and be not entangled **again with the yoke of bondage**.

- **Hebrews 2:14-15**
Forasmuch then as the children are partakers of flesh and blood, he also himself likewise took part of the same; that through death he might destroy him that had the power of death, that is, the devil; And deliver them who through fear of death were all their lifetime **subject to bondage**.

Before we were saved we were in bondage and slavery, doing the will of another. We could do nothing for ourselves. Today people who are lost are in bondage to Satan and taken captive by him. There are many who are not only taken captive by legalism, the law, but also by drugs and many other sins. People who are not born-again are in bondage to the works of the devil. These people who were under the law of Moses were also in bondage under the elements of the world. The *"elements,"* STOICHEION, are the first or basic things. They are like the letters of the alphabet. They were under just the simple things of bondage. But the wonderful contrast is found in verse four.

Galatians 4:4

"But when the fulness of the time was come, God sent forth his Son, made of a woman, made under the law" God did not wait a minute later or a minute earlier than His planned time. Did you ever think why the Lord Jesus Christ came when He did? (We do not know the dates for sure.) They keep changing their calendars. At that proper time the Lord Jesus Christ was born at Bethlehem. Sin had risen to a certain level. People had rejected all of the prophesies of the Old Testament. Finally, *"in the fulness of the time,"* God sent forth--not an angel--but His own Son!

He was the Son of God and God the Son from all eternity past. There was never a time when the Lord Jesus was not God's Son. The Trinity--the Father, Son, and Holy Spirit, were from eternity past, without beginning and without ending. God the Father, God the Son, and God the Holy Spirit made a decision. I'm sure they discussed the whole plan of man's redemption. God the Father sent His Son. That Greek word for "sent" is EXAPOSTELLO. APOSTELLO means *"to send away."* The preposition, EX, means *"out from."* The entire compound term means *"to send away out from"* His glory." In a real sense *"God sent forth His Son."* You can still think that He sent away His Son. He sent His Son away from Heaven, away from a place of absolute perfection, away from a place of sinlessness, away from His eternal state to take upon Himself a body like unto our body, yet perfect and sinless. He was born from a virgin so God was His Father. No human male had any part of His incarnation and birth. *"God sent forth His Son, made of a woman."* This refers to Christ's virgin birth.

- Luke 1:35
  And the angel answered and said unto her, **The Holy Ghost shall come upon thee**, and the power of the Highest shall overshadow thee: therefore also **that holy thing which shall be born of thee shall be called the Son of God.**

This was God's antidote to Adam's sin. The first Adam got us into trouble, and the last Adam will get us out of trouble if we trust Him as Saviour and Redeemer. God made provision for all to be saved. That is where we part company with the hyper-Calvinists who say that Christ died only for the elect and not for the sins of the whole world. The Scriptures teach us that God sent forth His Son for the whole world that we may be saved if we trust Him by faith. Obviously this provision is of no value to us unless we receive Christ as our own Saviour.

- John 1:12
  But as many as received him, to them gave he power to become the sons of God, *even* **to them that believe on his name**:

Christ was *"made under the law."* The law was still in affect. The Lord Jesus came while the law was still in effect. He came to abolish the law while He was still under that law. That is why He came.

Some people believe that you can still be saved and not believe in the virgin birth of Christ. My problem with those people would be this: If you do not believe that the Lord Jesus was born of a virgin, then that means He was born just like the rest of us. That would mean He has the sin nature inherited from Adam and passed down to all of his sons, right down to all of us. If you believe that, then Jesus cannot be your Redeemer because He would have His own sins inherited from Adam's line. The only way that Jesus could escape the sin nature inherited from Adam was not to be born through Adam's line. That was precisely what God did. *"God sent forth his Son, made of a woman."* Joseph was not the father of Jesus. No, God Himself was the father of Jesus Christ the sinless Son of God.

Galatians 4:5

"To redeem them that were under the law, that we might receive the adoption of sons." He sent His son *"to redeem them that were under the law."* This was done for us Gentiles too. We Gentiles were grafted in, as it were, so that we, along with the Jews who believe in Christ, might receive the *"adoption"* as mature, full-grown sons. Remember from verse one that only a full-grown son received the inheritance from his father. In this verse, we learn that the Lord Jesus came to redeem us, to buy us back from the slave market of sin that we might become the heirs of Christ.

Galatians 4:5

When we accept Christ, we have everlasting life and are made mature and complete sons. No longer are we babies under tutors or governors like the law of Moses. We are full-grown sons. There is not a single person who trusts Christ as Saviour and Redeemer who does not receive a full-fledged adoption as Sons. Even though there are baby Christians as far as growth in this life is concerned, there is not a single Christian who is not a full and mature son able to partake of all of the promises from the God of Heaven. They can partake of eternal life. That is why He sent forth His Son *"to redeem"* us. There are many verses on God's redemption.

- **Luke 1:68**
  Blessed *be* the Lord God of Israel; for he hath visited and **redeemed** his people,
- **Luke 24:21**
  But we trusted that it had been he which should have **redeemed** Israel: and beside all this, to day is the third day since these things were done.
- **Galatians 3:13**
  Christ hath **redeemed** us from the curse of the law, being made a curse for us: for it is written, Cursed *is* every one that hangeth on a tree:
- **Titus 2:14**
  Who gave himself for us, that he might **redeem** us from all iniquity, and purify unto himself a peculiar people, zealous of good works.
- **1 Peter 1:18-19**
  Forasmuch as ye know that **ye were not redeemed with corruptible things**, *as* silver and gold, from your vain conversation *received* by tradition from your fathers; **But with the precious blood of Christ**, as of a lamb without blemish and without spot:

John MacArthur and his followers do not believe that we are redeemed by the literal blood of Christ. He says that blood does not mean blood. This verse is clear. We are redeemed *"with the precious blood of Christ."* Yes, He died for our sins, but in His death He shed His blood. It was the blood, God says, that *"redeems"* us as we trust in the Lord Jesus Christ as our Saviour.

There is another man, Mr. Harold Camping of Family Radio, who has followed this error that John MacArthur follows. In his book on baptism, he said that the blood of Christ does not save us but it was just His death. This is just like the heresy of John MacArthur. MacArthur says that blood is a metonym for death. He says that every time you see the word blood, it just means death. There is a word for death in the Greek. It is THANATOS. The word for blood in the Greek is HAIMA. These are totally different words.

Christ did die for our sins, but the Bible is clear that the forgiveness of our sins is based upon the shedding of Christ's blood. I am very sorry that Mr. Camping has gone the way of John MacArthur. Harold Camping has a world-wide radio ministry where he is teaching the false doctrine and heresy that it is not the blood of Christ that saves us.

- **Romans 3:24-25**
  Being justified freely by his grace **through the redemption that is in Christ Jesus**: Whom God hath set forth *to be* a propitiation **through faith in his blood**, to declare his righteousness for the remission of sins that are past, through the forbearance of God;
- **1 Corinthians 1:30**
  But of him are ye **in Christ Jesus**, who of God is made unto us wisdom, and righteousness, and sanctification, and **redemption**:

Jesus was made unto us redemption.

- **Ephesians 1:7**
  In whom we have redemption through his blood, the forgiveness of sins, according to the riches of his grace;

The blood of Christ is again involved in redemption.

- **Colossians 1:14**
  In whom we have redemption through his blood, *even* the forgiveness of sins:

This is why He came. He came so that all of us might believe in Christ and receive the redemption of our souls and the *"adoption of sons."* This is the tremendous purpose for Christ's redeeming all who trust Him. Everyone is not redeemed automatically. That would be universalism. I do not agree with that false and unscriptural doctrine. God made provision for the whole world, but it is up to each person to receive Christ as their Saviour by faith.

If I had a ten dollar bill, and I offered it to you. It would not be yours until you received it. Right? It is the same with salvation. God the Father, God the Son, and God the Holy Spirit offer the whole world redemption, forgiveness, eternal life, and a home in Heaven. But you do not get it until you receive it. You must, in genuine saving faith, say something like *"Yes, I receive the Lord Jesus as my Saviour and believe on His Name as the One who took all my sins upon Himself in my place."* Only then have you "received" God's gift of eternal life which He wants so much to bestow upon you.

Galatians 4:6

"And because ye are sons, God hath sent forth the Spirit of his Son into your hearts, crying, Abba, Father." In this verse, the word, *"sent forth,"* is the same word as in verse four where it said *"God sent forth his Son."* It is the same word, EXAPOSTELLO. We are related to the Father. We are adopted. That expression, *"Abba, Father,"* is found in two other places.

- **Mark 14:36**
  And he said, **Abba, Father**, all things *are* possible unto thee; take away this cup from me: nevertheless not what I will, but what thou wilt.
- **Romans 8:15**
  For ye have not received the spirit of bondage again to fear; but ye have received the Spirit of adoption, whereby we cry, **Abba, Father**.

"Abba" is the word for father in Hebrew. When my wife and I were in the Holy Land we had to cross over in cable cars to see one of the sights at Masada. As we were riding, we overheard a little frightened infant trying to communicate with his father. I pointed out to my wife that the child called his father *"Abba."* It conveyed some of the same meaning as our word, "daddy." There is a very close and intimate relationship between a child and a father. We have been adopted and have received the *"adoption of sons."*

- **Ephesians 1:5**
  Having **predestinated us unto the adoption of children by Jesus Christ** to himself, according to the good pleasure of his will,

He has predestined us to the *"adoption of children."* There is a song that we sing in our hymnbook that begins, *"I'm adopted, I'm adopted, I'm one of His own."* It is a beautiful thing that we are adopted by faith in Christ so that we may cry *"Abba Father."*

Galatians 4:7

"Wherefore thou art no more a servant, but a son; and if a son, then an heir of God through Christ." A son is an *"heir."* We are mature, so we can be legitimate heirs now. We are not babies like we were while we were under the law. Christ has come. He has redeemed us from the curse of the law. Now He has made us adopted sons and daughters. We are full-fledged heirs. God is not slighting the women when he uses the word *"son."* That is just how God is. Whether we are male or female, He refers to us as sons.

- **Romans 4:13**
  For the **promise**, that he should be the heir of the world, *was* not to Abraham, or to his seed, through the law, but **through the righteousness of faith**.

This was the promise to Abraham. We are not an heir to the law.

- **Romans 8:17**
  And if children, then heirs; **heirs of God, and joint-heirs with Christ**; if so be that we suffer with *him*, that we may be also glorified together.

Those of us who have been saved by trusting Christ are heirs and joint-heirs with Christ.

- **Hebrews 1:2**
  Hath in these last days spoken unto us by *his* Son, **whom he hath appointed heir of all things**, by whom also he made the worlds;

If we are in Christ and saved, then we are heirs of all things with Him. We are going to have an inheritance. We already have been made heirs. Eternal life starts when we trust Christ as Saviour.

Galatians 4:8

"Howbeit then, when ye knew not God, ye did service unto them which by nature are no gods." That word for did service is the verb, DOULEUO. This word has as its root DOULOS, which means *"a slave."* We were slaves. Before any of us were saved, we were in bondage. We did service to those that *"are no gods."* It might have been religious bondage or drug bondage or any other kind of slavery. We were the slaves to the devil.

Galatians 4:9

"But now, after that ye have known God, or rather are known of God, how turn ye again to the weak and beggarly elements, whereunto ye desire again to be in bondage?" God saved these Jews from their old ways. Remember, Galatians was written for a two-fold purpose. First: it was written to tell these former barbarians of Galatia that they were not saved by the law of Moses. Secondly: it was written to tell them that they were not sanctified or made holy by the law of Moses. They were neither saved or sanctified by the law.

The law could not save them. Why did they go back to it? No works of ours can save us. Why do we revel in them? We can please the Lord with our works after we are saved, but these works cannot save us. He is telling these Jews that they have been saved by grace. Then he asks why are they going back to the *"weak and beggarly elements."* Do you know what *"beggarly,* [PTOCHOS] *elements* are? They are elements that are *"destitute of wealth, influence, position, or honor"* They are elements that are *"lowly, afflicted, destitute of Christian virtues and eternal riches"* They are elements that are *"helpless, powerless to accomplish an end."* That is what beggarly means.

You have seen beggars. We have many of them in Philadelphia. I go to teach every Monday evening at the Bible Baptist Institute at the Christ Independent Baptist Church in Philadelphia. When I come back over the Ben Franklin Bridge, I sometimes see the homeless people sleeping underneath the shelter of that bridge. Some beggars have nothing, and some have a few things.

We heard also about the blind Christian who was converted. He used to go out and beg with his tin cup in Atlantic City, New Jersey. He made out better than those who work for a living. It was a good living. It was good business. He looked like a beggar, but he was not a beggar.

That is the trouble with some of us. We look like beggars, but we have all the riches of God in Christ Jesus. Why would you want to be a slave again? I don't want to be. In Christ I am free. I don't want to go back into the things that enslaved me. The Jews should not go back into the law of Moses. Paul was really ashamed of that.

Galatians 4:10

"Ye observe days, and months, and times, and years."
Here Paul mentions that some of the Galatians observed special days.

- **Romans 14:5-6**
  One man **esteemeth one day above another:** another **esteemeth every day** *alike*. Let every man be fully persuaded in his own mind. He that **regardeth the day**, regardeth *it* unto the Lord; and he that **regardeth not the day**, to the Lord he doth not regard *it*. He that eateth, eateth to the Lord, for he giveth God thanks; and he that eateth not, to the Lord he eateth not, and giveth God thanks.

These people were going back to the various days of the Jewish celebration.
Leviticus chapter twenty-three outlines the seven feast days of Israel:
1. The feast of passover (Leviticus 23:5)
2. The feast of unleavened bread (Leviticus 23:6-8)
3. The feast of first fruits (Leviticus 23:9-14)
4. The feast of Pentecost (Leviticus 23:15-22)
5. The feast of trumpets (Leviticus 23:23-26)
6. The feast of atonement, (Leviticus 23:32) and
7. The feast of tabernacles (Leviticus 23:33-37).

They had a special feast on the first of every month and so on. They were worshiping all these things. They had special days, special weeks, and special years such as the year of jubilee. Paul says that is all past. We do not have to do that.

As I said before, that is what many of the Messianic Jews are doing. That is what many of the "Jews for Jesus" people are doing. They are getting Jews who have accepted Christ to segregate into their own churches. They are not integrating into Gentile churches. Paul said we are now neither Jews nor Gentiles, but we are all one in Christ. We are Christians. Once you are saved, you are part of the church and a Christian. These groups in our day often try to get these Messianic Jews to keep these old laws and dietary ways. Paul chastised these Jewish Christians who were going back to the law of Moses. That word for *"observe,"* PARATEREO, means *"to stand beside and watch, to watch assiduously, observe carefully, to watch, to attend to with the eyes."* The Galatians were watching and observing these special days also.

No, there is no special day to be remembered except the day we were redeemed by genuine faith in Christ. I hope you can all know that there was a day when you were saved. You may not know the exact day, but I hope you know there was a day that you were saved. I hope you know that there was a month you were saved. You may not remember the exact month you were saved, but I hope you know there was a month you were saved. I hope that you can know that there was a year when you were saved. There has to be a time you can point to and say, *"That was the time that I opened my heart and accepted Christ as Saviour."*

I was talking to a man recently who told me that there had never been a time that he was not a Christian. God says all of us are born in sin. All of us have gone astray. There must be a time when you knew that you were not a Christian. Maybe his mind does not remember, I do not know. Can we become a Christian by osmosis? No, there has to be a time and a place where we trusted Christ as our Lord and Saviour. That is the day we ought to remember.

Galatians 4:11

"I am afraid of you, lest I have bestowed upon you labour in vain." Why is Paul saying that? When you do something for the Lord are you saying, *"Lord, I did all this for you. Now what are you going to do for me?"* No! Paul was worried. He was afraid. He did not want to labor without any purpose. He did not want to do this in vain. That word *"labor,"* KOPIAO, means *"to grow weary, tired, exhausted with toil or burdens or grief, to labor with wearisome effort, to toil"* This is very toilsome labor. This is the kind of wearisome labor that most of us never engage in for any cause. He says I have labored and worked hard. Is it in vain? The Lord has a number of things to say about doing things *"in vain."* Christian work is labor if done right. Sad to say, some preachers and even missionaries are lazy. This is not right.

- **Psalms 127:1**
  Except the LORD build the house, they labour in vain that build it: except the LORD keep the city, the watchman waketh *but* in vain.

The Lord must build that house and keep that city.

- **Matthew 15:9**
  But **in vain they do worship me**, teaching *for* doctrines the commandments of men

- **1 Corinthians 15:58**
  Therefore, my beloved brethren, be ye stedfast, unmoveable, always abounding in the work of the Lord, **forasmuch as ye know that your labour is not in vain** in the Lord.

Our labor is never *"in vain"* if it is in the Lord. No matter what we do. No matter what we say. No matter what we give. If it is in the flesh, it is *"in vain."* But if it is in the Lord, it is not *"in vain."* We should examine ourselves to be sure we are serving the Lord with the right motives.

- **2 Corinthians 6:1**
  We then, *as* workers together *with him*, beseech *you* also **that ye receive not the grace of God in vain.**

- **Galatians 2:22**
  I do not frustrate the grace of God: for if righteousness *come* by the law, **then Christ is dead in vain.**

If you can get righteousness by the law then why did Christ have to die?

- **Philippians 2:16**
  Holding forth the word of life; that I may rejoice in the day of Christ, **that I have not run in vain, neither laboured in vain.**

Paul wanted to be sure that the Philippian Christians were established, growing, and mature.

- **1 Thessalonians 3:5**
  For this cause, when I could no longer forbear, I sent to know your faith, lest by some means the tempter have tempted you, **and our labour be in vain.**

Paul was always aware if his labor would be *"in vain"* it would be worthless. He wanted the Christians in the churches that he had founded to go on with Christ. Is that how you are? When you bring up your children, you hope it will not be in vain. You sacrifice for them. You save for them. Perhaps you help to put them through college, and you hope it is not *"in vain."* The Lord hopes that our salvation is not *"in vain."* He has saved us. He hopes that we have not wasted and squandered our life when we get to the end of the line. As the saying goes, *"Only one life, 'twill soon be past. Only what's done for Christ will last."* May our lives not be lived *"in vain."*

Galatians 4:12

"Brethren, I beseech you, be as I am; for I am as ye are: ye have not injured me at all." Paul was free from the law of Moses. He was not in bondage to that old law, and he didn't want them to be in bondage either. Paul hoped that he had not run in vain. He knew that they had not physically *"injured"* him. But I think by what he says here, he is saying something is wrong. Paul wants them to be as he is in all respects. He is implying that these Galatian Christians were not what they ought to be.

Galatians 4:13

"Ye know how through infirmity of the flesh I preached the gospel unto you at the first." Paul was infirmed. We do not know exactly the nature of his problem. In a way, that is good because then all of us who have infirmities can plug right into Paul's infirmity. It might have been his eyes because later in this letter (Galatians 4:15) he mentions his eyes. It might have been a speech impediment. Perhaps it was a limp like Jacob had from wrestling with the angel (Genesis 32:24). We do not know for sure what it was, but they knew. Even though Paul was sick, he could still preach the gospel. Some of you have come to church this morning even though you are not feeling good. You may stay home and still be able to work and serve the Lord from your home. Paul was faithful in every circumstance and we should be faithful also.

Galatians 4:14

"And my temptation which was in my flesh ye despised not, nor rejected; but received me as an angel of God, even as Christ Jesus."

"And my temptation which was in my flesh ye despised not" The Galatians did not despise Paul's *"temptation"* or his testing or infirmity. Some people *"despise"* their pastors. They don't want a preacher who is ugly or who weighs four hundred pounds. They do not want a preacher who is skinny or who cannot talk properly. It is difficult to please people. The bigger the crowd, the harder it is to please everyone. The point is, are we trying to please the people or the Lord? We may try to please both, but if we have to please just one, we should want to please the Lord.

"nor rejected; but received me as an angel of God, even as Christ Jesus" Paul was received even as *"an angel of God."* They did not despise him. They did not reject him. That word, *"reject,"* EKPTUO, is an example of onomatopoeia. This is a word that sounds like what it means. EK means *"out"* and PTUO means *"to spit."* When you say PTUO, it sounds like you are spitting. They received him as if he were *"Christ Jesus."* They received him well. He is now asking them why they did not obey him when he told them to forsake the law.

Galatians 4:15

"Where is then the blessedness ye spake of? for I bear you record, that, if *it had been* possible, ye would have plucked out your own eyes, and have given them to me."

"Where is then the blessedness ye spake of?" The Galatian believers were ready to receive him. They were happy as a lark, as we say. When a pastor first comes to a church, that is often called a honeymoon period. The church likes him. Then soon he might be cast out of the church. When Paul went to this church in Galatia they had *"blessedness."* They received him well.

"for I bear you record, that, if *it had been* possible, ye would have plucked out your own eyes, and have given them to me" Maybe Paul's infirmity had to do with his eyes. Paul talked about *"how large a letter"* he had written (Galatians 6:11). If you can't see well, you might write with larger letters so you can see what you are writing. Those of you who need to wear glasses, try taking them off a while and write a letter without your glasses. You might write with larger letters so you could see what you were writing. My sermon notes are not in the normal twelve-point type. Just to be sure I can see them because I do not wear glasses, I put them in sixteen-point type. These people cared so much for Paul that if it were possible, they *"would have plucked out their own eyes"* for him.

This could have been just an expression illustrating how much they cared for Paul. That word, "pluck," EKORUSSO, means *"to dig out."* We can have eye transplants these days. Dr. Ray Adams, now retired, was a very skilled ophthalmologist. He did a lot of eye-surgery. If somebody were willing to take out their own eyes and give them to you, then you would assume that they really loved you. We heard about a fairly young man who died and donated his eyes at death. Two people are now able to see because of this.

Galatians 4:16

"Am I therefore become your enemy, because I tell you the truth?" Have you ever made an enemy by speaking *"the truth"*? I think all of us here have experienced that. These Galatians at first would have plucked out their eyes for Paul. They were all for him. Now all of a sudden he is no good because he told them the truth. He told them that they did not need the law of Moses. All they needed was Christ, not Christ plus the law of Moses.

I have made many enemies telling the truth about the King James Bible and the Hebrew Masoretic and Greek Textus Receptus texts which underlie it. It is not my purpose to make enemies, but they are made when I try to preach and speak the truth. I hope that you do the same. If enemies come, they just come. I do not know why this happens. Paul had the same experience. Aren't you glad that we can enter into his experience? Someone has rightly said: *"The enemies you make by telling the truth will have more respect for you than the friends you make by compromising."* There are a number of verses that talk about *"truth."*

- **Matthew 22:16**
  And they sent out unto him their disciples with the Herodians, saying, Master, we know that thou art true, and **teachest the way of God in truth**, neither carest thou for any *man*: for thou regardest not the person of men.

The Lord Jesus taught these people truth.

- **John 1:14**
  And the Word was made flesh, and dwelt among us, (and we beheld his glory, the glory as of the only begotten of the Father,) **full of grace and truth**.

- **John 1:17**
  For the law was given by Moses, *but* **grace and truth came by Jesus Christ**.

- **John 4:23**
  But the hour cometh, and now is, when the true worshipers shall **worship the Father in spirit and in truth**: for the Father seeketh such to worship him.

Many churches teach false doctrine rather than true doctrine. That is not the way to worship *"in truth."*

- **John 8:32**
  And ye shall **know the truth**, and the **truth shall make you free**.

That is what we need.

- **John 8:44**
  Ye are of *your* father the devil, and the lusts of your father ye will do. He was a murderer from the beginning, and **abode not in the truth, because there is no truth in him**. When he speaketh a lie, he speaketh of his own: for he is a liar, and the father of it.

Galatians 4:16

- John 14:6
  Jesus saith unto him, **I am the way, the truth**, and the life: no man cometh unto the Father, but by me.
- John 14:17
  Even the **Spirit of truth**; whom the world cannot receive, because it seeth him not, neither knoweth him: but ye know him; for he dwelleth with you, and shall be in you.

That is a reference to and a name of God the Holy Spirit.

- John 17:17
  Sanctify them through thy truth: thy word is truth.

The truth is what I try to preach from this pulpit in every service. Oh, I tell a few stories here and there, but not skyscraper stories. (Do you know what a "skyscraper sermon" is? It is a sermon with one tall story after another.) Some preachers preach tall stories, believe me. Now, I am not saying we should not use illustrations. We have to have illustrations to let in the light. But we need to preach the light and preach and teach the Scriptures. I need to know what this Bible teaches in order to do this effectively.

- John 17:19
  And for their sakes I sanctify myself, **that they also might be sanctified through the truth.**
- John 18:37
  Pilate therefore said unto him, Art thou a king then? Jesus answered, Thou sayest that I am a king. To this end was I born, and for this cause came I into the world, **that I should bear witness unto the truth.** Every one that is of **the truth** heareth my voice.
- Romans 1:25
  Who changed the truth of God into a lie, and worshiped and served the creature more than the Creator, who is blessed for ever. Amen.
- 1 Corinthians 13:6
  Rejoiceth not in iniquity, **but rejoiceth in the truth**;

You may say that you are a very loving person. Many modernists and liberal preachers claim to love everybody, but they neglect to preach the truth. If you really have charity, AGAPE, or love, you will rejoice in the truth. What we need is not "sloppy AGAPE" (as they say), but real, genuine love. The truth will set us free. The truth is found in the Words of God.

- 2 Corinthians 4:2
  But have renounced the hidden things of dishonesty, not walking in craftiness, nor handling the word of God deceitfully; **but by manifestation of the truth** commending ourselves to every man's conscience in the sight of God.

- **Galatians 2:5**
  To whom we gave place by subjection, no, not for an hour; **that the truth of the gospel might continue** with you.
- **Galatians 5:7**
  Ye did run well; **who did hinder you that ye should not obey the truth**?
- **Ephesians 4:15**
  But **speaking the truth in love**, may grow up into him in all things, which is the head, *even* Christ:

Many of us who speak the truth are told that we do not speak the truth in love. I do not know how else to speak the truth, but to speak it. Quite often those who do not like the truth that is spoken might say that it is not spoken *"in love."* When your house is on fire, how else can you phrase it than *"Your house is on fire"*? Is that *"in love"*? Frankly, if my house were on fire, I wouldn't care how the words were spoken. I would need desperately to know that my house were on fire in order to do something about it. Recently our house had a small fire set by an outside person. I detected it first by smelling the smoke. Fortunately I was able to put it out quickly with minimal damage.

- **Ephesians 5:9**
  (For the fruit of the Spirit *is* in all goodness and **righteousness and truth**;)
- **Ephesians 6:14**
  Stand therefore, **having your loins girt about with truth**, and having on the breastplate of righteousness;
- **2 Thessalonians 2:10**
  And with all deceivableness of unrighteousness in them that perish; because **they received not the love of the truth**, that they might be saved.

The church is *"the pillar and ground of the truth"* (1 Timothy 3:15). In the last days people will be destitute of the truth. We must stick by the truth. If you listened to MacDonald Martin's interview with me on "Halloween and the Cults," you heard him ask me what I thought about people who make laws against Christians and think that we are crazy. I said that there are people that think we are crazy, nuts, stupid, ignorant mossbacks and neanderthals. They think we do not know anything. I told him, *"Sticks and stones will break my bones, but names will never hurt me."* But sometimes they do hurt us.

Regardless what the world thinks of us, we must speak the truth. If we make enemies by speaking that truth, we must still speak it. After spending so many years teaching these Galatian Christians, Paul's great disgust with them was, *"Am I therefore become your enemy because I tell you the truth?"*

I want the truth in my life. If I am wrong, I want somebody to set me straight. If I preach error, please set me straight. I want the truth. I do not want any error or false teaching to go forth from this pulpit! I want the truth in my life. Someone has written *"Truth forever on the scaffold, wrong forever on the throne. . . . "* This often seems to be the case, sad to say.

Galatians 4:17

"They zealously affect you, *but* not well; yea, they would exclude you, that ye might affect them." He is speaking now of these Judaizers. Remember, we have said that there were two reasons that Paul has given for writing this book. The first reason was that these people thought that you could be saved and go to Heaven by keeping the law of Moses. The second reason was that these people thought that they could be sanctified by keeping the law of Moses. Both of these are false. These Judaizers, as we call them, are people who came into the Christian community and tried to make these born-again Jews observe the law of Moses. They wanted them to be circumcised and keep all the feast days. That simply was not the way to go. We have some people today who want us to go back to a works-system. They say that we can be sanctified by what we do. This teaching would affect all of the works-people as well as these Judaizers.

People who do not agree with us many times exclude us from fellowshiping with them. If we are not a Baptist or a Presbyterian or whatever group, they want to keep us out of their circle. That word, *"exclude,"* EKKLEIO, means *"to shut out, to turn out doors, to prevent the approach of one."* There are some people who think they are *"holier than thou."* They think they are so *"sanctified"* that they seem to be no good for Heaven as well as no good for earth. And they are proud of it. They say that they are perfect, and they do nothing wrong. They say *"If you cannot match what we do, we do not want anything to do with you."* If we are saved by God's grace, through genuine faith in Christ, we are all sinners and none of us are able to be perfect. This is a battle between works and grace. These are opposites.

Galatians 4:18

"But *it is* good to be zealously affected always in a good *thing*, and not only when I am present with you." We have called our message, "Zealous always in a good thing." We do not want to be zealous in a bad thing. Paul said this about his life.

- **Acts 22:3**
    I am verily a man *which am* a Jew, born in Tarsus, *a city* in Cilicia, yet brought up in this city at the feet of Gamaliel, *and* taught according to the perfect manner of the law of the fathers, and **was zealous toward God**, as ye all are this day.

Paul was talking to the Jews. Paul was zealous in the wrong direction. That word for *"zealous,"* ZELOO, means *"to burn with zeal, to be heated or to boil with envy, hatred, or anger."* That is what Paul was before he was saved. He had only one speed but in different directions--full speed ahead or full speed astern. He was going full speed astern when he was following the law of Moses and rejecting Christ. As soon as he came to know the Lord Jesus Christ as his Saviour, he went full speed ahead. Now he was *"zealous"* in the pursuit of good with zeal in a good sense.

- **Romans 10:2**
  For I bear them record that **they have a zeal of God, but not according to knowledge**.

This is also true in many churches today. There is zeal with fire. God wants us to be zealous and on fire, but He does not want us to be burning for the wrong cause. Some people have the fire and the zeal, but they have very little knowledge of the Word of God.

I think that Charismatic extremists fit into this category. They are emotional, but have very little knowledge. My wife and I were at the "Toronto Blessing" as reporters for the Bible For Today. We took video pictures of some of the service. These people were yelling, screaming, crying and falling down. After this service there were about five lines of people with about fifty people in each line "smitten in the Spirit." They had someone lay hands on them. They had a "catcher" behind them. When they were so called "slain in the Spirit," they would fall over. Then the next one would come up and have this happen to them. Nowhere in Scripture do I see this mentioned! This whole meeting was emotion and zeal. There was lots of zeal, but not according to knowledge. Paul was like this before he was saved. He was zealous but not according to the word of God.

- **Philippians 3:6**
  Concerning zeal, persecuting the church; touching the righteousness which is in the law, blameless.

Paul's kind of zeal before he was saved was persecuting the church.

- **Titus 2:14**
  Who gave himself for us, that he might redeem us from all iniquity, and purify unto himself a peculiar people, **zealous of good works**.

God wants everybody who is saved to be *"zealous of good works."* The *"good,"* KALOS, means

> *"beautiful, handsome, excellent, eminent, choice, surpassing, precious, useful, suitable, commendable, admirable, genuine, approved, beautiful by reason of purity of heart and life, honorable and affecting the mind agreeably, comforting and confirming."*

These are the things that we are to be zealous of. We are to be *"zealous"* always in good things. The Lord Jesus wants us to be zealous for Him. We are not to be slothful for that which is good. Bible reading, prayer, purity, witness for the Lord with our life and lips, fellowship with others are examples of how the Lord wants us to live zealously for Him.

Galatians 4:19

"My little children, of whom I travail in birth again until Christ be formed in you" Here Paul calls them his *"little children"* because they are learning and are Paul's pupils. They are children in the sense of immaturity. *"Of whom I travail in birth again until Christ be formed in you"* means he wonders if they are even saved. Are they even Christians? Are they even born-again yet? If they are still insisting that they can be saved by their good works by keeping the law of Moses, they are not trusting in Christ alone. It is important to remember what Paul said earlier in Galatians 2:21. *"For if righteousness come by the law, then Christ is dead in vain."* If man can be righteous by keeping the law, then Jesus did not have to die. If anyone is insisting that they can save themselves by their own righteousness, then there is something wrong. They are not born-again.

The minute that we come to Christ and are saved by genuine faith, the Lord Jesus Christ and the Holy Spirit and God the Father enter into our bodies. Our bodies become the temple of the Holy Spirit which is in us.

- **1 Corinthians 6:19-20**
  What? know ye not that **your body is the temple of the Holy Ghost *which is* in you**, which ye have of God, and ye are not your own? For ye are bought with a price: therefore glorify God in your body, and in your spirit, which are God's.

Christ is also in us.

- **Colossians 1:27**
  To whom God would make known what *is* the riches of the glory of this mystery among the Gentiles; which is **Christ in you**, the hope of glory:

Normally we think of the Holy Spirit indwelling the body of the believer. This is true. But here, the Bible says that Christ is also in the saved people.

- **John 14:23**
  Jesus answered and said unto him, If a man love me, he will keep my words: and my Father will love him, and **we will come unto him, and make our abode with him.**

So comparing these verses, we see that the entire Triune God, Father, Son, and Holy Spirit are indwelling the saved born-again Christians.

These Galatians were anything but Christlike in their actions. Paul wondered if they were even saved. It is not easy to lead a soul to Christ. It was not easy for Paul to go to the Galatians who were formerly heathen and tell them about Christ. It was not easy for Paul to give his life, his time, his effort, and his energy for these barbarians. He probably did not have much sleep or food. Now, he thought he would have to repeat the same things he told them before. Paul felt like he was going through the agony of giving birth. Many women know a mother's travail in the birth of a first child, a second child, a third child, and even a fourth child or more. This is what Paul felt like he was going through with these Galatians. He went through the birth pangs before and now he had those pains repeated over and over again. This is what his spiritual agony was like to Paul.

Galatians 4:20

"I desire to be present with you now, and to change my voice; for I stand in doubt of you." Paul wonders if they are saved. He is in doubt if they are really saved. If you think that you can save yourself just by being good and nice, you have to wonder if you are saved. This is what all of the human religions teach. You cannot trust in your own merits or your own works to be saved. Paul stood in doubt of these Christians.

We know all about boys changing their voices. When they get older, their voices get deeper. This is not what Paul is talking about. What *"voice"* did he use when he led them to Christ? He was no doubt very gentle, nice, and kind. He tried to encourage them. How is he going to change his voice? I think he is going to let them have a good loud salvo of blame. I think that is what he means. Maybe he wants to scream at them. They say that screaming does the person who is screaming some good. How about the one being screamed at? That might be so, just as long as we do not scream at the wrong person or scream out of line! He wants to vent his emotions. Sometimes people do not listen to us if we are talking quietly and nicely. When you shout at them, all of a sudden they wonder what you are talking about. Well, Paul wanted to change his *"voice"* in order for them to hear his message. You know hearing is one thing. Doing is another. God says this in the book of Ezekiel.

- **Ezekiel 33:31**
  And they come unto thee as the people cometh, and they sit before thee *as* my people, and **they hear thy words, but they will not do them**: for with their mouth they shew much love, *but* their heart goeth after their covetousness.

James also remarks about this.

- **James 1:22**
  But **be ye doers of the word, and not hearers only**, deceiving your own selves.

Paul says he is in doubt. He is *"without resources."* He is *"embarrassed."* That is what that word, *"doubt,"* APOREO, means. He does *"not know which way to turn."* He does *"not know how to decide."*

Galatians 4:21

"Tell me, ye that desire to be under the law, do ye not hear the law?" Paul is going to give an illustration from the law. It is the same with us today. Do we really want to be living with our works? Do we really want to trust our works to save us instead of grace through faith? Paul says if you desire to be under the law, listen to what the law says. Some people think that you must be under certain rules in order to be saved. The Church of Christ believes you cannot be saved unless you are baptized by immersion. That is their doctrine. Their salvation hinges on that. When I was with the Marines in Okinawa as a Navy Chaplain, I had an assistant who was a member of the Church of Christ. He told me that you had to enter into water baptism or you cannot be saved. This would be salvation by some work that we do. Some people believe you cannot be saved unless you are a member of a church.

Galatians 4:22

"For it is written, that Abraham had two sons, the one by a bondmaid, the other by a freewoman." Here is that expression again, *"it is written."* Whenever this expression is written, I like to comment on its significance. This is in the perfect tense in the Greek language. People these days are doubting that every Hebrew and Greek Word has been preserved. They say that just the message, ideas, thoughts, or concepts in general have been preserved, but not every Word.

The perfect tense of the Greek language is a very ingenious tense. *"It is written"* refers to something that has been written down in the past. Moses wrote it down. It also means that the action continues up to the present time. It stands written today. The letters have not changed. The words are still there. It also means that which has been written and preserved to the present time will also continue in that same way, preserved way on into the future. There is no question about the past, present, and future of the Hebrew and Greek Words of the originals..

Many Fundamentalists today deny that God even **promised** to preserve His Words. These people say they believe that God promised to preserve His "Word," but they do not believe that He actually preserved His "Words." They re-define "Word" to include only God's thoughts, concepts, ideas, or message, but not His actual Hebrew and Greek "Words." If we do not have God's Words preserved in His Hebrew Text and His Greek Text, we are of all men most miserable. Words are very important. Words make up thoughts. Without accurate Words, there can be no accurate thoughts.

Abraham had two sons, Ishmael and Isaac. He had Ishmael by his bondmaid, Hagar, and Isaac by the freewoman, Sarah. Abraham was promised an heir. That heir was to be Isaac. The mother of that son was to be Sarah, his wife. Abraham was impatient like many of us. The Bible says we have need of patience.

- **Hebrews 10:36**
  For **ye have need of patience**, that, after ye have done the will of God, ye might receive the promise.

How we need patience. We just do not want to wait too long for anything. After we have done the will of God, we often get a little jumpy. We might want to interfere with the timing of God. Sarah probably said something like this: *"Maybe you can go in unto my handmaid, Abraham. You can have a child by her, and that will fulfill the promise."* Abraham was glad about that. He got a son from that bondmaid named Ishmael. But that was not the promised son. The bondmaid was a servant who worked in the kitchen. She was an Egyptian slave named Hagar.

- **Genesis 16:15**
  And **Hagar bare Abram a son**: and Abram called his son's name, which Hagar bare, Ishmael.
- **Genesis 21:1**
  And the LORD visited Sarah as he had said, and **the LORD did unto Sarah as he had spoken**.

God kept His promise. God always keeps His promises. I say when God promises to preserve His Words He has kept that promise. He has preserved His Hebrew and Greeks Words.

There are three different places in the gospels where the Lord Jesus Christ Himself says, *"Heaven and earth shall pass away, but my words shall not pass away."* (Matthew 24:35, Mark 13:31, Luke 21:33) I will take the Lord Jesus Christ's word for it over all of these professors in Fundamentalist schools who say that Christ's Words were not preserved, just His message. No! The Lord Jesus Christ did not say that. He said His Words shall not pass away. I believe that He is the author of all the New Testament Words and all the Hebrew Old Testament Words. God keeps His promises. The Lord did unto Sarah as he had spoken.

Here's another promise God has given us concerning salvation.

- **John 3:16**
  For God so loved the world, that he gave his only begotten Son, **that whosoever believeth in him should not perish, but have everlasting life**.

If we trust in Him, receive Him, and believe in Him, He will keep this promise. Sarah conceived and bare a son to Abraham at the set time. Abraham did not

want to wait long enough for the set time. Abraham said he would get a son his way, the way of the flesh instead of the spirit, the way of works instead of grace.
- **Genesis 21:10**
Wherefore she said unto Abraham, Cast out this bondwoman and her son: **for the son of this bondwoman shall not be heir with my son,** *even* **with Isaac.**

The two sons were born. One is Ishmael and one is Isaac.

Galatians 4:23

"But he *who was* of the bondwoman was born after the flesh; but he of the freewoman *was* by promise." Ishmael was *"born after the flesh."* That word, *"flesh,"* SARX, is after the human desire. One of the meanings of this word is *"the animal nature with cravings which incite to sin."* Abraham "jumped the gun." When runners start a race, they get all set, and the gun goes off. Then they go, but they wait for the gun to signal the start of the race. Abraham said he was not going to wait for the set time. He said he was going to go ahead. So he had this son born of a bondwoman. Ishmael was born from the desires of the flesh and not of the spirit. Abraham could not wait in faith. God promised a son by Sarah. Abraham's flesh did not believe that. Here is the battle again between the works of the flesh and salvation by grace through faith. Remember that the promised son was the Lord Jesus Christ.
- **Galatians 3:16**
Now to Abraham and **his seed were the promises made.** He saith not, And to seeds, as of many; but as of one, **And to thy seed, which is Christ.**

The Lord Jesus Christ was the "Seed" to Whom all the promises of Abraham were made.

Galatians 4:24

"Which things are an allegory: for these are the two covenants; the one from the mount Sinai, which gendereth to bondage, which is Agar." This is an *"allegory,"* a story, or a figure of speech that people can understand. The Sinai Desert is the lower part of the Arabian Desert. The children of Israel left Egypt, crossed the Red Sea, then went to the borders of Canaan, the land of promise. Ten of the twelve spies thought that Israel could not enter into Canaan because there were giants who lived there. So, Israel wandered for forty years. This answers to bondage. The law brings bondage. There are two covenants. The one from Mount Sinai is the bondage of Hagar. The other of promise by God to Sarah and Abraham.

I believe that the bondage of works is a very serious bondage. We cannot do things by our own selves. Instead, we must do things by the Lord's will and with the Word's purpose. You cannot minister by the flesh or by works. You must minister by the Spirit of God. You cannot preach and be effective except by the Spirit of God. You cannot live your life to please the Lord except it is by faith and promise, not by works.

Galatians 4:25

"For this Agar is mount Sinai in Arabia, and answereth to Jerusalem which now is, and is in bondage with her children." Paul wrote to these Galatian Christians in about 60 A.D. As he wrote, Jerusalem was in bondage. That is what he is saying. Jerusalem rejected the Son of promise, rejected the Messiah, rejected the Lord Jesus Christ. They crucified *"the Lord of Glory"* (1 Corinthians 2:8). All the Jews, both in Paul's time and in our day, who rejected Christ are in bondage. Any Gentile who rejects the Lord Jesus Christ and His provision of salvation by genuine faith is in bondage to the devil.

Many people are in bondage. Some people are in bondage to homosexuality, pornography, drugs, gambling, swearing, uncontrolled behavior, and other things. I do not know what possesses a man to shoot a policeman in the face here in South Jersey and then kill himself. This is craziness. He is in bondage to something. All of the other people who commit crime are in bondage of some sort. Only the Lord Jesus Christ can get us out of bondage and make us free.

- John 8:36
  If the Son therefore shall make you free, ye shall be free indeed.

Whether it is the law of Moses in Paul's day or the law of works today, it is still bondage. Without Christ all of us are in bondage.

Galatians 4:26

"But Jerusalem which is above is free, which is the mother of us all." This speaks, I believe, of the new Jerusalem, the Heavenly Jerusalem. It speaks of the Lord Jesus Christ and His freedom.

- John 8:36
  If the Son therefore shall make you free, ye shall be free indeed.
- John 8:32
  And ye shall know the truth, and the truth shall make you free.

There is no One who can free us from the shackles of sin but the Lord Jesus Christ. The Lord Jesus Christ came to deliver us from bondage whether it is smoking, narcotics, drinking, pornography, lying, stealing, or whatever it is. Just like Moses came to deliver his people out of the bondage of slavery, Jesus came to deliver us out of the bondage of sin. The Lord Jesus Christ is the Deliverer and is able to deliver us. The question is do we want Him to deliver us from our bondage. He is able. We simply have to ask the Lord to help us. We have to trust in Him so that He can free us from this bondage.

The *"Jerusalem which is above"* speaks of the Heavenly or new Jerusalem (Revelation 21:1). The Jerusalem which is above is free. That speaks of the Lord Jesus Christ who is in this Heavenly Jerusalem. One day there will be a new Jerusalem. In the millennial reign of Christ, there will be a Heavenly Jerusalem which will be above the city of Jerusalem. The Scriptures speak of it in the book of Revelation. It is a city foursquare. It is just as high as it is wide and long. Apparently, believers will inhabit the new Jerusalem during either the Millennium or for all eternity. The former Jews who have become Christians who are on the earth during the Millennial reign of Christ will be in the Jerusalem that is below. It will be a time of genuine peace. The Lord Jesus Christ will be reigning in Jerusalem. So, there is a Heavenly Jerusalem which is above and an earthly Jerusalem which is below.

Galatians 4:27

"For it is written, Rejoice, *thou* barren that bearest not; break forth and cry, thou that travailest not: for the desolate hath many more children than she which hath an husband." Again, we see that phrase, *"it is written."* This is the Greek perfect tense. He is saying it was written back in Isaiah 54:1, which is the verse he is quoting. The perfect tense of the Greek language also says that it is still preserved today in the present. The perfect tense also means that in the future it will still stand preserved. This is Bible preservation, the preservation of the Hebrew and Greek Words of Scripture.

"It is written" comes from GRAPHO from which we get the word graphite like in pencils. Phonograph is the writing of sound. Mimeograph is the writing of same things. Graphic arts is the writing or drawing arts. GRAPHO means *"to delineate or form letters on a tablet, parchment, paper, or other material."* When God uses *"it is written,"* GRAPHO, in His Word, it is in the perfect tense. It is talking not only about Words but about letters also. You cannot write words without writing letters, can you? Whether you are typing, using the computer, or handwriting, you still need letters to make up words. The Lord Jesus Christ promised that neither the Words, nor the letters, nor the parts of the letters will pass away.

- **Matthew 5:18**
  For verily I say unto you, **Till Heaven and earth pass, one jot or one tittle shall in no wise pass from the law**, till all be fulfilled.

The jot is the smallest letter in the Hebrew alphabet. It is like a little comma or apostrophe. The tittle is a part of a Hebrew letter distinguishing it from another letter. I do not see how you can get any clearer than that.

Dan Wallace from Dallas Seminary, my school, does not believe it means that. Over in Biblical Seminary outside of Philadelphia, Douglas Chinn and Dr. Newman do not believe it means that. They do not believe the Hebrew Words and Greek letters are going to be preserved. They say it just means some kind of fulfilled prophecy. In fact this is what Dr. Glenny says in a book, *One Bible Only?* printed by Central Baptist Seminary. He says that it does not mean that the Words or letters will be preserved. He says that it is only fulfilling prophecy. He calls himself a Fundamentalist. I could understand if a Roman Catholic would say such a thing. I could understand if the modernist, apostate, liberal, or the neo-evangelical compromiser would say this. But a Fundamentalist is supposed to believe the Bible and all of its promises.

Three of my sons, one son-in-law, and one daughter-in-law are graduates of Bob Jones University. That school does not believe in the preservation of the Words of Christ either. They believe only in the preserved *"message."* In fact, Dr. Samuel Schnaiter, one of the Greek teachers who taught my son at Bob Jones, wrote his doctoral dissertation on this subject. I have a copy of it and have answered it on the radio. He says very clearly that we are not required to believe that the Words of Scripture are preserved but only the *"message."*

All of these things are written in this new book, *From the Mind of God to the Mind of Man*. My answer to this upsetting book is called *Fundamentalist Mis-Information on Bible Versions*. It is **BFT #2974** for a gift of **$7.00 + $4 S&H**. This *Mind of Man* book is a product of Bob Jones University personnel, graduates, and friends, though this is not admitted anywhere in the book. Eighty-six per cent of the committee who wrote the book are in some way connected with Bob Jones University. Various authors in this book also say that Bible preservation involves just the "message," rather than the Hebrew and Greek "Words." This battle involves semantics. It involves a re-defining of terms. I have said before that I believe they are playing "antics with semantics." This is exactly what they have done in this area. They say proudly that they believe that God has preserved His **"Word"** but are very careful not to say that He has preserved His Hebrew and Greek **"Words."**

This is what Bob Jones University teacher, Thurman Wisdom, has said in a video. Yet, just before he said this, his fellow Bob Jones teacher, Dr. Jaegli, from the Hebrew department, pointed out a series of "scribal errors" in the Hebrew text in one of the Old Testament books. After the scribal errors were pointed out, Dr. Wisdom said that shows that *"God preserved His **Word**."* He is not talking about preserving the "**Words**," but only preserving the "**Word**" which means merely the message, thoughts, ideas, or concepts. The reason these two men say this is because they believe that there are "scribal errors" in the Hebrew Old Testament text. Dr. Thurman Wisdom signed the doctrinal dissertation of Dr. Samuel Schnaiter. So did Dr. Marshal Neal and Dr. Stewart Custer. By signing it, they are approving of that dissertation and that position that stated clearly that God has only preserved the "message" and not the Hebrew and Greek Words of Scripture.

Getting back to the verse in question, Paul is quoting from the book of Isaiah.

- **Isaiah 54:1**
  Sing, O barren, thou *that* didst not bear; break forth into singing, and cry aloud, thou *that* didst not travail with child: for **more *are* the children of the desolate than the children of the married wife**, saith the LORD.

What he is saying is there are more children of the Hagar and Ishmael variety than there are of Isaac's seed. What he is saying also to us is there are more that are after the flesh than are after the spirit. There are more that are children after works than after promise. This is true today. The Ishmaelite Muslims are fighting the Israelite Jews in Palestine.

The children who are children after the works of the flesh only have their works. They do not have faith in Christ. They are lost trying to save themselves with their good works. If you ask them if they are going to Heaven, they might say, *"Oh sure. I'm doing the best I can."* The best you can is not going to get you saved and take you to Heaven. Christ is the only One who can take you to Glory. Faith in Christ is the only way you can get to Heaven. There are many people who are of the flesh like Hagar. They are just working their way to Heaven. They will be most disappointed when they get to the end of the road and the Lord Jesus Christ will say, *"I never knew you: depart from me."* (Matthew 7:23) There are going to be some surprises at death. The woods are full of those who are after Hagar's desolation. There are very few who are the children of the promise and of genuine faith

Galatians 4:28

"Now we, brethren, as Isaac was, are the children of promise."

- **Ephesians 2:8-9**
  For by grace are ye saved through faith; and that not of yourselves: *it is* the gift of God: **Not of works**, lest any man should boast.

Salvation is by grace through faith plus nothing but minus nothing.
- **Ephesians 2:10**
  For we are his workmanship, **created in Christ Jesus unto good works**, which God hath before ordained that we should walk in them

This is after we are saved. After we are saved, then we can walk in the works that the Lord has for us. Before we were saved, we do not have the power to do good. It is like a locomotive without an engine. It may be a beautiful locomotive, but it cannot go anywhere. When we are saved, then God gives us an engine. God gives us the power to serve Him and do good works. We are not saved by those works, but after we are saved, the Lord expects us to do them.

Galatians 4:29

"But as then he that was born after the flesh persecuted him *that was born* after the Spirit, even so *it is* now." Ishmael constantly was battling and fighting with the sons of Isaac. They argued over wells, land, and everything. Those people who say they are saved by their works are going to argue with you and me. You cannot tell them anything. They will persecute you. That is what it says happened with Ishmael and Isaac in this verse. Paul was persecuted severely because he preached this truth.
- **Galatians 4:16**
  Am I therefore become your enemy, because I tell you the truth?

Paul was an enemy because he spoke the truth. As I said before, many of us make enemies and get into trouble because we speak the truth. There are probably people who listen to me on the radio, on the Internet, or reading this book who will be angry because I am saying that they cannot be saved by their own good works. There is no such thing as "bootstrap religion." Only Christ can take you to Heaven.
- **Ephesians 2:8-9**
  For by grace are ye saved through faith; and that not of yourselves: *it is* **the gift of God: Not of works**, lest any man should boast.

The Lord Jesus Christ died for us on the cross of Calvary. You will be persecuted if you insist that salvation is by God's pure grace and by our pure and sincere faith in Christ. You will be persecuted. People might fight and argue with you. They will tell you they are good enough. They will tell you that they do not need your Christ. They will say that. As Paul said, *"if righteous-*

ness come by the law, then Christ is dead in vain" (Galatians 2:21). Christ did not die in vain.

He is the only One Who can take us to Heaven. It is like a fireman who is pulling you out of a burning building. Suppose this house was burning completely and you were trapped on the third floor with no way out. What would you do? You could jump from the window and die from the fall. Now suppose that you see a fireman up on a ladder ready to take you out of the burning house. There is nobody else who can help you. If you jump, you might die. This was the case at the World Trade Towers buildings in New York City on September 11, 2001. After the planes hit those towers, some people around the 100th floor were seen jumping out of the windows to their death on the street rather than dying in the painful flames. There was no one able to rescue them.

The Lord Jesus is the only one who can get us out of our burning fire which is all of our sin and wickedness. That is what salvation is. It is a rescue. It is a rescue of us who needed rescuing. It is like someone that is in water over his head. There is a pool next door to us that is eight feet at the deep end. If there were a little child who does not know how to swim in the deep end, there would be no hope unless someone were able to rescue that child. This is how it is with Christ. All of that drowning child's futile paddling and thrashing to save himself is like our futile efforts of work to save ourselves. The Lord Jesus is the only One Who can rescue us from certain death which is Hell and the lake of fire. By genuine faith in Him, He can take our hand and save us. His hand is a grip of steel which can never let us go into the burning flames of the lake of fire. Jesus never fails.

Galatians 4:30

"Nevertheless what saith the Scripture? Cast out the bondwoman and her son: for the son of the bondwoman shall not be heir with the son of the freewoman." This is a reference to the narrative in Genesis.

- **Genesis 21:10**
  Wherefore she said unto Abraham, **Cast out this bondwoman and her son**: for the son of this bondwoman shall not be heir with my son, *even* with Isaac.

Sarah finally came to her senses. Sarah, who brokered the deal in the first place with Hagar and Abraham, finally woke up to the fact that Ishmael was not the son of promise. Abraham was a little surprised.

- **Genesis 21:11**
  And **the thing was very grievous in Abraham's sight** because of his son.

Abraham loved Ishmael. Maybe Ishmael, the son after the flesh, was Abraham's favorite. Sarah finally got it right. Often, though not always, our wives do get it right. As a matter of fact, quite often they get it right. Sometimes we husbands do not listen to our wives. Occasionally, they get it wrong, like Eve and Sarah at first, and so do we husbands. In this case Sarah got it right, and God told Abraham to listen to her voice.

- **Genesis 21:12**
  And God said unto Abraham, Let it not be grievous in thy sight because of the lad, and because of thy bondwoman; **in all that Sarah hath said unto thee, hearken unto her voice**; for in Isaac shall thy seed be called.

The Seed that was to come, Jesus Christ, was in Isaac and the son of Isaac. Throw out the bondwoman and her son. Throw out the law of Moses and works. Let us throw out all of circumcision and everything that you do yourself. Cling to the Lord of promise who is Jesus Christ. That is what Paul is saying. Cast out the works of the law. Cast out the sins and the wickednesses, and look to Christ.

Galatians 4:31

"So then, brethren, we are not children of the bondwoman, but of the free." If we are saved by genuine faith in Christ, we are children *"of the free."*

- **John 8:36**
  If the Son therefore shall make you free, ye shall be free indeed.

Slavery no longer needs to engulf us. Slavery to sin and corruption no longer should reign in us because Christ has made us sons and children of the Lord Jesus Christ. Christians are not sons of Ishmael. Christians are sons of Isaac.

Galatians Chapter Five

Galatians 5:1

"Stand fast therefore in the liberty wherewith Christ hath made us free, and be not entangled again with the yoke of bondage."

"Stand fast therefore in the liberty wherewith Christ hath made us free" God wants us to be zealous in a good thing always. Remember I said that the Galatian Christians were saved by grace through faith. Paul led them to the Lord. Then and all of a sudden, those Judaizers came down from Jerusalem and said that they could not be saved by genuine faith alone, but rather by the keeping of the law. They also said that they could not grow in grace or be sanctified by the Spirit of the Lord but only by the keeping of the law of Moses. Paul's preaching refuted these false notions.

Paul said to *"stand fast."* Christ has set us free from the law of Moses. Standing fast is a practice which is almost forgotten in most churches today. Christians today do not know anything about standing fast. They are moving from every imaginable position like the drifting river. It is difficult to believe or understand it. There is a man who is supposed to be an "evangelical" Christian on the same radio station that I am on. This is a "freedom of speech" station that takes all various religious views. This man says that there is not a bodily resurrection for anybody. He does not believe that Christ arose. He does not believe that we will rise again. He believes that it is just spiritual. He says that as soon as we are saved, we are resurrected. I say that is serious drift from the truth. We need to *"stand fast."*

That expression of standing fast is used at least five times in the New Testament.

- **1 Corinthians 16:13**
  Watch ye, **stand fast in the faith**, quit you like men, be strong.

There is to be no wavering, no moving, no motion! Dr. John F. Walvoord, one of my teachers while I was a student at Dallas Theological Seminary and now one of the Chancellors, said about ten years ago that "theology changes." I do not believe that at all. It is difficult for me to comprehend that he believes that, yet he wrote it in a bulletin to Dallas Seminary graduates. How could he say that theology changes? If it is Biblical, it does not change. *"Stand fast"* in theology. When this sermon was delivered, Dr. Walvoord had several professors at Dallas Seminary that were believers in "progressive dispensationalism" rather than the original dispensationalism of the founder of Dallas Seminary, Dr. Lewis Sperry Chafer. Dr. Chafer taught our class from 1948 through 1952. He died in the summer of 1952.

- **Philippians 1:27**
  Only let your conversation be as it becometh the gospel of Christ: that whether I come and see you, or else be absent, I may hear of your affairs, **that ye stand fast in one spirit**, with one mind striving together for the faith of the gospel;

We have to be united by Bible doctrine.

- **Philippians 4:1**
  Therefore, my brethren dearly beloved and longed for, my joy and crown, **so stand fast in the Lord,** *my* dearly beloved.

- **1 Thessalonians 3:8**
  For now we live, **if ye stand fast in the Lord.**

The Lord Jesus Christ is *"the same yesterday and today, and forever."* We must *"stand fast"* in the Lord. He stands fast, and we ought to stand fast. He does not change. The Lord says in Malachi 3:8, *"For I am the Lord, I change not."* That is it. You might say, *"You have to stay with the times."* That is the trouble with the motto of "Youth For Christ" It was *"Geared to the Times, But Anchored to the Rock."* I never liked that slogan. I know what they are saying, but the Lord Jesus Christ wants us to *"stand fast"* in the Lord. We are not to be moving, not to be *"gearing to the times."* We may have new cars that change their models. That is one thing. We may have new clothes and new styles. The Word of God never changes, and we are to stand fast.

"and be not entangled again with the yoke of bondage"

Christ has made us free from bondage. We are not to be *"entangled again."* The Israelites were entangled in the land of Egypt.

- **Exodus 14:3**
  For Pharaoh will say of the children of Israel, **They are entangled in the land**, the wilderness hath shut them in.

Pharaoh thought he had them and would be able to kill them. That is the idea of entanglement.

- **2 Peter 2:20**
  For if after they have escaped the pollutions of the world through the knowledge of the Lord and Saviour Jesus Christ, **they are again entangled** therein, and overcome, the latter end is worse with them than the beginning.

We cannot be entangled again with the bondage that had bound us. We must not be entangled in any kind of sin whether it is the sin of alcohol, drugs, sex, etc., going back under the law of works, or any other sin.

- **Galatians 2:4**
  And that because of false brethren unawares brought in, who came in privily to spy out our liberty which we have in Christ Jesus, **that they might bring us into bondage**:

These Judaizers wanted to bring these Jews back under the law of Moses. They wanted them to practice all the sacrifices, all the ordinances, and all the offerings. The Christian believer does not have to be in bondage to the Devil's power.

- **Hebrews 2:14**
  Forasmuch then as the children are partakers of flesh and blood, he also himself likewise took part of the same; that through death **he might destroy him that had the power of death, that is, the devil**;

We do not need to be in Satan's bondage anymore.

- **2 Peter 2:19**
  While they promise them liberty, they themselves are the servants of corruption: **for of whom a man is overcome, of the same is he brought in bondage**.

Men are not the only ones who are in bondage these days. We have women who are bound up in all kinds of sins. Let us not be overcome. When these things come along, just stand fast in the Lord and in the power of His might. We need to stay out of the *"yoke of bondage."* This word *"yoke,"* ZUGOS, is *"a yoke that is put on draft cattle. It is used of any burden or bondage."* This bondage is slavery. That Greek word for **"entangled,"** ENECHO, is in the present tense. If this were an aorist tense prohibition, it would mean do not even begin to do be *"entangled."* The present tense prohibition used here means to stop an action already in progress. He is saying *"stop being entangled again"* in this.

These Galatian Christians were up in what we now call Turkey. They were free in the gospel as Paul led them to the Lord. He was telling them to stop being entangled in the yoke of bondage. Christ has made you free. You do not have to be circumcised. You do not have to keep the law of Moses. You do not have to keep the sacrifices.

Galatians 5:2

"Behold, I Paul say unto you, that if ye be circumcised, Christ shall profit you nothing." If you say that every person who becomes a Christian has to go under the Old Testament law, *"Christ shall profit you nothing."* What is he saying? Does that mean that Christ could not possibly save them? No! I think he means if you are resting the whole weight of your salvation and sanctification on your works, Christ will not profit you. You are on your own. I do not want to be on my own. My works are no good. *"All our righteousnesses are as filthy rags"* as it says in Isaiah 64:6. I cannot save myself.

Galatians 5:3

"For I testify again to every man that is circumcised, that he is a debtor to do the whole law." Circumcision was just one part of the Law of Moses. Paul simply says, in effect, *"Do you want to start on that journey? Do you want to begin that chapter of your book? Then keep the whole law."* If we once start down that long road of keeping the law, we have to keep everything about it. Keep the Sabbath day, the sacrifices, the morning and evening burnt offerings, all of the feasts of Jehovah, the Passover feast, the feast of unleavened bread, the feast of the firstfruits, the feast of Pentecost, the feast of trumpets, the feast of atonement, the feast of tabernacles-- all seven feasts of Jehovah, and much, much more. He says go ahead and keep them all if you start to keep just one.

- **James 2:10**
  For whosoever shall keep the whole law, and **yet offend in one *point*, he is guilty of all**.

If you are trying to keep the whole law and fail to keep just one point, then you are guilty of all. This is like two people jumping across a canyon. If you are trying to jump across a fifty-foot chasm, you might jump just three feet and fall into the canyon. A world class athlete might jump forty-nine feet across the same canyon, but he would still fall into the canyon. Whether it was one foot short or forty-seven feet short, both would fall short. Any amount of sin makes us fall short of God's glory.

- **Romans 3:23.**
  For all have sinned, and come short of the glory of God;

Some of us are tall and some of us are short, but as far as our ability to keep the law, we are all short. No matter how wide or narrow your chasm is you cannot make it on your own. God's righteousness is only available through genuine faith in the Lord Jesus Christ. He alone can give us righteousness. We cannot earn it, and we do not deserve it.

There was a man who came up to the Lord and asked Him what he must do to inherit eternal life. Jesus said that he must keep the commandments. The young man told Him that he had kept the commandments from his youth. The Lord said that he lacked one thing. Then the Lord told him to sell all that he had, give it to the poor, and follow Him. Then he would have treasure in Heaven. Well, he could not do that. (Mark 10:17-22) We have to trust the Lord Jesus Christ and consider Him to be more worthy than everything we could name. The Lord Jesus Christ and His Salvation is worth more than all of the gold, silver, or rubies of the world. If you start keeping the law, you are obligated to keep it all. It is your duty. That is what a *"debtor,"* OPHEILETES, is. It is *"one held by some obligation, bound by some duty."*

Galatians 5:4
"Christ is become of no effect unto you, whosoever of you are justified by the law; ye are fallen from grace."

I would like to review, for your consideration, some verses on justification.
- Luke 16:15
And he said unto them, **Ye are they which justify yourselves before men**; but God knoweth your hearts: for that which is highly esteemed among men is abomination in the sight of God.

How can you justify yourself? We sinners cannot justify ourselves. Our hearts are as black as coal.
- Acts 13:39
And by him **all that believe are justified** from all things, from which **ye could not be justified by the law** of Moses.

The law of Moses cannot justify us. We are only justified by genuine believing in the Lord Jesus Christ.
- Romans 3:20
Therefore **by the deeds of the law there shall no flesh be justified** in his sight: for by the law *is* the knowledge of sin.
- Romans 3:24
Being justified freely by his grace through the redemption that is in Christ Jesus:

He is the only One Who can declare us righteous.
- Romans 3:26
To declare, *I say*, at this time his righteousness: that he might be just, and **the justifier of him which believeth in Jesus**.

That is the way to get justified, by believing genuinely in the Lord Jesus.

- **Romans 3:28**
  Therefore we conclude that **a man is justified by faith without the deeds of the law**.
- **Romans 4:5**
  But **to him that worketh not, but believeth on him that justifieth the ungodly**, his faith is counted for righteousness.

That is a good gospel verse.

- **Romans 5:1**
  Therefore **being justified by faith**, we have peace with God through our Lord Jesus Christ:
- **Romans 5:9**
  Much more then, **being now justified by his blood**, we shall be saved from wrath through him.

John MacArthur says it is not Christ's blood that justifies, just His death. No, this verse says it is *"by His blood."* God says it. I believe it. And that is the end of the argument.

- **1 Corinthians 6:9-11**
  Know ye not that the unrighteous shall not inherit the kingdom of God? Be not deceived: neither fornicators, nor idolaters, nor adulterers, nor effeminate, nor abusers of themselves with mankind, Nor thieves, nor covetous, nor drunkards, nor revilers, nor extortioners, shall inherit the kingdom of God. And **such were some of you**: but ye are washed, but ye are sanctified, **but ye are justified in the name of the Lord Jesus**, and by the Spirit of our God.

I am glad that is in the past tense. God goes on to say that we are washed, sanctified, and justified in the name of the Lord Jesus and by the Spirit of our God. God can take a Hell-bound sinner who is dirty and wash him and make him clean and just in the court of Heaven by the blood of the Lord Jesus Christ.

- **Galatians 2:16**
  Knowing that **a man is not justified by the works of the law**, but by the faith of Jesus Christ, even we have believed in Jesus Christ, **that we might be justified by the faith of Christ, and not by the works of the law**: for by the works of the law shall no flesh be justified.
- **Galatians 3:11**
  But that **no man is justified by the law** in the sight of God, *it is* evident: for, The just shall live by faith.
- **Galatians 3:24**
  Wherefore the law was our schoolmaster *to bring us* unto Christ, **that we might be justified by faith**.

Galatians 5:4-5

Some of our Arminian friends who believe that they can lose their salvation point to the last part of this present verse which says *"ye are fallen from grace."* This word for *"fallen"* means *"to fall from a position."* I believe that they have fallen from a position of grace to a position of law. We cannot fall out of our spiritual birth anymore than anybody sitting in this room can decide not to be born. You cannot do it. When you are born-again by genuine faith in Christ, there is no way you can be unborn. You may not walk in the Spirit and have a carnal life, but if you are God's child and have ever been saved in the first place, you cannot lose your salvation.

- John 10:27-29
  My sheep hear my voice, and I know them, and they follow me: And I give unto them eternal life; and they shall never perish, **neither shall any** *man* **pluck them out of my hand.** My Father, which gave *them* me, is greater than all; and **no** *man* **is able to pluck** *them* **out of my Father's hand.**

We have a double lock on our salvation. We have the hand of our Lord Jesus Christ. This hand is much stronger than our hand in securing our salvation. Then we have the hand of God the Father which is stronger than the Son's hand also securing our salvation. *"Fallen from grace"* means that these Christians have taken away the principle of grace and have gone back to the law of Moses. Trying to secure your own salvation with your own works will lead you to a dead-end street. If you are trying to keep the law, you cannot do it.

Galatians 5:5

"For we through the Spirit wait for the hope of righteousness by faith." I hope that we know how to *"wait."* Some of us are so impatient. We do not want to wait for anything. Young people today want to be full grown and mature when they are only fourteen or fifteen. They want to be adults, now. We want to be millionaires, now. We do not want to wait. That is why we have the fast food restaurants. That is why we go to "Wendys." We have to wait for the hope of righteousness. Here are five verses on that.

- Romans 8:23
  And not only *they*, but ourselves also, which have the firstfruits of the Spirit, even we ourselves groan within ourselves, **waiting for the adoption,** *to wit***, the redemption of our body.**

Many of these bodies of ours are creaking, gnawing, and groaning with different kinds of pains. If we are born-again Christians, one day we are going to have new bodies, but we just have to wait until we get the redemption of our bodies.

We will have no arthritis, no pain of any kind, no death, and no sorrow. The former things will pass away.
- **Romans 8:25**
  But if we hope for that we see not, *then* do we with patience wait for *it*.
- **1 Corinthians 1:7**
  So that ye come behind in no gift; **waiting for the coming of our Lord Jesus Christ**:

These are the same Corinthian Christians whom Paul mentioned earlier. We do not know when the Lord is coming back, but we must wait patiently.
- 1 Thessalonians 1:10
  And to wait for his Son from Heaven, whom he raised from the dead, *even* Jesus, which delivered us from the wrath to come.

That is expectation.
- **2 Thessalonians 3:5**
  And the Lord direct your hearts into the love of God, and into **the patient waiting for Christ**.

It is not simply waiting, it is *"patient waiting."* There is a difference. Put yourself in the most difficult situation you can imagine. Can you be patient in that waiting? Pray unto the Lord that He may answer your prayers and may give you your requests. Christ will appear. He promised to appear, and He will not let us down. The rapture of the saved ones will happen first, then the seven-year tribulation, and then Christ, our Heavenly Bridegroom, will come back to rule and reign for a thousand years.

Galatians 5:6

"For in Jesus Christ neither circumcision availeth any thing, nor uncircumcision; but faith which worketh by love." *"In Jesus Christ,"* it is not a question of circumcision or uncircumcision, but faith. Faith works by love. Faith is made perfect and energized by love. You cannot see my faith, and I cannot see your faith if you are saved. Faith, if it is by the Spirit of God, has a working and energizing ability. Saving faith will lead to the working out of the love of the brethren and the love of the Word of God. We can see the working on the outside but not the working of faith on the inside. Faith works and is operative.

Galatians 5:7

"Ye did run well; who did hinder you that ye should not obey the truth?" These Christians at Galatia used to be all right. They did *"run well."* They were on the right track. Salvation is by genuine faith through grace plus nothing and minus nothing. Let us look at a few verses that talk about running.

- **Isaiah 40:31**
  But **they that wait upon the LORD** shall renew *their* strength; they shall mount up with wings as eagles; **they shall run, and not be weary**; *and* they shall walk, and not faint.

There is our waiting again.

- **1 Corinthians 9:24**
  Know ye not that **they which run in a race run all, but one receiveth the prize**? So run, that ye may obtain.

This is a Christian race.

- **1 Corinthians 9:26**
  I therefore so run, not as uncertainly; so fight I, not as one that beateth the air:

- **Philippians 2:16**
  Holding forth the word of life; that I may rejoice in the day of Christ, **that I have not run in vain**, neither laboured in vain.

Paul did not want the Philippian Christians to end up in the waste basket. He did not want his preaching to be empty.

- **Hebrews 12:1-2**
  Wherefore seeing we also are compassed about with so great a cloud of witnesses, let us **lay aside every weight**, and the sin which doth so easily beset *us*, and **let us run with patience the race that is set before us**, Looking unto Jesus the author and finisher of *our* faith; who for the joy that was set before him endured the cross, despising the shame, and is set down at the right hand of the throne of God.

"Lay aside every 'Waite.'" That is what the janitor used to tell my wife at Dallas Theological Seminary. We were newly married. We don't believe in divorce, so we took that comment as a joke, but perhaps he was serious. We all have our own races to run. I cannot be in your shoes, running your race. And you cannot be in my shoes, running my race.

- **1 Peter 4:4**
  Wherein they think it strange **that ye run not with *them* to the same excess of riot**, speaking evil of *you*:

We do not want to continue to run with the old wicked world. That should be in our past. We want to run with the saints of Glory.

Galatians 5:8

"This persuasion *cometh* not of him that calleth you."
That word, *"persuasion,"* can either have a good sense or a deceptive sense. These Galatian Christians were involved with the deceptive persuasion. These Judaizers said not to trust Christ alone but also go back under the law. Paul never told them to go back under the law. There are many people today who are trying to persuade us to get off base in some way, either by our lifestyle or by our doctrines.

There are all kinds of cults. I was talking to someone the other day who said he would like to talk to the Jehovah Witnesses who come to his door. I said that he better be careful. 2 John 10-11 says of such heretics who try to convince you of their error: *"neither bid him God speed: for he that biddeth him God speed is partaker of his evil deeds."* There are all kinds of people who want us to get off the track. All of these cults are looking for Bible-believing Christians to get off the doctrinal track. One lady told me that she was hired by a woman who was a Jehovah Witness. The Jehovah Witness told this lady that the Lord Jesus Christ is not God. That made this woman sick. She almost wanted to quit. These cultists are very strong in what they believe. The Lord Jesus Christ is God the Son, but he is also the Son of God. He is perfect Deity as well as perfect Humanity. *"Beware let him that thinketh he standeth take heed lest he fall"* (1 Corinthians 10:12). It is better not to discuss Biblical things with known heretics. It is especially better not to let them into your house where other family members who are listening might be persuaded to embrace their errors, even though you yourself might not be convinced.

Galatians 5:9

"A little leaven leaveneth the whole lump." I do not bake bread, but I understand that you put yeast in it. Yeast is leaven. It does not take long for that yeast to permeate the entire lump. It does not take long for wickedness and sin, even in our local church, to permeate. It would only take a little poison to poison our entire church. It could be a poisonous doctrine. It could be poisonous and corrupt activities. Or it could even be poisonous attitudes. Pretty soon it would shoot all through the congregation and spoil it.

When I came out of the Navy, I was pastor at Immanuel Baptist Church in Newton, Massachusetts. It was a good-sized church. We had about three hundred and fifty coming in the morning service. Little did I know what was awaiting me. I just began to preach and teach the Bible. Lo and behold about two weeks after I got there, the head deacon and his brother-in-law came to our parsonage and told me that I was moving too fast. I did not know I was moving too fast. I was just preaching the Bible. Apparently, there were some things I was preaching that did not set too well with many in the congregation. The long and the short of it was that I learned that once there is a disaffection with the preacher for preaching too straight, it is an uphill battle.

I came out of the Navy a neo-evangelical. I was not even a separatist Fundamentalist. I learned my Fundamentalism the hard way after I got out of that church. I became a separatist. I became a Fundamentalist. Even a neo-evangelical could not please the people at Immanuel Baptist Church. I just preached the Bible. I taught the gospel of John in the morning, and the book of Acts in the evening. I guess I made my mistake on a Wednesday night preaching a sermon on "the little foxes that spoil the vines" (Song of Solomon 2:15). When I started talking about those little foxes, I started stepping on toes. I did not have any idea I was doing that. I was just preaching the Word. I did not think I was moving too fast. I was just trying to conform us all to the image of Christ. (Romans 8:29)

Before long the head deacons wanted to get rid of me. I called a business meeting to see what the church wanted. There needed to be a two-thirds vote to get rid of a pastor. At that meeting there was a vote of about seventy-five in favor of my continuing as Pastor, and about twenty against my continuing. That was not even a majority vote, much less two-thirds. The twenty became angry and called another meeting. They still did not have enough for a two thirds vote. We finally just left that church and started another church, Faith Baptist Church. Forget the leaven. You cannot stop it from spreading no matter how much you try. Once you start disbelieving in a person, it just spreads fast.

- **Matthew 16:6**
  Then Jesus said unto them, Take heed and **beware of the leaven of the Pharisees and of the Sadducees.**

This was a leaven of poison and false doctrine.

- **1 Corinthians 5:6**
  Your glorying *is* not good. Know ye not that **a little leaven leaveneth the whole lump**?

This refers to an incestuous person in the Corinthian congregation. Paul said to get him out until he repents and comes back in faith. Purge him out. We want to keep everything straight. There is sin in all of us, preacher and people included. But we want to keep that sin confessed before the Lord and cleansed.

- **1 John 1:9**
  If we **confess our sins**, he is faithful and just to **forgive us** *our* sins, and to **cleanse us** from all unrighteousness.

That is what we all need to do on, not only a daily basis, but a moment by moment basis as soon as we sin in thought, word, or deed.

Galatians 5:10

"I have confidence in you through the Lord, that ye will be none otherwise minded: but he that troubleth you shall bear his judgment, whosoever he be." Paul is confident in the Lord that the Galatians would get rid of the legalism. That word for *"trouble,"* TARASSO, means *"to agitate."* I hope none of us are agitators or have anybody agitating us. It also means *"to disquiet, make restless, to stir up, to render anxious or distressed, to perplex the mind of one by suggesting doubts."* Paul did not know who was going to trouble him, but he certainly knew Who was going to judge those false teachers. The Lord is going to judge whomever is troubling Christians. I know that does not help us now while we are in the trouble, but one day it will. We have to *"put on the whole armour of God"* so that we will be able to withstand against the wiles, the onslaughts, the wickednesses, and the strategies of the devil. We must have Christ's righteousness, not our own. We have to be armed against anyone who would trouble us.

If we have to stand alone, then stand alone! Was not the Lord Jesus alone on the cross of Calvary. John was the only apostle who was with him. Eleven-twelfths of the disciples did not make it to the crucifixion. They were probably scared to death that they might be next. The Lord Jesus knew how to stand alone. There is song we sing sometimes.

> *"Dare to be a Daniel,*
> *Dare to stand alone,*
> *Dare to have a purpose firm,*
> *Dare to make it known."*

Standing alone is a lonely place to be because all we have is ourselves and the Lord Jesus Christ. *"If God be for us, who can be against us?"* (Romans 8:31) One with God is a majority. One of the early church fathers was told that the whole world was against him. This church father replied, **"Then I am against the world."** That was it. I have stood alone, all by myself, in many issues throughout my life of ministry. I know what it is like to stand alone. I have been there. So have my wife and children.

Galatians 5:11

"And I, brethren, if I yet preach circumcision, why do I yet suffer persecution? then is the offence of the cross ceased." If Paul preached circumcision, then he would have blended in with the rest of them. Then he would not be persecuted anymore. If those in the world want us to compromise our Biblical position in order for them to be happy with us, the temptation is for us to join them, compromise our principles,

Galatians 5:11

and blend into the woodwork. That is not how God wants us to do. Paul did not do that. Paul was persecuted. Note some of these verses about persecution.

- **Matthew 5:10-12**
  Blessed *are* they which are **persecuted for righteousness' sake**: for theirs is the kingdom of Heaven. Blessed are ye, when *men* shall revile you, and persecute *you*, and shall say all manner of **evil against you falsely, for my sake**. Rejoice, and be exceeding glad: for great *is* your reward in Heaven: for **so persecuted they the prophets** which were before you.

Make sure that men are saying evil things *"falsely"* about you.

- **John 15:20**
  Remember the word that I said unto you, The servant is not greater than his lord. **If they have persecuted me, they will also persecute you**; if they have kept my saying, they will keep yours also.

The servant is not above his Lord.

- **Romans 8:35**
  Who shall separate us from the love of Christ? *shall* tribulation, or distress, or **persecution**, or famine, or nakedness, or peril, or sword?

Persecution will never separate us from *"the love of Christ."* If we're saved, Christ still loves us even when we are surrounded by persecution.

- **2 Corinthians 4:8-9**
  We are troubled on every side, yet not distressed; *we are* perplexed, but not in despair; **Persecuted, but not forsaken**; cast down, but not destroyed;

The Lord Jesus never forsakes His own.

- **2 Corinthians 12:9-10**
  And he said unto me, **My grace is sufficient for thee**: for my strength is made perfect in weakness. Most gladly therefore will **I rather glory** in my infirmities, that the power of Christ may rest upon me. Therefore **I take pleasure in** infirmities, in reproaches, in necessities, in **persecutions**, in distresses for Christ's sake: for when I am weak, then am I strong.

Paul took pleasure in his persecution. That is so opposite to how we think. Paul felt the sufficient grace of the Lord Jesus Christ.

- **Galatians 6:12**
  As many as desire to make a fair shew in the flesh, they constrain you to be circumcised; only **lest they should suffer persecution for the cross of Christ**.

- 2 Timothy 3:12
  Yea, and **all that will live godly in Christ Jesus shall suffer persecution.**

All Christians who want to live godly **WILL** suffer persecution of one sort or another and of one severity or another. Do you want to live godly? I hope that you do. Your persecution may be different from mine, and mine might be different from yours. It is a promise from God's Word that we will suffer persecution. Do you know what that word for persecution means? DIOKO means *"to make to run or flee, put to flight, drive away."* Persecution is someone running swiftly after you. Persecution makes you turn, run, and flee. It puts you to flight. It drives you away. That is persecution. God wants us to stand fast and just stay put.

Galatians 5:12

"I would they were even cut off which trouble you."

That Greek word for *"cut off,"* APOKOPTO, means *"to amputate."* That is a little drastic, is it not? When Paul saw the believers he had led to the Lord going down the drain into the law of Moses, he was very angry. He had godly anger, I am sure. He wanted to cut off somebody.

- Romans 11:22
  Behold therefore the goodness and severity of God: on them which fell, severity; but toward thee, goodness, if thou continue in *his* goodness: **otherwise thou also shalt be cut off.**

Here "cut off" is in the sense of not being used again or not being prominent.

You can see the intensity of that verse. That word for "trouble," ANASTATOO means *"turn upside down, make an uproar."* You cannot always control the people who are making an uproar in your life. There is very little you can do. You just have to let nature take its course, and let it come as it will. We do have to *"be strong in the Lord, and in the power of His might"* (Ephesians 6:10).

Galatians 5:13

"For, brethren, ye have been called unto liberty; only *use* not liberty for an occasion to the flesh, but by love serve one another."

"For, brethren, ye have been called unto liberty; only *use* not liberty for an occasion to the flesh" Do you remember how this chapter started out in verse one? Paul told the Galatians to *"Stand fast therefore in the liberty wherewith Christ hath made us free, and be not entangled again with the yoke of bondage."* We are not under the yoke of bondage with works or the law, but we are called unto liberty. We have liberty to do that which is right. He says do not use that liberty for an *"occasion to the flesh."* Some people say *"I am saved by grace so I can live any way I want to."* Yes, you can. But if you have been genuinely saved by the grace of Christ, you have a different *"want to"* than before you were saved. As Dr. M. R. DeHaan used to say on the Radio Bible Class, *"Once you are saved, you can do anything you want to, but after you are saved, you have a different 'want to.'"* That is true. I question the salvation of those who say they are born-again and then go out and live for the world, the flesh, and the devil. I just question their salvation. Maybe they are saved, but I cannot see it. The Lord can see all our conditions. I could not see that Lot was saved. I would never in the world have called him *"just,"* but God did (2 Peter 2:7). He delivered him from that wicked city of Sodom. Lot was a disgraceful father. He seemed to be almost as wicked as those who lived in Sodom. God sees the heart, and we do not.

"but by love serve one another" That word for *"serve,"* DOULEUO, has in it the word, DOULOS, or *"bond slave."* That means *"doing the will of another."* Can we serve one another here in our local church? I think we can try to please and help one another. That is a service. Paul in that very first verse says to *"stand fast."* The doctrine in churches is moving a mile-a-minute in this wicked day. Churches are moving from their moorings and shifting like shifting sand. I do not like it, and I am against it. They are leaving our Bible, the King James Bible, and its underlying Hebrew and Greek Texts. They are leaving our doctrines. They are leaving our faith. I do not like it at all. Paul says to *"stand fast."* We need to be steeled and firm against movement.

Does that mean we are stick-in-the-muds? I guess it does, according to some people at least. Does that mean we do not want to change? We do not change when it comes to doctrine. Now, we might change in different things, but not in the Word of God and its sound doctrine. I do not think we should change our old-fashioned-hymns and start singing those choruses. There was a man who used to preach in the Tenth Presbyterian Church, Dr. Donald Gray Barnhouse. He used to be a Fundamentalist but changed into a new-evangelical in later years. He spoke to us in a chapel service at Dallas Theological Seminary. I remember what he said about these meaningless choruses. He called them *"an abomination **not** spoken of by Daniel the Prophet."* We have to *"stand fast in the liberty wherewith Christ hath made us free."*

Galatians 5:14

"For all the law is fulfilled in one word, *even* in this; Thou shalt love thy neighbour as thyself." This is quoted from the law of Moses in Leviticus 19:18. Paul saw that the law can be fulfilled in one phrase, *"love thy neighbor as thyself."* We are not for salvation through good works. That is not what Paul is saying. Nobody is going to put you in jail for loving your neighbor like you love yourself. That is the fulfillment of the law. If you want to eat, and you feed your neighbor because he wants to eat, then you are loving your neighbor as yourself. If you do for your neighbor what you want to do for yourself, then you are fulfilling the law of Moses.

Who is your neighbor? That is the question that the man asked Jesus in the book of Luke (Luke 10:29-36). Then the Lord Jesus told the story about the man who was beaten by thieves while he was on his way to Jericho. A priest came by and saw that man bruised and ready to die. He just walked by *"on the other side."* Then a Levite came. He also walked by *"on the other side"* and did not help. Finally, a Samaritan, one of those half-breeds that the Jews did not like, came by and bound the man up, put him on his own beast, and took him to an inn. He told the innkeeper to put him up and whatever he owed, he would pay. That is what the Lord Jesus Christ has done for us. We are the poor beaten individuals lost and in sin. The law represented by the priest and the Levite could not save us. The love that the Samaritan showed toward that man is like the love the Lord Jesus had for us. He died for our sins. He loved us and gave Himself for us. The Samaritan was the *"neighbor"* to the man who fell among thieves.

- **John 3:16**
  For **God so loved the world, that he gave his only begotten Son**, that whosoever believeth in him should not perish, but have everlasting life.

The whole law is fulfilled in love. That is the motivation, the propelling force that caused the Son of God to leave Heaven's glory to come into this wicked, sin-cursed world. That is the wonderful word that propelled Paul. Paul said the *"love of Christ constraineth us"* (2 Corinthians 5:15).

Galatians 5:15

"But if ye bite and devour one another, take heed that ye be not consumed one of another."

"But if ye bite and devour one another" Apparently there was trouble in this Galatian church. (Remember, the Galatians were in what is present-day Turkey.) To *"bite,"* DAKNO, means metaphorically *"to wound the soul, cut, lacerate, rend with reproaches."* They were arguing, bickering, and fighting with one another in that church. That is what the law does. That is what the works of the law does. There is no grace involved in that. If one did not do right, the other one bit him, not literally, but figuratively. Then they would *"devour,"* KATESTHIO, one another. That word means *"eat up, devour up, to consume by eating."* It also means metaphorically *"to squander, waste."* It is essentially trashing each other's personality.

"take heed that ye be not consumed one of another"
If they were going to eat each other up and devour each other, they were going to wipe each other out. Is not that what you do when you eat an apple. You wipe it out and consume it. Watch yourself, or you may completely destroy the other person. Now, you may be strong but some of you may not be as strong as others. Not everyone can take bickering, squabbling, and fighting. After so many years, they may just leave because they cannot take it. They want the Spirit of grace and the Spirit of God and not the spirit of fighting. That is the trouble with some of our churches. If you go to a business meeting, you will know what I am talking about. Be careful because pretty soon you will not have a church because everybody will be gone. The ones who stay in the church and bicker are the biggest sharks in the church. And they will devour one another. Sharks will go after a body in the water, but they will also feed on one another. That is a frightening description. Praise God that we do not have anything like that in our little church.

Galatians 5:16

"This **I say then, Walk in the Spirit, and ye shall not fulfil the lust of the flesh."** There are seven verses I would like to point out on this idea of *"walk."*
- **Romans 13:13**
  Let us walk honestly, as in the day; not in rioting and drunkenness, not in chambering and wantonness, not in strife and envying.
- **1 Corinthians 3:3**
  For ye are yet carnal: for whereas *there is* among you envying, and strife, and divisions, are **ye not carnal, and walk as men**?

The carnal Christians walk just about like the unsaved people of the world.
- **2 Corinthians 10:3**
  For **though we walk in the flesh, we do not war after the flesh**:

We who are saved are still in the flesh, but we do not have to war after the flesh.
  Ephesians 2:2
  Wherein **in time past ye walked according to the course of this world**, according to the prince of the power of the air, the spirit that now worketh in the children of disobedience:
- **Ephesians 2:10**
  For we are his workmanship, created in Christ Jesus unto good works, **which God hath before ordained that we should walk in them**.

God wants us to walk in good works after we are saved.
- **1 Thessalonians 2:12**
  That ye **would walk worthy of God**, who hath called you unto his kingdom and glory.
- **1 John 1:6**
  If we say that we have fellowship with him, and walk in darkness, we lie, and do not the truth:

This is the idea of walking in the Spirit or walking by the power of the Holy Spirit. The new versions wrongly translate PERIPATEO which means literally *"to walk around."* They mistakenly translate it as *"live."* There is a big difference between walking and living. Walking is an accurate translation. That is exactly what the Christian life is, a walk. Dr. Lewis Sperry Chafer, my teacher for four years at the Dallas Theological Seminary, used to say, *"Every step of this walk is an incipient fall"* Incipient means in the first stage or the beginning of something. If that other foot does not come down, then you stumble. The Christian life is a walk. We are to walk by means of the Spirit moment by moment. The only ones who have that power to walk in the Spirit are those who are saved and are indwelt by the Holy Spirit. The rest of the world cannot walk in the Spirit of God. The Spirit of God can overcome the lust of the flesh if we walk in His power.

- **1 Corinthians 6:19**
  What? **know ye not that your body is the temple of the Holy Ghost** which is in you, which ye have of God, and ye are not your own?

The Holy Spirit of God wants us to have the victory over our flesh. Born-again Christians have three enemies: the world outside of us, the flesh inside of us, and the Devil who, through his demons, is all around us. I believe that the flesh that is within us is the most serious enemy because it is within us. We are the enemy. Who wants to fight with one's self? The flesh is the sensuous nature of each man and woman. It is the animal nature. That is what SARX is, *"the flesh."* It is *"the animal nature with cravings which insight to sin."* Everyone of us has this flesh whether we are three years old or ninety- nine years old. We all have this corrupt flesh. The only way that God can deal with it is to give us a new nature by the Holy Spirit of God. We get this new nature when we are saved. The Holy Spirit of God has the power to fight that flesh.

Galatians 5:17
"For the flesh lusteth against the Spirit, and the Spirit against the flesh: and these are contrary the one to the other: so that ye cannot do the things that ye would." Here is the internal battle. The believer's *"flesh"* is lusting after the Spirit of God. The Spirit of God is fighting against the flesh. They are *"contrary the one to the other."* If you are saved, you just cannot make peace between the flesh inside of you and the Spirit of God inside of you. There is no peace treaty. They are on other sides of the spectrum. These two natures are opposites. It is like two ends of a teeter-totter. You often cannot do the things that you really purpose to do because of the battle that is within you. Unsaved people have no battle. They just have flesh. They have no Holy Spirit of God indwelling them. Before you were saved, you just did what you wanted to do. There was no conflict within you. They have a little conscience here and there that the Lord has given to them, but most consciences these days are *"seared with a hot iron"* (1 Timothy 4:2). They cannot even feel their conscience. For the believer, however, there is a continuous conflict that we must understand and confront.

Galatians 5:18
"But if ye be led of the Spirit, ye are not under the law." This word, *"led,"* AGO, means *"to lead by laying hold of, and this way to bring to the point of destination of an animal."* For instance, *"you lead a horse to water,"* as they say, *"but you cannot make him drink."* By the same token, it is also true that *"you can send a kid to college, but you cannot make him think."* After you lead a person to the Word of God, you cannot force that person to partake of it and obey it. If you are led by the Spirit of God, you *"are not under the law."* There is no law of Moses or law of anything that is going to bind you if you are led by the Spirit of God. The leading of the Spirit of God is always in line with the Word of God. Never does the Holy Spirit lead contrary to the Bible. You must have the Bible's instruction at all times. If someone is led to do something prohibited by a Scripture verse, then he is not being led by the Spirit but by the flesh. It is very important to see that the Holy Spirit of God never leads contrary to the Word of God. If we are saved, we should want to be led by the Spirit of God. Our desire should be to do what God wants us to do. We should want to serve Him, and it is by the Spirit of God that we can do that.

Galatians 5:19

"Now the works of the flesh are manifest, which are these; Adultery, fornication, uncleanness, lasciviousness," Here is the beginning of a list of seventeen specific sins which are *"works of the flesh."* These Galatians wanted to go back under the works of the law. So Paul just simply said, in effect, *"All right. Here are the works that your flesh will produce."* These works are open and manifest. Everyone can see them.

"Adultery" can be seen on every hand in our country, including the former President of the United States, Bill Clinton. Reportedly, there were many women in his life. I heard a program about the presidents on C-Span. This week they were reviewing President John F. Kennedy. The historian who was reporting said that President Kennedy was the most wicked man who ever lived in the White House. He slept with all kinds of women. I was glad to see the truth finally publicly revealed about the morality of President Kennedy. He was a playboy. This is adultery. People today think there is nothing wrong with it and even make it known in public with little or no embarrassment about it. That is the work of the flesh.

- **Hebrews 13:4**
  Marriage *is* honourable in all, and the bed undefiled: **but whoremongers and adulterers God will judge**.

That includes the priests of Rome, the pope of Rome, and everyone else.

"Fornication" involves unmarried persons. This is also a work of the flesh, and young people think nothing of it. Many of the new Bible versions do not even use the word "fornication." They use *"immorality,"* or some other term. They do not even name the name. There is fornication even in Christian schools, and people seem to think nothing of it.

"Uncleanness," AKATHARSIA, is, in a moral sense, *"the impurity of lustful, luxurious, profligate living."* Uncleanness is also a work of the flesh.

"Lasciviousness," ASELGEIA, is *"unbridled lust, excess, licentiousness, wantonness, shamelessness, and insolence."* This kind of behavior is all over in our high schools, in our colleges, and even in our grade schools. What do you expect when they teach sex education in the schools that says anything goes? They say that there is nothing wrong with an alternative lifestyle of homosexuality or anything else. This is a work of the flesh.

Galatians 5:20

"Idolatry, witchcraft, hatred, variance, emulations, wrath, strife, seditions, heresies," All of these "works" are serious indeed and should not be taken lightly. Here are nine more items on the list of seventeen works of the flesh.

Galatians 5:20

"Idolatry," EIDOLOLATREIA, is made up of EIDO, *"to see,"* and LOLATREIA, *"divine service."* Idolatry is simply the worship of things that are seen. False gods are just one kind of idol. We can make a false god out of anything or anybody. We can worship people. God forbid that we would worship any individual. We need to follow the Lord Jesus Christ and the Word of God. Some people bow down to money. Everybody is glad when the stock market is doing wonderfully, but what happened in 1929 when the stock market was not doing wonderfully? Some of those who lost their wealth committed suicide. If you have Christ as your Saviour, you have the most important Person in all the world. As Martin Luther wrote in his hymn "A Mighty Fortress," *"Let goods and kindred go. This mortal life also."*

"Witchcraft" is a translation of the Greek word, PHARMAKEIA. We get the English word, "pharmacy" from that word. People sometimes ask me what about drugs? *"Witchcraft,"* PHARMAKEIA, means *"the use or the administration of drugs, sorcery, magical arts, often found in connection with idolatry and fostered by it."* Drugs are closely associated with witchcraft. Halloween is a night where the witches are out in force. They believe it is the devil's birthday and on that day they honor the one that they are worshiping. All of the covens of witches are out on that Satanic high holy day. On that day they have animal sacrifices like a cat or a dog, but also have human sacrifices according to ex-witches. Witchcraft is a work of the flesh, and the Spirit of God has nothing to do with it.

"Hatred" is a word that we all understand. From time to time, we have all hated things and people. The only thing that God wants us to really hate is sin. Do you know where God wants us to hate sin the most? He wants us to hate sin the most right inside of us. That is where God wants us to hate sin. If we hate and detest sin, then we will not have any part of it.

"Variance," ERIS, means *"contention, strife, and wrangling."* That is good for these Galatian Christians because they were devouring one another. Variance is a work of the flesh.

"Emulations," ZELOS, means *"an envious and contentious rivalry, jealousy."* Someone might say, *"Well, I know more Scripture than you do and I want to teach this Sunday School class."* You could be envious that some person makes more money then you do or has something that you do not have. This is a burning zeal. It is an ardor and a fervency of spirit which envies and contends against someone else in a spirit of rivalry.

"Wrath," THUMOS, is *"passion, angry, heat, anger forthwith boiling up and soon subsiding again."* Wrath often manifests itself in loud voices, cursing, or beating something or someone. This is not Christian wrath or righteous indignation. It is a work of the flesh.

"Strife," EIRITHEIA, means *"electioneering or intriguing for office, a desire to put one's self forward, a partisan and fractious spirit which does not

disdain low acts." In Aristotle's time, it was used to denote *"a self-seeking pursuit of political office by unfair means."* I read a book many years ago about the election to the Congress of former President Lyndon Johnson. It was called *A Texan Looks at Lyndon.* The point of the book was that it was a rigged election. This is what strife is--a self-seeking pursuit of political office by unfair means. Sometimes we hear about stuffing ballot boxes. This is what the word strife conveys. Sometimes people do not get elected into an office at church. There is strife and battling in this. We used to be members of a certain church. When they had elections, we would wait a long time until the ballots were counted. Finally, on the same night as the elections, the ballot totals were given. Then, when Sunday morning came, they would give different numbers. So it was always a mystery as to what the true totals were. Finally, someone asked if the men who counted the ballets could count. Well, the men who counted the ballets got all angry about this with many accusations flying around the room. One of the counters resigned, as I recall.

"Seditions," DICHOSTASIA, means *"division and dissensions."* This would include the splitting of churches. I was talking to a man the other day who told me he would rather not split a church. He said if he did not agree with what the church was doing, he would rather just leave than split the church. That was admirable.

"Heresies," HAIRESIS, means *"a choosing or a choice, the holding of doctrines contrary to the Word of God."* This term has been used recently in a false way by the Fundamental Baptist Fellowship (FBF) in commenting on Titus 3:10. It was given at their 81st Annual Meeting and titled *"Schismatic 'Brethren.'"* The quotation marks around the word, *"Brethren,"* indicates that the FBF really didn't know whether or not to call those who disagreed with them on Bible texts and translations *"Brethren."* In effect, they were doubting or at least questioning their salvation. The resolution wrongly used the word *"schismatics"* to translate this word, *"heresies."*

The same error was made by Dr. Kevin Bauder, a teacher at Central Baptist Seminary, Minneapolis, Minnesota,. He is one of the general editors of a book entitled *One Bible Only?* On page 167 of this book, Bauder is content to use any one of three wrong translations of *"heretic"* to urge his readers to reject those of us who stand for the King James Bible and its underling Hebrew and Greek texts. He used *"divisive man"* from the New King James Version, *"factious man"* from the New American Standard version, and *"divisive person"* from the New International Version. All three of these terms are distortions of the true linguistic and historical meaning of HAIRESIS, which is one of the works of the flesh.

Galatians 5:21

"Envyings, murders, drunkenness, revellings, and such like: of the which I tell you before, as I have also told you in time past, that they which do such things shall not inherit the kingdom of God."

"Envyings, murders, drunkenness, revellings, and such like" Envying of people is wanting something that someone else has. This is a work of the flesh. They have a hat. We want that hat. They have a car. We want that car.

We have had an influx of murders in recent years. The multiple shootings in the schools are horrible. They are a work of the flesh.

We have drunkenness all over school campuses, both in high school and college.

"Revelling," KOMOS, means

"a nocturnal and riotous procession of half drunken and frolicsome fellows who after supper parade through the streets with torches and music in honor of Bacchus [the god of wine and revelry] or some other deity, and sing and play before houses of male and female friends; hence used generally of feasts and drinking parties that are protracted till late at night and indulge in revelry."

That is all involved in that word, *"revellings."* They are works of the flesh.

The Lord does not stop there. He says, *"and such like."* There is no end to the works of the flesh.

"of the which I tell you before, as I have also told you in time past, that they which do such things shall not inherit the kingdom of God" *"They which do such things"* is in the present tense which means they which continuously practice such things. The ones who practice and live in the flesh do not have the Spirit of God living in them. They are unsaved. You might ask, *"Can a Christian manifest the works of the flesh?"* There are some hyper-Calvinists and others who say no. They would say if one manifests the works of the flesh, they are lost. I believe that a carnal Christian can manifest the works of the flesh. Why do you think Paul wrote this letter? He wrote it to Galatian Christians to warn them about the works of the flesh. I do not advocate Christians following the works of the flesh, but I will tell you that we all have the flesh. Our flesh is not going to be completely put out of commission until the Lord Jesus Christ redeems our bodies. Some of this Arminian teaching is wrong. They teach that it is possible after we are saved to be entirely sanctified and become sinlessly perfect, without the ability to do any of the works of the flesh. I say just ask their spouses, their children, other relatives or friends. They will tell you whether or not they have obtained the status of being sinlessly perfect!

Galatians 5:22

"But the fruit of the Spirit is love, joy, peace, longsuffering, gentleness, goodness, faith" The Spirit and the flesh are constantly in a battle. *"The joy of the Lord is your strength."* (Nehemiah 8:10) This is one of the fruits of the Spirit. The fruit of the Spirit is manifested when we are filled with the Spirit or controlled by the Spirit of God. As Dr. Lewis Sperry Chafer has stated in his book, *He That is Spiritual*, there are three things to keep in mind when thinking about being controlled by the Spirit of God. Two are negative, and one is positive.

Three Requirements For the Spirit's Filling

First: we are told to *"grieve not the Spirit"* (Ephesians 4:30). We grieve the Spirit when we sin. We need to confess all known sin, and stop sinning in order to stop grieving the Spirit of God.

Second: we are told to *"quench not the Spirit"* (1 Thessalonians 5:19). We quench the Spirit when we say "no" to the will of God.

Third: we are told to *"walk in the Spirit"* (Galatians 5:16). We walk in the Spirit when we depend on the Holy Spirit of God as we live our life day by day.

If these things are true in my life and in your life, then we can be filled with the Spirit of God. When we are controlled by the Spirit of God, we will manifest the fruit of the Spirit of God.

Love

The *"love"* mentioned here is not human love. It is God's love. That is how we are able to love the people who are unlovely. It is the Spirit of God that can empower us to love others.

What do you think God did when He sent His Son to save you and to save me? We were the most unlovely creatures in the whole world. Those of this wicked world crucified *"the Lord of glory."* But He loved them, and He loved you.

Someone said to me recently that they do the will of God and try to do what is right, but they have no joy. I told that person that joy is a fruit of the

Spirit of God. He can give you joy. After we have done the will of God, trust Him to give us joy which is part of the fruit of the Spirit. He will bring us Divine joy.

Joy

The joy of the Lord is not human joy. It is not happiness. Happiness is dependent on happenings. If the happenings are bad, it makes us unhappy. But no matter what the happenings are, the Lord can give us His joy.

The Lord also gives us peace.

Peace

"Peace," EIRENE, is *"the tranquil state of a soul assured of its salvation through Christ, and so fearing nothing from God and content with its earthly lot, of whatsoever sort that is."* Peace is also *"exemption from the rage and havoc of war."* It is *"security and safety."*

Longsuffering

"Longsuffering" is MAKROTHUMIA. It comes from two Greek words, MAKROS, which means *"large, long, or far."* THUMOS means *"passion, angry, heat, anger forthwith boiling up and soon subsiding again."* So longsuffering means that our boiling point is still a long-ways off. **It refers to putting up with people.**

Patience is putting up with things. We remember the patience of Job. He lost his friends, his children, his possessions, and almost his wife. All of us have boiling points. When that boiling point is reached, there is a boiling over. Longsuffering means that your boiling point is still a long way off. You can get a lot hotter before you boil over. That grace is from the Spirit of God. That is not human. We all know that people can be unpleasant, horrible, and ugly. How in the world are you going to put up with these people? You just have to ask the Lord to give you longsuffering which is a part of the fruit of the Spirit of God.

Gentleness

"Gentleness" is kindness. It means to be as gentle as a lamb.

Goodness

The Greek word for *"goodness"* is AGATHOSUNE. In commenting on this synonym of the Greek language, goodness means something similar to what we might call today *"righteous indignation."*

Goodness does not come over that way in the English, but that is what the Greek term means. The Lord Jesus Christ manifested goodness when he took the whip and drove the money changers from the temple. You might ask, "Was he angry?" Yes, He had righteous anger and righteous goodness in respect to His Father's house which was turned into a *"house of merchandise"* (John 2:16). This *"goodness"* is part of the fruit of the Spirit. Some people believe in order to display the fruit of the Spirit you have to be soft and not firm on anything. That may be debatable in some areas, but certainly not in this one part of the fruit of the Spirit. This is manifested when you stand firm and appeal to Caesar or do whatever is necessary for the sake of the Lord. You are not going to deny Christ. You are going to be firm and nobody is going to move you.

- 1 Corinthians 15:58
  Therefore, my beloved brethren, **be ye stedfast, unmoveable**, always abounding in the work of the Lord, forasmuch as ye know that your labour is not in vain in the Lord.

When you are *"stedfast and unmovable"* you are displaying this fruit of goodness.

Faith

The Holy Spirit of God gives us *"faith"* also. *"Now faith is the substance of things hoped for, the evidence of things not seen."* (Hebrews 11:1)

Sometimes we might be able to believe that God is still on the throne. Sometimes our lives and our troubles in this life are so great. But if we are filled with and controlled by the Holy Spirit of God, He can give us faith to believe the Bible is still true and our salvation is still true. We do not have to worry because God is still on His throne, and prayer changes things.

Galatians 5:23

"Meekness, temperance: against such there is no law."

"Meekness, temperance" The eighth and ninth part of the fruit of the Spirit is meekness and temperance, respectively.

Meekness
"Meekness" is a *"mildness that is noticeable."*

Temperance
"Temperance," EGKRATEIA, means *"self control, the virtue of one who masters his desires and passions, especially his sensual appetites."*

When the Spirit of God is filling and controlling us, all the parts of the fruit of the Spirit are present. It is one fruit with nine different parts. It is just like an orange. You open it up, and you have this part and that part. If you have *"temperance,"* you have control of yourself. When the flesh wants to get angry in a sinful manner, there is that battle between the Spirit of God and the flesh. If the Spirit of God is in control, you will have self-control and will not get angry in a sinful manner.

"against such there is no law" Nobody can ever properly make a law against any one of the nine parts of the fruit of the Spirit, *"love, joy, peace, longsuffering, gentleness, goodness, faith, meekness, temperance."* There is no Old Testament law *"against"* these nine Christian virtues.

Galatians 5:24

"And they that are Christ's have crucified the flesh with the affections and lusts." This is positional *"crucifixion"* rather than a literal crucifixion. This is mentioned in several places in the New Testament.

- **Romans 6:6**
  Knowing this, that our **old man is crucified with *him***, that the body of sin might be destroyed, that henceforth we should not serve sin.

Positionally everyone who is a believer in the Lord Jesus Christ has died with Christ, has risen with Christ, and is seated with Christ in Heaven. We who are saved are in Christ. That is positional.

- **Galatians 2:20**
  I am crucified with Christ: nevertheless I live; yet not I, but Christ liveth in me: and the life which I now live in the flesh I live by the faith of the Son of God, who loved me, and gave himself for me.
- **Galatians 6:14**
  But God forbid that I should glory, save in the cross of our Lord Jesus Christ, **by whom the world is crucified unto me**, and I unto the world.

Paul says that they that are Christ's have *"crucified the flesh with the affections and lusts."* Positionally, the flesh is crucified. What about practically? I do not want to crucify my flesh. That is painful. Crucifixion is very painful. If you are crucifying your flesh even metaphorically, it is also a painful situation. You want to do what you want to do. I want to do what I want to do in the natural sense. To crucify the flesh with the lusts and affections and all of the desires is painful. There is an engine inside of us that Satan is very happy to work with. God is displeased with it. It is called the flesh. That engine wants to go. That engine wants to move. That engine wants to do its thing and manifest its seventeen works of the flesh. There is another engine inside of us. It is the Holy Spirit of God which has a nine-fold fruit of the Spirit. Here are nine qualities against seventeen sins. The question is "Who wins?" If you walk by means of the power of the Holy Spirit of God, you will not fulfill the lusts of the flesh. The one who is stronger is the one who will win. Those of us who are saved have crucified the flesh.

Galatians 5:25

"If we live in the Spirit, let us also walk in the Spirit." The only ones who *"live in the Spirit"* are those who are saved.
- **1 Corinthians 6:19**
  What? know ye not that **your body is the temple of the Holy Ghost which is in you**, which ye have of God, and ye are not your own?
- **Romans 8:9**
  But ye are not in the flesh, but in the Spirit, if so be that the Spirit of God dwell in you. Now **if any man have not the Spirit of Christ, he is none of his**.

If we do not have the Spirit of God in us we are not one of Christ's. We are lost and bound for Hell if we have not trusted the Lord Jesus Christ as our Saviour and our Redeemer. Then we must live in the Spirit and also walk in the Spirit. Just because you have food in your house does not mean you are eating. You have to go get the food and use it. Just because you have the Spirit of God in your body does not mean that you are walking by means of and in the power of the Spirit of God. God wants us all walking in the Spirit of God.

If we are walking in the power of the Spirit of God, then we can manifest His fruit. Now, if you were to take a test and I were to ask you on this test which of these two would you prefer-- the works of the flesh or the fruit of the Spirit, which would you choose? I do not think there would be anyone in this room who would choose the works of the flesh with all its wickedness. You would want the fruit of the Spirit of God. These new versions such as the New International Version, New American Standard Version, and New King James Version often change the word, *"walk"* to *"live."* They do not like that word walk. Walking is the figure of speech that God wants us to see because it is a step by step process.

Galatians 5:26

"Let us not be desirous of vain glory, provoking one another, envying one another." This is a prohibition in the Greek present tense. It means to stop something that is already in progress. There are two forms of negative prohibitions in the Greek language. There is a prohibition in the aorist tense and a prohibition in the present tense. An aorist tense prohibition tells you not even to begin the action in question. *"Do not even begin to have a desire for vain glory."* But that is not the form here. It is a prohibition in the present tense. This means to stop an action already in progress. These Galatians were desiring vain glory and provoking one another. Paul tells them to stop it. Paul did not know why they were fighting and bickering, but he said to stop it.

What is *"vain glory"*? Vain glory is glory that is empty. Vanity is emptiness. Ecclesiastes says, "Vanity of vanities, saith the preacher, vanity of vanities, all is vanity." (Ecclesiastes 1:2). Let us not be desirous of vain glory. The flesh wants vain glory. The word, *"provoke,"* PROKALEOMAI means *"to call forth especially to challenge to a combat or contest with one."* The flesh will provoke one another in the sense of having a contest or combating. It's as if we say, *"Here is a chip on my shoulder. I dare you to knock it off."* Then as soon as it is knocked off, there is a fist fight. They were challenging, irritating, and envying one another. Paul says, "Stop it." These are the works of the flesh and not the fruit of the Spirit of God.

The internal battle I have been talking about this morning will never cease. It is the battle between the Holy Spirit of God Who indwells the Christian and the flesh that also lives within them. This is a constant, moment by moment, day by day, week by week, and year by year, battle. You have heard the story about the two dogs, the black dog (the flesh) and the white dog (the new nature). Which one wins this fight? The one you feed the most will win.

We have a small church. We are a little dog so-to-speak. But remember the old saying, *"It is not the size of the dog in the fight that counts, but the size of the fight in the dog."* We are a church meeting in our home, but praise God our services can be heard on several national radio stations, and, both by short wave and the Internet, our message is sounding out all around the world. This technology is truly amazing! At this time, we also help support five foreign missionaries and four home missionaries. Yes, we are a little dog in the fight but we have a great deal of tenacity and a great deal of unity which God will honor and bless. He wants us to manifest the fruit of the Spirit of God in our lives and also in our church.

Remember, the only way to walk in the Spirit is step-by-step. It is a moment-by-moment situation. One time we may have the Spirit reigning and controlling us, and then at the next moment the flesh erupts. God wants us to walk every step by means of the Spirit of God. *Walk in the Spirit, and ye shall not fulfil the lust of the flesh.* (Galatians 5:16)

Galatians Chapter Six

Galatians 6:1

"Brethren, if a man be overtaken in a fault, ye which are spiritual, restore such an one in the spirit of meekness; considering thyself, lest thou also be tempted."

"Brethren, if a man be overtaken in a fault, ye which are spiritual, restore such an one" In this local church in Galatia there was a situation, no doubt, in which a person was being *"overtaken in a fault."* God gives us a remedy for this. Those who are *"spiritual"* should be the ones who take care of the situations, not the ones who are carnal and walk by the flesh, exhibiting the seventeen sins of the flesh listed in the last chapter. Those who are *"spiritual"* should be the ones who restore such a person. That word *"restore,"* KATARTIZO, means *"to mend what has been broken or rent, to repair."* Some people's lives are in disrepair, and they need to be brought back. They need to be mended and brought close to the Lord Jesus Christ. Ethically, the term means *"to strengthen, complete, make one what he ought to be."*

This Greek word, *"overtaken,"* is in the aorist tense which means that it is just a once and for all overtaken. This is not talking about people who are living in constant sin. This must be dealt with as well. But this *"overtaken in a fault"* seems to be just one fault. There is a difference in being overtaken and taken-over. If you are being overtaken, somebody is after you. This is a person who is in serious trouble whatever that sin of the flesh might be. The spiritual ones who are walking by means of the Spirit of God are the ones who are to restore the one who has fallen down.

"in the spirit of meekness; considering thyself, lest thou also be tempted" The people who are mending the net of those who have fallen into some sin must be careful and *"consider"* themselves. The person who is helping someone else to overcome a sin could be tempted to commit the very same sin. Let us look at some verses regarding temptation.

- **Matthew 4:1**
  Then was Jesus led up of the Spirit into the wilderness **to be tempted of the devil.**

The devil is one of the tempters who tries to tempt us.

- **Matthew 6:13**
  And **lead us not into temptation,** but deliver us from evil: For thine is the kingdom, and the power, and the glory, for ever. Amen.

- **Luke 8:13**
  They on the rock *are they,* which, when they hear, receive the word with joy; and these have no root, which for a while believe, and **in time of temptation fall away.**

There is no fruit.

- **1 Corinthians 7:5**
  Defraud ye not one the other, except *it be* with consent for a time, that ye may give yourselves to fasting and prayer; and come together again, **that Satan tempt you not for your incontinency.**

- **1 Corinthians 10:13**
  There hath no temptation taken you but such as is common to man: but God *is* faithful, who **will not suffer you to be tempted above that ye are able; but will with the temptation also make a way to escape,** that ye may be able to bear *it.*

This is probably the key verse on temptation.

- **1 Thessalonians 3:5**
  For this cause, when I could no longer forbear, I sent to know your faith, **lest by some means the tempter have tempted you,** and our labour be in vain.

- **1 Timothy 6:9**
  But **they that will be rich fall into temptation** and a snare, and *into* many foolish and hurtful lusts, which drown men in destruction and perdition.

A desire to have wealth more than anything else will lead a person into temptation. That is the only thing they think about. They do not think about the Lord, the Word, or the church.

- **James 1:12**
  Blessed *is* the man that endureth temptation: for when he is tried, he shall receive the crown of life, which the Lord hath promised to them that love him.

- **James 1:13-14**
  Let no man say when he is tempted, I am tempted of God: for God cannot be tempted with evil, neither tempteth he any man: But **every man is tempted, when he is drawn away of his own lust, and enticed.**

Do not blame God for the temptations. They come from the devil, the world, and the flesh.

- **James 1:15**
  Then when lust hath conceived, it bringeth forth sin: and sin, **when it is finished, bringeth forth death.**

This is what yielding to temptation brings--sin and death.

- **2 Peter 2:9**
  The Lord knoweth how to deliver the godly out of temptations, and to reserve the unjust unto the day of judgment to be punished:

This restoration of the brother who has fallen into sin must be made very carefully to avoid multiple catastrophes.

Galatians 6:2

"Bear ye one another's burdens, and so fulfil the law of Christ." We are to help one another. We have a small church, but I hope that we will continue to care one for another. When somebody needs something, we hope we can help. Our burdens are all different. The Lord Jesus told us to come to Him and He will give us rest.

- **Matthew 11:28**
  Come unto me, all *ye* that labour and are heavy laden, and I **will give you rest.**

We are to help one another whatever the sin or addiction may be. These *"burdens"* are pressures. The Lord wants all His children to be in good shape. When you have a burden that is too hard to bear, give me a call. I hope that everyone of us in our church will do the same thing. If we have burdens, let us share our burdens so that we can pray for each other. Remember that is one of the characters in John Bunyan's *Pilgrim's Progress*. As Pilgrim was walking the journey, he had a big pack on his back, his load of sin. As he began walking up to the Cross of Calvary, that burden rolled away. We have some people who have the burden of sin. They need Christ as their Saviour and Redeemer. We are to help lead them to Christ and to bear their burden.

Galatians 6:3

"For if a man think himself to be something, when he is nothing, he deceiveth himself." There are many people who think they are something when they really are nothing. Now, that does not mean that we should think that we are nothing. With the Lord's help, we are somebody, but not in our own strength. There are some people who are egotists. Paul is saying here that a man should not think himself *"to be something."* It says in Scripture that you should let another praise you and not your own lips.

- **Proverbs 27:2**
  Let another man praise thee, and not thine own mouth; a stranger, and not thine own lips.

I do not agree with the people who say that we should be absolute nothings. On the other hand, I do not think we should go along with Robert Schuller who thinks that we should have such high self-esteem that we believe we have no sins. That is false. We are born in sin. We have the sin nature, and we must recognize it. We should not be puffed toads and think that we are something when we are nothing. We only deceive ourselves. It is a mental deception. Some people think they can run the one hundred-yard dash in seven seconds. They are deceiving themselves in their own mind. Paul is cautioning us to not be overly impressed with ourselves.

Galatians 6:4

"But let every man prove his own work, and then shall he have rejoicing in himself alone, and not in another."

"But let every man prove his own work" There are two words for *"prove."* We saw the first one in the first verse of this chapter when it said *"considering thyself lest thou also be tempted."* This word for *"tempt"* is PEIRAZO. It has the idea of tempting with the hope that they will fall. That is what the devil was doing to the Lord Jesus Christ. He was tempting with a hope that he would fall and fail and deny the Father.

The word used here for *"prove"* is DOKIMAZO. It is a different word for tempt or prove. It has the idea of testing with the hope that it will pass inspection. It is like when a parachutist packs his own chute. You can be sure that he is going to be careful because when he tests that chute, he could endanger his own life. That is a test with the hope that it will pass. That is the word used here. We are to *"prove"* our own work to see if it is genuine or not. We have to test and try our own works. We have to walk in the power of the Holy Spirit.

"and then shall he have rejoicing in himself alone, and not in another" It is good to have fellowship and Christian friends, but there is a time when we are all by ourselves. What happens when we are by ourselves? There is something to being self-contained. That was a criticism that my senior chaplain had of me when I was a Naval Chaplain stationed at Corpus Christi, Texas. This senior chaplain was a modernist unbeliever. He said that Chaplain Waite was not a team-player. If he meant that I did not want to be teaming up with the wrong people, then he was right. I did not take a "coffee break" with them. I don't even drink coffee. I am not a team-player with the devil's crowd and with unbelievers.

Furthermore, when they had communion service, I would not participate because, like the Roman Catholics, they used the intinction method. They took the wafer, dipped it in the grape juice and placed it on the person's tongue. I would not be a part of it. In one of his fitness reports, the senior chaplain wrote that I would not cooperate and was not a team-player, but self-contained. That is a compliment as far as I am concerned. We have to be self-contained. With us and the Lord, we ought to be on our own. It was not that I was a loner and was not friendly. It was that I would not cooperate with their devilment.

That is why if I were ever to join the service again, I would never again go into the Navy. It would be better to go into the Army where each chaplain is his own chaplain in his own chapel where no other chaplain could horn in and try to make it a modernistic service. In the Navy when all the ships at sea came back to shore, many chaplains were in one base. Sometimes there were five chaplains in the same location. You had to take your turn and go with the modernists and liberals. I would never do that again. That is compromise. The Lord can give us His joy, and that is what we need. Joy is one of the parts of the fruit of the Holy Spirit.

Galatians 6:5

"For every man shall bear his own burden." Some people see this as a contradiction, but it is not. This verse means that you cannot blame your sin on your mother, your father, or your grandfather. This principle is found in the Old Testament as well.

- Ezekiel 18:20
  The soul that sinneth, it shall die. **The son shall not bear the iniquity of the father, neither shall the father bear the iniquity of the son**: the righteousness of the righteous shall be upon him, and the wickedness of the wicked shall be upon him.

I think that this is teaching us that it is not the environment that causes us to sin, but it is the sin nature. We are to bear our own burden.

If we are saved and have trusted the Lord Jesus Christ as our personal Saviour, we will stand before the Judgment Seat of Christ. This will take place at the coming of the Lord Jesus Christ in the rapture when He takes the saved believers who are then living home to Heaven. This is when He will take His bride, the church, home to be with Him. At that Judgment Seat of Christ, we are not going to be able to hide behind our spouse, our mother, our father, or anybody else. We are going to be there on our own, and we must bear our own burden. Believers will have to answer for the unconfessed sins that we have committed after we have been saved. God wants us to confess our sins and stay in fellowship with Him.

- **1 John 1:9**
  If we confess our sins, he is faithful and just to forgive us our sins, and to cleanse us from all unrighteousness.

That is a verse for saved believers only. It is not written for the unsaved people.

Now, if you are an unbeliever, you must appear before the Great White Throne Judgment. This judgment is for all the unsaved of all generations. There again they cannot blame anyone for how they turned out. I realize that people do this all the time. They blame others for their own problems. When you stand before the Lord of Heaven and earth, you will not have any excuses. We are each on our own. God will say, *"You did it. You are responsible for your own actions."* We must bear our own burdens. This is why we must accept the invitation of the Saviour.

- **Matthew 11:28**
  Come unto me, all ye that labour and are heavy laden, and I will give you rest.

Jesus Christ is the only One Who can give us rest from our sins. If you yoke up with the Lord Jesus Christ, He does the pulling. We just sit there and do nothing and let Him pull. His burden is light. People might ask, *"Am I going to go to Hell if I reject Christ?"* Yes, you are going to go to Hell if you reject Christ. You might ask, *"Can't I bear my own burden, bear my own sin, and die for myself?"* No, not at all.

I remember my Speech Teacher at Southern Methodist University. I gave a speech which was a gospel message. After I finished, Dr. Harold Weiss got up and said that he did not agree with that. He said, *"I do not have to have someone else forgive me. I forgive myself."* He sounded as if he were God. We cannot bear our own sins. Christ bore our sins on the cross of Calvary. Christ is our Saviour and our substitute. If we have Him as our substitute, then He has borne that burden. When we stand before Him, we will be free.

Galatians 6:6

"Let him that is taught in the word communicate unto him that teacheth in all good things."

"Let him that is taught in the word" We are teaching the Word of God in the 𝕭𝖎𝖇𝖑𝖊 𝕱𝖔𝖗 𝕿𝖔𝖉𝖆𝖞 𝕭𝖆𝖕𝖙𝖎𝖘𝖙 𝕮𝖍𝖚𝖗𝖈𝖍. We believe that this is our mission and our goal. That is why I wanted to get back-in-the-saddle and be a preacher once again. I was out-of-the-saddle for twenty-six years. Yes, I had my Bible For Today ministry, preached in churches, and taught at different schools, but I just felt burdened to get back into the preaching situation. To do what? To tell stories, or to read poetry, or to tell about biographies? No, to preach the Word of God. And I do it in a verse-by-verse method, taking half-a-chapter each Sunday morning. That is what I was called and trained to do and I believe that is what Christians need desperately and are not getting in most churches in our land. I make no apologies. You are here today because you wanted to hear the Word of God taught and preached. That is why we are assembled here. I praise the Lord that there are some people still left in this world who are still interested in hearing the Word of God. We try to make it practical and applicable.

"communicate unto him that teacheth in all good things" What are we to do if we are taught in the Scriptures? We are to *"communicate unto him that teacheth in all good things."* That includes money, support, and prayer. I am very glad, as I told my electrician yesterday, that I am able to preach the Word without having the need to receive a salary for myself. The Lord has supplied our needs so everything that goes into that box in the back can go for the needs of the ministry of radio and Internet, printing of books, and support for our current nine missionaries (including five foreign and four here at home). I am interested in proclaiming the Word of God to as many as I can. I am interested in getting God's message out and am happy not to have to receive a salary. There is another man in Scripture who had the same position as I have. His name is the apostle Paul.

- **1 Corinthians 9:18**
  What is my reward then? *Verily* that, when I preach the gospel, **I may make the gospel of Christ without charge**, that I abuse not my power in the gospel.

Paul was a tentmaker.

- **1 Corinthians 9:9**
  For it is written in the law of Moses, **Thou shalt not muzzle the mouth of the ox that treadeth out the corn**. Doth God take care for oxen?

The preacher is like the ox in this verse. That ox should be fed by what he is doing. Preachers should be supported by the people they preach to. That is what he is teaching.

- **1 Corinthians 9:13-14**
  Do ye not know that they which minister about holy things live *of the things* of the temple? and they which wait at the altar are partakers with the altar? **Even so hath the Lord ordained that they which preach the gospel should live of the gospel.**

They did not give Paul a penny for all of his preaching. Occasionally, churches would give him gifts for his preaching but not on a regular basis. Paul taught that every church from then on should support its pastor and its missionaries. Churches should give, but do not give anything to Paul lest people think he was just feathering his own nest. Paul did not take any money except for certain gifts on his missionary journeys. The Old Testament priests ate from the offerings that the people brought to the temple. That is the way it works. The preachers who preach the gospel should live of the gospel as the offerings are received from the people.

I am also preaching these things not so it would be done unto me either. The Lord has supplied our needs and we are thankful for that. We are happy to preach. I enjoy preaching. I told the electrician that I have to study and know what these Greek words mean and what they do not mean. It gives me great joy to dig into the Scripture.

The rule is let him that is *"taught in the word."* Notice, Paul wrote *"in the word."* It is important that we use the right Word. That is why we use the King James Bible here in our **Bible For Today Baptist Church**. This is the right Scripture with the right Old Testament Masoretic Hebrew Text and the right New Testament Textus Receptus Greek Text. Our King James Bible is founded on these proper texts and it is accurate in its translation. The new versions that people are using are not the Words of God. They are founded on a different New Testament text. It is different in 5,604. Dr. Jack Moorman has found over 7,000 differences in his current research. The New International Version and the New American Standard Version and these other new versions do not give us the correct Words of God. They add their own words, they subtract Words, and they change Words in other ways. Let me give you one example.

- **John 6:47**
  Verily, verily, I say unto you, He that believeth **on me** hath everlasting life.

The false Greek text of the apostates Westcott and Hort (as well as the texts of Nestle-Aland and the United Bible Society) leaves out two words, *"on me."* Therefore, the New American Standard Version, the New International Version and most other new versions leave out these two words also. The two words are *"on me."* Those other modern versions just say "he that believes has everlasting life." This would lead us to believe that you do not have to trust in the Lord Jesus Christ to have everlasting life. That is not the gospel. There are three hundred and fifty-six doctrinal errors in these new, modern versions because they have used the Westcott and Hort false Greek New Testament Text. We have a battle on our hands to try to get the right Bible into the hands of the right people.

We have a tape of what even some of the Fundamentalists are doing in regard to the Bible. We look at some of the arguments and changes they are making. They wrote a whole book about this, *From the Mind of God to the Mind of Man*. These are Fundamentalist men who have said that all the versions are fine, and do not worry about it. Go back to sleep. I do not believe we ought to go back to sleep when the Words of God are in peril. As Dean John William Burgon has written,

> *"When the Words of Inspiration are seriously imperilled, as now they are, it is scarcely possible for one who is determined effectually to preserve the Deposit in its integrity, to hit either too straight or too hard."* [Dean John William Burgon, *The Revision Revised*, p. viii]

This was written in 1883 and it is still true today.

Galatians 6:7

"Be not deceived; God is not mocked: for whatsoever a man soweth, that shall he also reap."

"Be not deceived" We should not deceive ourselves. This is a present tense prohibition. As I have mentioned before, in the Greek language whenever you have a negative prohibition in the present tense, it means to stop a thing already in progress. Whenever you have it in the aorist tense, it means do not even begin to do a thing. Here it is present tense and means *"stop being deceived."* These Galatians were deceived. Paul says, "Stop it."

"God is not mocked: for whatsoever a man soweth, that shall he also reap" God is not mocked or is not made a fool of. We harvest what we plant. This is the law of sowing and reaping. When considering sowing and reaping, I think about five things.

(1) First: the size of what you reap is larger than the size of what you sow. You put a tomato seed in the ground, and you get a whole plant. It is larger than what you have sown.

- Hosea 8:7
  For they have sown the wind, and they shall reap the whirlwind: it hath no stalk: the bud shall yield no meal: if so be it yield, the strangers shall swallow it up.

(2) **Second:** the amount of what you reap is in proportion to the amount that you sow.
- 2 Corinthians 9:6
  But this *I say*, He which soweth sparingly shall reap also sparingly; and he which soweth bountifully shall reap also bountifully.

(3) **Third:** you reap the same thing that you sow.
- Matthew 7:17
  Even so every good tree bringeth forth good fruit; but a corrupt tree bringeth forth evil fruit.

You reap the same material that you sow. You do not put in a banana and come up with an orange.

(4) **Four:** you can't reap something different from what you sow.
- Matthew 7:18
  A good tree cannot bring forth evil fruit, neither *can* a corrupt tree bring forth good fruit.
- James 3:12
  Can the fig tree, my brethren, bear olive berries? either a vine, figs? so *can* no fountain both yield salt water and fresh.

Figs do not bear olives. They do not bear something different from that which was sown.

(5) **Five:** you do not reap immediately what you sow. There is a delay in the production of the fruit to be reaped. You may say I can sow a little bit of the flesh here. There is a delay, but down the line it comes back. It is the same way with the sowing of the Spirit. There is a delay, and that is why Paul says do *"not be weary in well doing"* in verse nine. There is always a delay.
- Mark 4:28
  For the earth bringeth forth fruit of herself; first the blade, then the ear, after that the full corn in the ear.

Five Laws of Sowing and Reaping

1. One, the size of that which is reaped is usually larger than that which is sown.
2. Two, the amount that we reap is proportional to that which we sow.

3. Third, the thing reaped is the same as that which is sown.
4. Four, the thing reaped cannot be entirely different from the thing that is sown.
5. Five, there is a delay in the production of the fruit to be reaped.

God is not mocked. He is not sneered at. He does not turn up His nose. That is what that word means. Whatsoever a man sows or continues to scatter as seed, that same thing he shall also reap. That is a law.

Galatians 6:8

"For he that soweth to his flesh shall of the flesh reap corruption; but he that soweth to the Spirit shall of the Spirit reap life everlasting."

"For he that soweth to his flesh shall of the flesh reap corruption" Here is the internal battle between the flesh and the Spirit.

- **Galatians 5:17**
  For the **flesh lusteth against the Spirit, and the Spirit against the flesh: and these are contrary the one to the other**: so that ye cannot do the things that ye would.

Remember the works of the flesh.

- **Galatians 5:19-21**
  Now the **works of the flesh** are manifest, which are *these*; **Adultery, fornication, uncleanness, lasciviousness, Idolatry, witchcraft, hatred, variance, emulations, wrath, strife, seditions, heresies, Envyings, murders, drunkenness, revellings**, and such like: of the which I tell you before, as I have also told *you* in time past, that they which do such things **shall not inherit the kingdom of God**.

If we sow to these works we will reap corruption. You cannot take any of those fleshly sins with you. God has barred them from Heaven. They are not there. They just go right into the ground, and that is the end of them.

"but he that soweth to the Spirit shall of the Spirit reap life everlasting" As the saying goes, *"Only one life 'twill soon be past. Only what's done for Christ will last."* You cannot take it with you. As they say, there are no pockets in the shroud. You have never seen a funeral procession with a U-haul trailer behind the hearse. There is no sense in packing all of your belongings in a trailer to take with you to the next life. Now, I realize that the Egyptians believed this. That is why they had these big pyramids made to house all of those things that they thought they could bring into the next life. The Pharaohs found out, only too late, that you can't take anything with you.

The things of this world will pass away. We should not love these things.
- 1 John 2:15-17
  Love not the world, neither the things *that are* in the world. If any man love the world, the love of the Father is not in him. For all that *is* in the world, the lust of the flesh, and the lust of the eyes, and the pride of life, is not of the Father, but is of the world. And **the world passeth away, and the lust thereof: but he that doeth the will of God abideth for ever.**

The sowing to the spirit will reap fruit that lasts forever. Remember the fruit of the Spirit.
- Galatians 5:22-23
  But the fruit of the Spirit is **love, joy, peace, longsuffering, gentleness, goodness, faith, Meekness, temperance**: against such there is no law.

That is why Paul wrote in 1 Corinthians 13:8 that love and charity *"never faileth."* They will go on and endure whereas other things in the flesh will not. The sowing to the flesh will reap corruption, but the sowing to the Spirit will reap life everlasting.

Galatians 6:9

"And let us not be weary in well doing: for in due season we shall reap, if we faint not." Here we have once again a present tense prohibition in the Greek Text which means *"stop being weary and tired out."* Stop doing an action that is already in progress. Do not give up. You might say, *"I am sowing to the Spirit. I am not sowing to the flesh, and look what has happened. Where is my reaping of life everlasting."* God says don't give up.
- Luke 11:9-10
  And I say unto you, **Ask**, and it shall be given you; **seek**, and ye shall find; **knock**, and it shall be opened unto you. **For every one that asketh receiveth; and he that seeketh findeth; and to him that knocketh it shall be opened**.

We will reap *"in due season."* It is in God's own time. That means that there is a delay in sowing and reaping. You cannot plant a kernel of corn today and tomorrow get the full stock.

- **1 Corinthians 15:58**
  Therefore, my beloved brethren, **be ye stedfast, unmoveable, always abounding in the work of the Lord, forasmuch as ye know that your labour is not in vain** in the Lord.
  This was one of the favorite verses of Mr. R. O. Sanborn, my father-in-law. Our labor is *"not in vain in the Lord,"* so we are to keep laboring for the Lord from the dawn to setting sun.
- **Luke 18:1**
  And he spake a parable unto them *to this end*, that **men ought always to pray, and not to faint**;

The Lord is not wearied when we come to Him and ask Him for things that are in His will. The word, *"weary,"* EKKAKEO, means *"to be utterly spiritless, to be wearied out, exhausted."* We are not to come to the point where we have no spirit left in us. If you are wearied out and exhausted, stop being weary in well doing.

What is *"well doing"*? Well the word for *"well"* here is KALOS. It means *"good, excellent in its nature, beautiful, handsome excellent, eminent, choice, surpassing, precious, useful, suitable, commendable, admirable."* *"Well doing"* is something that is good and excellent in nature. It is something that is choice and surpassing, useful, commendable, suitable, in things for the Lord. Stop being weary in it. Continue to do that which is *"well doing."* Keep at it, for in due season we shall reap if we faint not.

There are two words for *"season"* in the Greek. One is KAIROS which is a specific type of a season. The other is CHRONOS which is a particular time. Here we have KAIROS. This refers to a special season for reaping. I understand that when you plant there is a certain season for reaping. It does not come before and it does not come after that time. At the proper time God says you will reap if you do not faint.

He does not want us *"fainting."* That word for *"fainting,"* EKLUO, means *"to loose, unloose, to set free, to dissolve, to have one's strength relaxed, to be enfeebled through exhaustion."* Marie, one of our congregation, was quite exhausted when she went through her operation. We saw her in the hospital, and she was feeble. I saw Bernice, also one of our congregation, after her last operation, and she was feeble as well. When I went into the hospital for my cancer, I was very feeble. It exhausts a person even when he is staying in bed. God promises that you will reap. That is His promise, and He will do it. Praise God. He keeps His promises.

Galatians 6:10

"As we have therefore opportunity, let us do good unto all *men*, especially unto them who are of the household of faith." There is what is called the "social gospel" that has its followers all over the world. I am opposed to it, and do not agree with it. I believe that the Scriptures are against it. This is what the United Methodist Church and most mainline denominations believe. This is what the Salvation Army believes. I am all for people being fed, clothed, and housed, but I do not believe this is the ministry of the local church.

This verse says when we have the *"opportunity,"* we are to do good. But we are to do good especially to those who are believers. We want to look at ten different passages that I believe prove this.

- Acts 2:44-45
  And all that believed were together, and **had all things common**; And sold their possessions and goods, **and parted them to all *men*, as every man had need.**

Some people say that this is Communism. No, it is not. Communism is a forcible thing. These people were like a family. They were believers in the Lord Jesus Christ, and they were like a family. What do we do as a family? Do we not have meals together? Do we not help each other? This is how it is in the household of faith.

- 1 Timothy 5:8
  But **if any provide not for his own, and specially for those of his own house, he hath denied the faith**, and is worse than an infidel.

It is the household of faith. We should provide for our own families and our household of believers.

- Romans 12:13
  Distributing to the necessity of saints; given to hospitality.

These are believers. We must take care of our believers first.

- Romans 15:25-28
  But now I go unto Jerusalem to minister unto the saints. For it hath pleased them of Macedonia and Achaia **to make a certain contribution for the poor saints which are at Jerusalem**. It hath pleased them verily; and their debtors they are. **For if the Gentiles have been made partakers of their spiritual things, their duty is also to minister unto them in carnal things.**

These people took up a collection for the poor saints over one thousand miles away in Jerusalem. This is a gift to believers.

- **1 Corinthians 16:1-3**
  Now **concerning the collection for the saints**, as I have given order to the churches of Galatia, even so do ye. Upon the first *day* of the week **let every one of you lay by him in store**, as *God* hath prospered him, that there be no gatherings when I come. And when I come, whomsoever ye shall approve by *your* letters, **them will I send to bring your liberality unto Jerusalem**.

This is speaking of believers.

- **1 Corinthians 16:15**
  I beseech you, brethren, (ye know the house of Stephanas, that it is the firstfruits of Achaia, and *that* **they have addicted themselves to the ministry of the saints**,)

Here again we see that helping the household of faith is very important.

- **2 Corinthians 8:1-5**
  Moreover, brethren, we do you to wit of the grace of God bestowed on the churches of Macedonia; How that in a great trial of affliction the abundance of their joy and **their deep poverty abounded unto the riches of their liberality**. For to *their* power, I bear record, yea, and **beyond *their* power** *they were* willing of themselves; Praying us with much intreaty **that we would receive the gift, and *take upon us* the fellowship of the ministering to the saints**. And *this they did*, not as we hoped, but first gave their own selves to the Lord, and unto us by the will of God.

These were poor people who gave to the ministry of believers. They gave their gifts out of poverty. A lady called up this morning. She told me she was homeless and asked. *"Can you give me a home."* I told her we were a very little church, and were not able to provide a home. There are needs all around the world. If the believers gave one hundred percent of all their funds and personnel to deal with all the billions in need, it would be impossible for them to give the gospel and tell these people how they could be saved.

- **2 Corinthians 9:1**
  For as touching the **ministering to the saints**, it is superfluous for me to write to you:

He goes on to give some principles for giving in verses two to eight.

- **2 Corinthians 9:12**
  For the administration of this service not only **supplieth the want of the saints**, but is abundant also by many thanksgivings unto God;

Here again it is for the need of the saints.

- **Hebrews 6:10**
  For God *is* not unrighteous to forget your work and labour of love, which ye have shewed toward his name, **in that ye have ministered to the saints, and do minister.**

It is proper for the church to give to its members if they have needs. Some churches have deacons' funds which they use to minister to needy believers. Pastor Joah has many needs in Liberia, West Africa. He is preaching the gospel over the radio now on three stations. His people are Christian believers, and they are part of our family. When some people say we are narrow-minded, I believe we should follow the Scriptures. The Scriptures say to do good to all if we have opportunity, but we are primarily to do good to the household of faith.

I am opposed to missions such as ABWE (The Association of Baptists for World Evangelism) and Baptist Mid Missions for opening up big hospitals all over the world. I am not against hospitals, but here they are making use of the "social gospel" which is not taught in the Bible. I think they formerly had just clinics. I guess I could understand clinics to care for the needs of the church people and missionaries when sick, but now all of a sudden millions of dollars are poured into these foreign countries for social needs--not gospel needs. This is done even by Fundamentalist Baptist missionaries and missions. I am opposed to it. I understand that ABWE has one field open where they're sending missionaries. But they are forbidden by that government to preach the gospel. All they can do is teach them to read and write and have a hospital.

That is not primary missions. The Lord said, *"Go ye into all the world, and preach the gospel to every creature. He that believeth and is baptized shall be saved; but he that believeth not shall be dammed"* (Mark 16:15-16). I am not against people eating. I eat myself. I am not against people having a roof over their head. I have a roof over my head myself. I am not against having jobs or any of those things, but I believe that the primary purpose of the local church is the preaching of the gospel and bringing people to the knowledge of eternal life through genuine faith in the Lord Jesus Christ that cannot perish or pass away.

In the history of the church, we have seen this move toward the social gospel. Think of the original Salvation Army. In the early days, they only preached the gospel. They preached the Word of God. They saved the souls that were round about them. Then little by little they were saving souls and then feeding them. Pretty soon they were feeding them first and then doing a little saving of souls. Now, it is almost all feeding. Look at the YMCA. It started out as the Young Men's Christian Association. They started with Bible. They started with preaching and evangelism. Then all of a sudden they put in swimming pools. I am for swimming pools. I like to swim, but that is all they have now. There is no more gospel preached in the YMCA. The Methodist

Church started out preaching the gospel. Then all of a sudden they have turned into a huge social-gospel denomination feeding, clothing, and housing the world with very little gospel preaching.

Paul says, *"As we have opportunity, let us do good unto all men, especially unto them who are of the household of faith."* That word, *"household,"* OIKEIOS, means *"belonging to a house or family, related by blood."* We have a relationship with all the saints throughout all the ages through the blood of Christ Who cleanseth us from sin. As we can, we help those who are in need. But first, we help those in the world by preaching the gospel of Christ and teaching the Word of God.

Galatians 6:11

"Ye see how large a letter I have written unto you with mine own hand." There are two ways to interpret this. One way is that it refers to a large size letter. This is possible. Some people have speculated that poor eyesight was Paul's thorn in the flesh.

- 2 Corinthians 12:7
  And lest I should be exalted above measure through the abundance of the revelations, **there was given to me a thorn in the flesh**, the messenger of Satan to buffet me, lest I should be exalted above measure.
- Galatians 4:15
  Where is then the blessedness ye spake of? for I bear you record, that, if *it had been* possible, **ye would have plucked out your own eyes, and have given them to me.**

Maybe he needed an eye transplant because he had poor eyesight.

- 2 Corinthians 10:10
  For *his* letters, say they, *are* weighty and powerful; **but *his* bodily presence *is* weak**, and *his* speech contemptible.

Maybe he has shrunk down to be a little person and was ugly and in poor health. If you are blind or cannot see very well, maybe you would write in large letters. I do not have perfect twenty-twenty vision. Sometimes when I do not have enough light, it helps me to write a little bit larger. Paul did not have a secretary on this occasion. Usually he dictated his epistle and another person wrote for him. To the Galatians, he wrote with his own hand. It was personal. Paul wanted these Galatians to get off the band wagon of the law of Moses and get on with the grace of Christ by faith alone both for salvation and for sanctification.

Galatians 6:12

"As many as desire to make a fair shew in the flesh, they constrain you to be circumcised; only lest they should suffer persecution for the cross of Christ."

"As many as desire to make a fair shew in the flesh, they constrain you to be circumcised" This is what these Judaizers did. They wanted the Galatian Christians to be circumcised so that they could have a *"fair shew in the flesh."* That is all the Law of Moses was, that which appealed to *"the flesh."* All they had was that which was on the outside. They desired to *"constrain"* these people. That means to obligate them. In the book of Acts, it says that they were teaching that you cannot be saved unless you are circumcised. The Church of Christ teaches that you cannot be saved except you are baptized by immersion in water. Was the thief on the cross baptized by immersion after he was saved? No. Water baptism does not save you. The Church of Christ is in serious error to teach this. So is any other denomination that teaches salvation plus baptism is necessary to save one's soul,

"only lest they should suffer persecution for the cross of Christ" Their motive for teaching this was to avoid *"persecution for the cross of Christ."* Paul was an old-hand at persecution for the cross of Christ. He knew all about that. The Lord Jesus mentions persecution many times. Let us look at some verses about persecution.

- Matthew 5:10

   Blessed *are* they which are persecuted for righteousness' sake: for theirs is the kingdom of Heaven.

Make sure it is for the Lord's sake.

- Matthew 5:44

   But I say unto you, Love your enemies, bless them that curse you, do good to them that hate you, and **pray for them which despitefully use you, and persecute you**;

- Mark 10:29-30

   And Jesus answered and said, Verily I say unto you, There is **no man that hath left house, or brethren, or sisters, or father, or mother, or wife, or children, or lands**, for my sake, and the gospel's, **But he shall receive** an hundredfold now in this time, houses, and brethren, and sisters, and mothers, and children, and lands, **with persecutions**; and in the world to come eternal life.

Because you love the Lord Jesus Christ, you are going to be in line for persecution.

- **Romans 8:35**
  As it is written, **For thy sake we are killed all the day long; we are accounted as sheep for the slaughter.**
Christ loves us no matter what. The world thinks that Christians are worthless people.
- **Romans 12:14**
  Bless them which persecute you: bless, and curse not.
That is hard talk, but that is what God expects of us if we are led by the Spirit of God.
- **1 Corinthians 4:9-13**
  For I think that God hath set forth us the apostles last, as it were appointed to death: for we are made a spectacle unto the world, and to angels, and to men. **We *are* fools for Christ's sake**, but ye *are* wise in Christ; **we *are* weak**, but ye *are* strong; ye *are* honourable, but **we *are* despised**. Even unto this present hour **we both hunger, and thirst, and are naked, and are buffeted, and have no certain dwelling-place**; And labour, working with our own hands: **being reviled**, we bless; **being persecuted**, we suffer it: **Being defamed**, we intreat: **we are made as the filth of the world, *and are* the offscouring of all things** unto this day.
Let persecution come.
- **2 Corinthians 12:9-10**
  And he said unto me, My grace is sufficient for thee: for my strength is made perfect in weakness. Most gladly therefore will I rather **glory in my infirmities**, that the power of Christ may rest upon me. Therefore **I take pleasure in infirmities, in reproaches, in necessities, in persecutions, in distresses for Christ's sake**: for when I am weak, then am I strong.
What kind of infirmities do you have? What kind of pain do you have? Do you take pleasure in them? Paul did. The Lord Jesus gave him these infirmities. He was in the center of the will of the Lord. So it was pleasure. This is difficult for us to understand. When I am sick or weak and flat on my back with a temperature, I turn to the Lord and He gives me the strength that I need. This is what Paul is talking about.
- **2 Timothy 3:10-11**
  But thou hast fully known my doctrine, manner of life, purpose, faith, longsuffering, charity, patience, Persecutions, afflictions, which came unto me at Antioch, at Iconium, at Lystra; **what persecutions I endured: but out of them all the Lord delivered me.**

Just one of the persecutions that came to Paul at Antioch would have stopped most of us. We might say, *"Let's go back to something else. Let us quit being a preacher, a missionary, and an evangelist."* Antioch persecuted Paul to the hilt. Then he went on to Iconium, and they persecuted him there. Then he went on to Lystra, and there they stoned him dragging him out of the city supposing that he was dead. I think he was dead because of what he mentions in 2 Corinthians.

- **2 Corinthians 12:2**
  I knew a man in Christ above fourteen years ago, (whether in the body, I cannot tell; or whether out of the body, I cannot tell: God knoweth;) **such an one caught up to the third Heaven.**

I think Paul went up to Glory when he was stoned and left for dead at Lystra (Acts 14:19). That is why he could write and comfort us about Heaven. The Lord did not deliver him out of that last persecution. Tradition says that they cut off his head after his second Roman imprisonment. He went Home to be with the Lord. When you think about it, the Lord delivered him there, too. He was delivered to Heaven. What they were really doing was threatening him with Heaven. Denounce Christ or I will kill you. Paul might have said, *"Let me see. Denounce Christ or I'll go to Heaven. I'm ready to go to Heaven. I'm not going to denounce Christ."*

- **2 Timothy 3:12**
  Yea, and **all that will live godly in Christ Jesus shall suffer persecution**.

That word for *"will"* is not just the sign of a future tense. It is all they who are willing or desirous to live godly in Christ Jesus will suffer persecution. So, the Jews were trying to avoid the persecution. For that reason they might have said, *"Let's just go ahead and have these people circumcised."* That word *"persecution,"* DIOKO, means *"to make to run or flee, drive away, to run swiftly in order to catch a person or thing, to harass, trouble, molest one."* This is what we can expect if we live a godly life. God will give us the strength and grace to be strong even in our weakness. His grace is sufficient for us.

Galatians 6:13

"For neither they themselves who are circumcised keep the law; but desire to have you circumcised, that they may glory in your flesh." Here you have these Jews who were wanting the Christians to be circumcised, yet they did not keep the law themselves. They are failing.

- **James 2:10**
  For whosoever shall keep the whole law, and **yet offend in one *point*, he is guilty of all**.

Paul says that these people are not doing themselves what they want others to do. They want to glory in the flesh of those Christians. There are many people who glory in the flesh whether it is movie-star flesh, sport's-star flesh, or even preacher flesh. This is a worshiping of flesh. They were hypocrites because they did not keep the law either.

Galatians 6:14

"But God forbid that I should glory, save in the cross of our Lord Jesus Christ, by whom the world is crucified unto me, and I unto the world."

"But God forbid that I should glory, save in the cross of our Lord Jesus Christ" Paul is saying may it never be said that I should glory in the flesh or anything else. Paul's only glory was in the cross of the Lord Jesus Christ. There are many verses about glory.

- Romans 5:3
  And not only *so*, but **we glory in tribulations** also: knowing that tribulation worketh patience;
- 2 Corinthians 5:12
  For we commend not ourselves again unto you, but **give you occasion to glory** on our behalf, that ye may have somewhat to *answer* **them which glory in appearance, and not in heart.**

It is nice to have a good appearance. You should have your hair combed and your clothes neat, but is that our only glory?
- 2 Corinthians 10:17
  But **he that glorieth, let him glory in the Lord**.
- 2 Corinthians 12:9
  And he said unto me, My grace is sufficient for thee: for my strength is made perfect in weakness. **Most gladly therefore will I rather glory in my infirmities**, that the power of Christ may rest upon me.

There is a hymn written by John Bowring that speaks about the glory of the cross.

> *"In the cross of Christ I glory*
> *Towering over the wrecks of time.*
> *All the light of sacred story*
> *Gathers round its head sublime.*

Another hymn written by the blind hymn-writer, Fanny Crosby, also talks about the cross:

> *In the cross, in the cross,*
> *Be my glory ever.*

> *Till my raptured soul shall find*
> *Rest beyond the river."*

What was a cross? Let me read the definition given in one reference source.

> *"It is a well know instrument of the most cruel and ignominious punishment. It was borrowed by the Greeks and Romans from the Phoenicians. To it were affixed among the Romans down to the time of Constantine the Great the guiltiest criminals particularly the bases slaves, robbers, the authors and abettors of insurrection, and occasionally in the provinces at the arbitrary pleasure of the governors upright and peaceable men also, and even Roman citizens themselves."*

That is the cross on which our Saviour was affixed with the vilest criminals. That was why those criminals were on either side. They were both insurrectionists and murderers. He was right in between them.

Why would Paul say he glories in the cross? The cross is not simply an emblem around a person's neck. That is not what Paul is getting at. Paul is glorying in what was accomplished on that cross on which the Lord Jesus Christ was crucified. On that cross He Who was both the Son of God and the Son of Man suffered, bled, and died. On that cross He carried in His own body the sins of the whole world. He carried my sins, your sins, the whole world's sins. That is what was accomplished on that cross. His blood was shed. That is what cleanses and gives peace and forgiveness. Paul gloried in the shed blood of the Lord Jesus Christ on that cross.

Nine Reasons Why Paul Gloried in the Cross

(1) **One**, it was the thing that turned his life from being a murderer. He was out killing Christians when Christ met him. The whole power and redemption of Christ is there on the cross.

(2) **Two**, it softened his heart. He was wicked and angry. He was full of hostility and bitter. The cross just softened his heart. Paul said, *"Who art thou, Lord?"* The Lord responded on that road to Damascus, *"I am Jesus whom thou persecutest."* (Acts 9:5)

(3) **Three**, It made him an evangelist of the gospel of Christ. It turned him from killing Christians to making Christians. He preached Christ to the world of lost people.

Galatians 6:14　　　　　　　　175

(4) **Four,** it redeemed his soul. He was lost. Oh, he was a religionist. He was brought up at the feet of Gamaliel. He knew the law of Moses. He was educated, but he was lost. What was done there on the cross of Christ redeemed his soul.

(5) **Five,** he got freedom from the power of sin. He received a new nature, and he no longer had to follow his old nature and do that which was wicked. He thought that he was doing God a service by killing Christians. Paul was on the road to Damascus to imprison and kill Christians. He was on the scene when the martyr Stephen was stoned to death. They laid their garments down at the young man's feet whose name was Saul. Saul or Paul was just a young man at that time when Stephen was stoned. Paul was like a shark who smelled blood and went after that source of blood to kill it.

(6) **Six,** the cross forgave his sins. That is what all of us need, the forgiveness of sins. Dr. Carl Elgena, one of my former pastors, used to comment that the man who led him to Christ had just one word on his tombstone. That word was *"FORGIVEN."* That is the only word on that stone. Forgiveness is the greatest thing that any one of us can have. To be forgiven by faith in the Lord Jesus Christ who died for our sins on that cross of Calvary is the greatest thing that we can ever possess.

(7) **Seven,** it regenerated his heart. It gave him a new life from within.

(8) **Eight,** it gave him a *"friend that sticketh closer than a brother."* The Lord Jesus Christ became his friend. He was his enemy before. Friends do leave us. Do they not? He will never prove untrue. He will never leave us. He will never forsake us. He will never fail us. This is what that verse in the Old Testament means when it says that the Lord Jesus is *"a friend that sticketh closer than a brother"* (Proverbs 18:24). He found that Friend in the cross of Calvary.

(9) **Nine,** it gave him an eternal home in Heaven where there will be no sickness, no sadness, no persecution, no pain, *"for the former things are passed away"* (Revelation 21:4).

To glory in an instrument of death is quite an interesting thing. But he gloried in the cross because of all that it gave him and all that it could give whomsoever will receive the Lord Jesus Christ as their Saviour. He gloried in the power of the cross. All of these things that Paul received can be yours and mine as well.

"by whom the world is crucified unto me, and I unto the world"

You know you can never upset a man lying in the coffin. You can say anything you want to that person. You could kiss that person. You could curse at him. You could slap him. Yet all of these things will never have any affect on him because he is dead. Paul says that *"the world is crucified unto me."* As far as Paul was concerned, he considered himself to be dead, so far as the influence of the world was concerned. There was no pull, no affection, no control, no desire. It is like trying to magnetize wood. It just will not be drawn up by a magnet. The wood is not attracted to the magnet. There is no attraction at all. There was nothing there as far as Paul is concerned that could pull him into the world. We all should be more like Paul. Oh, but that world is appealing to our flesh!

Paul had singleness of mind that the world was crucified to him and also he to the world. What does that mean? As far as the world is concerned Paul was dead as a door nail. The world does not like such Christians. You have heard the expression about someone who is sleeping, *"He is dead to the world."* That is what Paul is talking about. The world does not see anything appealing in the Christian life. The world is out there for pleasures. There are no rules. The worldlings can sin in any way they want. All is fair for the sinners. The Lord Jesus Christ says, *"Come unto me, all ye that labor and are heavy laden, and I will give you rest"* (Matthew 11:28). The world is saying that they do not need Christ's rest. They are going to live, live, live until they die. The sinner that is outside of Christ lives all right, but lives only for the world. Paul says, *"I am dead to the world, and the world is dead to me."* The worldlings think that we Christians have no fun, no money, no pleasures, nothing. So, many times people do not want to come to Christ because they think that Christians have an odd and different lifestyle. They do not want to change. Of course, we are not saved by works. But after the Lord saves us, we have a different desire and a different "want to."

Galatians 6:15

"For in Christ Jesus neither circumcision availeth any thing, nor uncircumcision, but a new creature." That is what is true about being *"in Christ Jesus."* We are a *"new creature."* It is not the question about circumcision or uncircumcision. We have newness of life.

- **2 Corinthians 5:17**
  Therefore **if any man *be* in Christ, *he is* a new creature**: old things are passed away; behold, all things are become new.

God creates something when He saves someone. We are made to be something new. It is not just dusting off the old flesh.

- **Romans 6:4**
  Therefore we are buried with him by baptism into death: that like as Christ was raised up from the dead by the glory of the Father, even **so we also should walk in newness of life**.

We should walk in the newness of life.

- **Romans 7:6**
  But now we are delivered from the law, that being dead wherein we were held; **that we should serve in newness of spirit**, and not *in* the oldness of the letter.

We should live in the newness of the Spirit. It is not the oldness of the law of Moses or anything of the kind. But when we are in Christ, we are saved and have a new life. We are a new creature and a new creation.

Galatians 6:16

"And as many as walk according to this rule, peace *be* on them, and mercy, and upon the Israel of God."

"And as many as walk according to this rule, peace *be* on them, and mercy" What *"rule"*? I think it is the rule Paul mentioned in a previous verse.

- **Galatians 6:14**
  But God forbid that I should glory, save in the cross of our Lord Jesus Christ, by whom the world is crucified unto me, and I unto the world.

There is peace **with** God when we are in Christ and redeemed.
- **Romans 5:1**
  Therefore being justified by faith, we have **peace with God** through our Lord Jesus Christ:

There is also the peace **of** God when we walk in victory by the power of the Holy Spirit.
- **Philippians 4:7**
  And **the peace of God**, which passeth all understanding, shall keep your hearts and minds through Christ Jesus.

This is the peace He is wishing upon those who follow the things of the Lord. Peace is *"the tranquil state of a soul assured of its salvation through Christ and so fearing nothing from God and content with its earthly lot of whatsoever sort it is."* That is peace, and that is what God has promised to those who come to the Lord Jesus Christ in genuine faith, receiving Him as their Saviour.

"and upon the Israel of God" This is not equating Israel with the church. Israel means those who are of faith just like Abraham was of faith. We are children of Abraham, not that we are Jews when we are Christians. Abraham was a man of faith and so are we when we trust Christ. Some of those who are Covenant theologians say that Israel's promises are fulfilled in the church. We dispensationalists do not believe that way at all. They say that the church is Israel, and that Israel is the church. Mr. Harold Camping, President of Family Radio, believes this error. We do not believe that way. In this verse Israel means those who are in the faith of the Lord Jesus Christ.

Galatians 6:17

"From henceforth let no man trouble me: for I bear in my body the marks of the Lord Jesus."

"From henceforth let no man trouble me" Here again is a prohibition. It is a negative, but instead of it being in the aorist tense, it is in the present tense. Therefore, it means to stop an action already in progress. People were troubling him on every side. People were begging Paul to teach circumcision and to keep the law of Moses. Paul said that he was not going to change his course of action. The Lord had stood with him all these years and in all his persecutions. Paul said he is not going to change. I feel the same way as Paul did. How about you? I do not know how old you are. But however many years you have been in Christ, you should not turn back regardless of what comes along. Paul is saying here, *"Stop troubling me!"*

"for I bear in my body the marks of the Lord Jesus" Paul put his life in hazardous situations for the Lord throughout his life. He was one of those spoken of in the book of Acts.

- **Acts 15:26**
  Men that **have hazarded their lives for the name of our Lord Jesus Christ**.

Paul had marks because of his service for the Lord Jesus Christ. He gives us a list of those marks in 2 Corinthians.

- **2 Corinthians 11:23-28**
  Are they ministers of Christ? (I speak as a fool) I *am* more; **in labours** more abundant, **in stripes** above measure, **in prisons** more frequent, **in deaths** oft. Of the Jews five times received I forty *stripes* save one. Thrice was I **beaten** with rods, once was I **stoned**, thrice I suffered **shipwreck**, a night and a day I have been in the deep; *In* **journeyings** often, *in* **perils of waters**, *in* **perils of robbers**, *in* **perils by** *mine* **own countrymen**, *in* **perils by the heathen**, *in* **perils in the city**, *in* **perils in the wilderness**, *in* **perils in the sea**, *in* **perils among false brethren; In weariness and painfulness, in watchings often, in hunger and thirst, in fastings often, in cold and nakedness**. Beside those things that are without, that which cometh upon me daily, **the care of all the churches**.

I believe that Paul was killed at Lystra, and the Lord took him to Heaven and brought him back. He kept on preaching. That would stop most of us. Would it not? If you were stoned to death for what you were doing, you would probably stop preaching that the Lord Jesus Christ is the only way to Heaven.

Galatians 6:17

Sometimes pastors have more trials from within than from without. That is a sad situation. Is it not? A pastor came to pick up six cases of our medium Bibles. When he came to pick them up, I commended his young people. They were the young people who were at the Christian camp where I preached last summer. There were about thirty young people who were obedient and well-behaved. The pastor said that he had been the pastor at his church for twenty-three years. In that church there was a good relationship. But recently he noticed a bad influence come into his church which was causing some problems. I told him that I knew exactly what he meant. People come in, and they do not know all the things that are going on. The pastor said he was going to try to put a stop to it. The Bible says to *"purge out therefore the old leaven, that ye may be a new lump"* (1 Corinthians 5:7). Any pastor is as happy as he can be to have peace and unity in the local church where he is preaching. Pray for our pastors.

That word for *"marks"* is STIGMA. The Roman Catholic Church talks about the phenomenon of stigmata. This supposedly happens when someone so identifies with the suffering of Jesus Christ that he shows the marks of Christ with bleeding on the hands or side or head. I do not believe all of that. STIGMA means

"a mark pricked in or branded upon the body. To ancient oriental usage, slaves and soldiers bore the name or the stamp of their master or commander branded or pricked {cut} into their bodies to indicate what master or general they belonged to, and there were even some devotees who stamped themselves in this way with the token of their gods."

Paul bore the marks of Christ in his body because of his service for Christ. What are you going to tell a man like that? How are you going to instruct a man like Paul? He has been through the mill. How are you going to make him quit? I do not think you can unless he loses his mind or something. He just went right straight on. Was Paul a fool? Paul says *"we are fools for Christ's sake"* (1 Corinthians 4:10). You see, the difference between the apostle Paul and most of us is that he met the Lord Jesus Christ face-to-face. Christ changed his life. He was without sight for three days, and he never forgot it. Christ Himself directed Paul as to what he should do. It were just as if Christ were seated right here in your room. Christ said that Paul would suffer many things for His sake. Christ said that Paul would be sent unto the Gentiles. Paul said that it did not matter, and he went ahead. Nothing stopped him. Paul went full speed ahead.

Galatians 6:18

"Brethren, the grace of our Lord Jesus Christ *be* with your spirit. Amen. *To the Galatians written from Rome.*"

"Brethren, the grace of our Lord Jesus Christ" It is interesting that Paul begins the book of Galatians writing to a people who wanted to practice the works of the law. After trying to straighten the Galatians out, Paul ends up leaving them with a word of grace. Grace is getting something we do not deserve.

- **2 Corinthians 8:9**
  For **ye know the grace of our Lord Jesus Christ**, that, though he was rich, yet for your sakes he became poor, that ye through his poverty might be rich.

This is grace. He leaves them with grace. *"Brethren, the grace of our Lord Jesus Christ be with your spirit. Amen."*

What is grace? The word, *"grace,"* CHARIS, means *"that which affords joy, pleasure, delight, sweetness, charm, and loveliness."*

Grace
Grace is *"of the merciful kindness by which God, exerting his holy influence upon souls, turns them to Christ, keeps, strengthens, increases them in Christian faith, knowledge, affection, and kindles them to the exercise of Christian virtues."*

That is what God's grace does. When God's grace comes into a person, there are some changes made for the better.

"be with your spirit. Amen. *To the Galatians written from Rome"* That word for *"spirit"* is interesting. God can give us the inner grace to our *"spirit,"* regardless of outer pain. We can have that. The poor saints in Liberia, West Africa, or anywhere else in the world can have God's grace if they have faith in the Lord Jesus Christ. That word for *"spirit,"* PNEUMA, can have many different meanings. One of them is *"the disposition or influence which fills and governs the soul of anyone."* This is what the Lord wants. We who are saved sinners can *"glorify God in your body, and in your spirit which are God's"* (1 Corinthians 6:20). That is what He wants.

We leave the book of Galatians. I hope that Paul has convinced all of us that we are not saved by the works of the law, but by grace through genuine faith. I hope Paul has convinced all of us that we are not sanctified and built up by the law of Moses, but by the Spirit of God as we walk step-by-step with the Lord Jesus Christ. May we abide in the grace of Christ.

Index of Words and Phrases

08108	i, 22
1 Corinthians	6, 17, 22, 35, 43, 44, 58, 60, 64, 66, 67, 87, 89, 90, 98, 103, 107, 111, 116, 123, 128, 130-133, 139, 140, 148, 150, 154, 159, 160, 164, 166, 167, 170, 179, 180
1,297	52
1,900	22
1,900 people	22
100th floor	121
1883	161
1971	80
1-800-JOHN 10:9	i
2002	i
60 A.D.	1, 116
7,000 differences	160
81st Annual Meeting of Fundamental Baptist Fellowship (FBF)	144
856-854-2464 (FAX)	i
856-854-4452 (PHONE)	i
90 or 100 A.D.	67
900 Park Avenue	i, 22, 27
A Texan Looks at Lyndon	144
abba	94, 99
abomination	127, 137
about the author	vi
Abraham	20, 25, 27, 68-71, 75, 76, 78-81, 84, 85, 91, 100, 113-116, 121, 122, 177
ABWE (Association of Baptists for World Evangelism)	168
accurate	56, 78, 114, 140, 160
accurate translation	140
accursed	7, 11, 12, 17, 72, 75
acknowledgments	iii, vi
Acts 15	33-35, 45, 178
Adams, Dr. Ray	105
advantage	42
Advocate	56, 84, 145
Africa	47, 48, 167, 180
agape	107
alcohol	40, 125
all over the world	v, 22, 30, 69, 75, 165, 168

Allah 30
ALLOS 9
alternative lifestyle 142
angel 11, 17, 95, 96, 104
angels 11, 82, 83, 91, 171
Annual Meeting of Fundamental Baptist Fellowship (FBF) 144
another gospel 11, 17
ANTI 59, 60
Antioch 48, 49, 51, 171
aorist tense prohibition 125, 151
apostasy 38, 47
apostate 118
apostle 1-3, 13, 17, 20, 21, 23, 35, 45, 48, 51, 53, 62, 63, 134, 159, 179
apostle Paul 13, 20, 21, 48, 63, 159, 179
apostles 2, 20, 22-24, 35, 37, 45, 67, 170
apostolic miracles 67
Arabia 23, 116
Arabian 17, 23, 24, 115
Arabian Desert 17, 23, 24, 115
Arminian 129, 145
Arminian teaching 145
Army 157, 166, 168
Asia Minor 18
Association of Baptists for World Evangelism (ABWE) 168
audio v
Author .... vi, 1, 2, 80, 114, 131
B (Vatican Manuscript) 1, 15
Babylonian captivity 27
bad habits 39
ballot boxes 144
ballots 144
baptism 12, 40, 89, 90, 97, 113, 170, 176
Baptist Mid Missions 168
Barbara Egan iii
barbarians 1, 63, 79, 94, 100, 112
Barnabas 33, 34, 45, 49, 51
Barnhouse, Dr. Donald Gray 137
battle 109, 115, 118, 133, 141, 146, 149, 151, 161, 163
Bauder, Dr. Kevin 144
beggars 101
believers 3, 6, 7, 11, 26, 29, 47-49, 58, 59, 64, 89-92, 105,

Index of Words and Phrases 183

117, 124, 136, 158, 166-168

Ben Franklin Bridge 101
Benjamin 27
Bethlehem 95
Beverly Grace Sanborn 85
BFT #1594-P 22
BFT #2974 118
BFT #595 40
BFT@BibleForToday.org (e-mail) i
Bible Baptist Institute 101
Bible For Today .... i, iii, v, 22, 27, 44, 110, 159, 160
Bible For Today Baptist Church .... v, 27, 44, 159, 160
Bible For Today Press i
Bible institute 22
Bible preservation 75, 81, 117, 118
Bible version issue 62
Biblical Seminary 118
Bill Clinton 142
Billy Graham 13, 48
bird 4, 5
Bishop Westcott 40
bishops 49
bite 138
blindness 2
blood 2, 8, 12, 15, 16, 21-23, 29, 34, 35, 38, 44, 48, 49, 53,
57, 58, 60, 63, 64, 69, 75, 78, 84, 95, 97, 98, 125, 128,
168, 169, 174
blood of Christ 8, 12, 15, 29, 38, 48, 57, 64, 69, 97, 98, 169
blotted out 6
Bob Jones University 73, 80, 118, 119
Bob Thieme 15, 16
bodily resurrection 35, 38, 58, 123
bondage 39-41, 44, 94, 95, 99, 100, 104, 115-117, 123-125,
136
bondwoman 115, 121, 122
books .... v, 17, 21, 23, 25, 49, 53, 55, 67-69, 72, 73, 86, 119,
159
books of heaven 55, 69, 86
born-again 8, 10, 16, 20, 26, 43, 47, 52, 53, 58, 59, 64, 87, 89,
95, 109, 111, 129, 137, 140
bought 43-45, 64, 75, 93, 111
bought with a price 43-45, 64, 111

broadcasts 22, 62
Burgon, Dean John William 161
buried 35, 58, 63, 176
cafeteria 88
California 21
called 2, 3, 7-9, 12, 18-22, 31, 33, 39, 43, 49, 51, 53, 59, 60,
         63, 64, 70, 71, 75, 77, 84, 87, 92, 96, 99, 105, 109, 110,
         114, 118, 122, 133, 136, 137, 140, 144, 150, 159, 165,
         167
Calvary 5, 8, 35, 36, 44, 58, 61, 63, 71, 73, 76, 78, 80, 121,
         134, 155, 158, 175
Calvary Baptist Seminary 73, 80
Calvinism 54
Camping, Harold 88, 91, 97, 98, 177
Canaan 115, 116
Canada 39
cancer 57, 165
canyon 126
Carl Elgena, Dr. 175
Carroll, Dick 9
cart before the horse 26
Catholic 19, 22, 24, 63, 83, 88, 118, 179
Central Baptist Seminary 73, 80, 118, 144
Chaplain 4, 19, 76, 113, 157
Chaplain Corps 4, 76
Charismatic extremists 110
charismatics 44, 90
chasm 126
cheap church politician 16
children .... v, 6, 25, 31, 32, 37, 40, 43, 56, 68-70, 75, 84, 86, 88,
         89, 93-95, 99, 100, 103, 111, 115-117, 119, 122, 124,
         125, 134, 139, 146, 147, 155, 170, 177
children of God 40, 88, 89
China 77
Chinn, Douglas 118
choruses 137
Christ 1-31, 35-66, 68-72, 74-76, 78-80, 82-86, 88-104, 106,
         108-139, 143, 145, 147-150, 153, 155, 156, 158, 159,
         161, 163, 166, 168-180
Christ Independent Baptist Church 101
Christian slavery 16
Christ's Person 13

Index of Words and Phrases

church	iii, v, 3, 4, 9, 13, 15-18, 23, 24, 27, 29-31, 34, 38-41, 44-48, 51, 59, 83, 87, 88, 91, 101, 102, 104, 105, 108, 110, 113, 132-134, 137-139, 144, 152-155, 158-160, 166-168, 170, 177-179
Church of Christ	40, 113, 170
church politician	16
chute	156
Cilicia	26, 109
circumcise	37
circumcision	34, 42, 43, 45, 50, 66, 122, 126, 130, 134, 176
cleansed	8, 67, 86, 133
clinics	168
Clinton, President Bill	142
Collingswood, New Jersey	i, v, 22, 27
Colossians	17, 23, 42, 75, 98, 111
commandments	14, 87, 103, 127
commentary	16
Commission	19, 47, 145
Communism	77, 166
Communist	77
Communist Russia	77
computer	iii, 56, 70, 118
concept	81
concepts	73, 81, 113, 119
conflict	26, 141
conflicts	25
Congress	77, 144
controlled	90, 146, 148
conversion	2, 16, 28, 44
Corinth	1, 3
Cosby, Dianne	iii
counsel	28
Counterfeit or Genuine?	16
court of heaven	55, 68, 128
covenant	69, 72, 76, 77, 79, 83-85, 177
Covenant theologians	69, 177
covens	143
covens of witches	143
co-equal	2
co-eternal	2
co-redemptrix	83
Crete	34, 37

crucified 58, 63, 116, 146, 149, 150, 172, 174, 175, 177
crucified with Him 58, 149
Cuba 77
cults 2, 108, 132
curse 6, 11, 17, 60, 70, 72, 74-76, 97, 99, 170, 175
Custer, Dr. Stewart 119
C-span 142
D. A. Waite .... i, v
Dallas 15, 16, 65, 80, 118, 124, 131, 137, 140
Dallas Seminary 118, 124
Dallas Theological Seminary 15, 16, 65, 80, 124, 131, 137, 140
Damascus 2, 18, 21, 23, 24, 26, 43, 174
Dan Wallace 80, 118
Daniel .... iii, 27, 134, 137
Daniel S. Waite iii
Day of Atonement 34
dead 1, 2, 24, 25, 30, 57, 58, 61, 63, 67, 70, 71, 75, 77, 87, 93,
                    103, 111, 121, 129, 130, 171, 172, 175, 176
Dean John William Burgon 161
death 7, 12, 21, 28, 29, 35, 36, 38, 58, 61, 70, 75, 79, 84, 95,
                    97, 105, 119, 121, 125, 128, 130, 134, 155, 171, 174-
                    176, 178
Defending the King James Bible 22
DeHaan, Dr. M. R. 137
Deliverer 117
desert 17, 23-26, 34, 115
Detroit Baptist Seminary 73, 80
Devil 28, 40, 41, 44, 94, 95, 100, 106, 116, 125, 134, 137,
                    140, 154-156
Dianne W. Cosby iii
Dick Carroll 9
different desire 176
different "want to" 137
dissertation 118, 119
divorce 131
doctoral dissertation 118
doctrinal errors 48, 81, 161
Douglas Chinn 118
DOULOS 16, 100, 137
Dr. Carl Elgena 175
Dr. Chafer, Lewis Sperry 124

Index of Words and Phrases

Dr. David Otis Fuller 16
Dr. Donald Gray Barnhouse 137
Dr. Fuller 16
Dr. Glenny 118
Dr. H. A. Ironside v
Dr. Harold Weiss 158
Dr. Jack Moorman 160
Dr. Jaegli 119
Dr. John F. Walvoord 15, 124
Dr. Kevin Bauder 144
Dr. Lewis Sperry Chafer 65, 124, 140, 146
Dr. M. R. DeHaan 137
Dr. Newman 118
Dr. Ray Adams 105
Dr. Samuel Schnaiter 118, 119
Dr. Stewart Custer 119
Dr. Walvoord 15, 16, 124
Dr. Wisdom 119
drugs 39, 40, 95, 116, 125, 143
dynamic equivalency 55, 56
eating pork 57, 87
Egyptians 163
elders 49
elect 5, 6, 12, 38, 54, 96
election 20, 21, 144
enemies 46, 106, 108, 120, 140, 170
enemy 105, 108, 120, 140, 175
entangled 94, 123-125, 136
Ephesians 7, 17, 23, 26, 36, 41, 43, 48, 60, 72, 98, 99, 108,
120, 136, 139, 146
Ephesus 22
equal power 4
errors 1, 9, 24, 48, 73, 76, 81, 119, 132, 161
essays 21
eternal Son of God 78
expositions v
extreme unction 12
extremists 110
e-mail: BFT@BibleForToday.org i
faint 131, 164, 165
faint not 164, 165
faith 1, 4, 9-12, 14, 16, 17, 20, 22, 25, 26, 28, 29, 31, 36, 38,

        39, 41, 42, 46, 47, 52-59, 61-64, 66-72, 74-76, 80, 85-89, 96, 98-100, 102, 103, 109, 111, 113, 115, 116, 119-124, 126, 128-131, 133, 137, 148-150, 154, 164-169, 171, 175, 177, 180
fallen from grace 127, 129
false brethren 37, 38, 94, 125, 178
false gospel 12-14
false teachers 10, 134
family 46, 47, 68, 88, 97, 132, 166, 168, 177
Family Radio 88, 97, 177
father-in-law 165
Father 1, 2, 4, 5, 7, 8, 21, 26, 35, 39, 40, 42, 56, 58, 66, 70, 78, 80, 84, 89, 93-96, 98, 99, 106, 107, 111, 129, 134, 137, 156-158, 164, 165, 170, 176
Fax: 856-854-2464 i
feast 46, 75, 88, 101, 109, 126
feast of atonement 101, 126
feast of tabernacles 126
feast of trumpets 101, 126
feasts 126, 145
February, 2002 i
feeding 46, 47, 168
feeding, clothing, and housing 47, 168
feminists 90
figure of speech 12, 38, 115, 151
filled 27, 90, 146, 148
first pope 24, 48
five thousand six hundred and four 81
flames 121
flesh 21-23, 26, 41, 43, 53, 54, 58, 59, 61, 64-66, 69, 95, 103, 104, 106, 115, 116, 119, 120, 122, 125, 127, 128, 135-137, 139-146, 149-153, 155, 162-164, 169, 172, 173, 175, 176
Florida 22
for .... i, iii, v, 1, 2, 4-31, 34-48, 50-112, 114-141, 143, 144, 146, 148, 150, 151, 153-156, 158-173, 175-180
for us 6-8, 14, 20, 35, 36, 44, 53, 54, 56, 59-61, 63, 69, 74, 75, 84, 90, 96, 97, 110, 120, 121, 134, 138, 171, 172
foreword .... v, vi
forgiven 86, 175
fornication 34, 66, 142, 163
four thousand examples 56

Index of Words and Phrases

fourteen years 33-35, 171
free 38-41, 50, 56, 75, 87-91, 94, 101, 104, 106, 107, 116,
  117, 122-125, 136, 137, 158, 165
freedom 116, 174
friend 28, 54, 175
From the Mind of God to the Mind of Man 81, 118, 161
fruit of the Spirit 59, 108, 146-152, 164
fulfilled prophecy 118
full speed 28, 110, 179
Fuller, Dr. David Otis 16
Fundamental 16, 31, 73, 144
Fundamental Baptist Fellowship (FBF) 144
Fundamental churches 16
Fundamental schools 73
Fundamentalist 48, 73, 81, 114, 118, 133, 137, 161, 168
Fundamentalist Mis-Information on Bible Versions 118
Galatia 1, 3, 4, 17, 94, 100, 105, 131, 153, 166
Galatians Chapter Five vi
Galatians Chapter Four vi
Galatians Chapter One vi
Galatians Chapter Six vi
Galatians Chapter Three vi
Galatians Chapter Two vi
Gamaliel 17, 43, 109, 174
gambling 40, 116
GARBC (General Association of Regular Baptist Churches) 16
Garden of Gethsemane 16
Gauls 1
genitive 54
Gentile 34, 39, 50, 52, 87, 88, 91, 102, 116
Gentiles 34-36, 42, 43, 45, 50, 52, 53, 57, 66, 76, 87, 89-91,
  96, 102, 111, 166, 179
genuine 14, 16, 26, 31, 36, 68, 72, 86, 88, 89, 98, 102, 107,
  109-111, 116, 117, 119, 121-123, 126, 127, 129, 131,
  156, 168, 177, 180
genuine faith 14, 36, 68, 72, 86, 88, 89, 102, 109, 111, 116,
  119, 121-123, 126, 129, 131, 168, 177, 180
Gertrude Grace Sanborn 27
Gethsemane 16, 28
gifts 44, 59, 67, 160, 167
giving 18, 19, 24, 82, 83, 91, 92, 112, 167
glasses 105

Glenny, Dr. W. Edward 118
glory 2, 5, 8, 22, 24, 29, 42, 66, 85, 92, 95, 106, 111, 119, 126,
         132, 135, 138, 140, 146, 150, 151, 154, 171-173, 175-177
God forbid 55, 85, 143, 150, 172, 177
God of the Hindus 30
God of the Muslims 30
God the Father 1, 2, 4, 5, 8, 35, 58, 95, 98, 111, 129
God the Son 4, 5, 8, 35, 58, 92, 95, 98, 132
godly 15, 16, 36, 136, 155, 172
good news 9, 13
good works 7, 12, 26, 36, 60, 97, 110, 111, 119, 120, 138-140
goodness 59, 108, 136, 146, 148, 149, 164
gospel 2, 8-14, 17, 21-25, 29-31, 34-36, 39-42, 47, 48, 52, 53,
         67, 69-71, 76, 104, 108, 124, 125, 128, 133, 158-161, 167-169, 174
grace 1, 4, 5, 8-10, 12, 14, 17, 20, 21, 24-27, 33, 36, 42, 44,
         45, 47, 52, 56, 59, 61, 63, 68, 76, 79, 83, 89, 93, 98,
         100, 103, 106, 109, 113, 115, 120, 121, 123, 127, 129,
         131, 135, 137-139, 147, 167, 169, 171-173, 179, 180
Graham, Dr. Billy 13, 48
Grand Rapids 16
Grand Rapids, Michigan 16
grandchildren v
graphic arts 117
GRAPHO 72, 73, 117
Greek .... v, 2, 4, 6, 9, 13, 22, 29, 37, 50, 52, 54-56, 59, 62, 68,
         72-75, 78-81, 86, 90, 91, 95, 97, 106, 113, 114, 117-
         119, 125, 136, 137, 143, 144, 147, 148, 151, 153, 160, 161, 164, 165
Greek Textus Receptus 106
Greek words .... v, 9, 55, 73, 80, 81, 86, 113, 117, 119, 147, 160
groaning 129
Guide 28, 80, 86
habits 39
Hagar 114, 116, 119, 122
HAIMA 97
HAIRESIS 144
Halloween 143
happiness 147
hard drugs 40
Harold Camping 88, 91, 97, 98, 177

Index of Words and Phrases

Harold Weiss 158
He That Is Spiritual 146
heathen 1, 21, 45, 48, 69-71, 112, 178
Heaven 5, 8, 11, 41, 53-55, 59, 68, 69, 79-81, 86, 88, 91, 95, 97, 98, 109, 118-121, 127, 128, 130, 135, 149, 158, 163, 170-172, 175, 178
Hebrew words 73, 80, 118
Hell-bound 12, 59, 128
Hell 12, 14, 17, 20, 22, 29, 30, 38, 39, 42, 59, 72, 75, 85, 121, 128, 150, 158
herald 36
heresies 40, 48, 142, 163
heresy 15, 37, 38, 97, 98
heretics 132
HETEROS 9, 10
Hindus 13, 30
Holy Spirit 4, 24, 27, 43-45, 49, 58, 59, 64, 68, 76, 78, 80, 89-91, 95, 98, 107, 111, 140, 141, 146, 148, 150, 151, 156, 157, 177
Holy Spirit of God 24, 27, 43-45, 64, 68, 78, 140, 141, 146, 148, 150, 151
homeless 101, 167
homosexuality 40, 142
homosexuals 90, 91
Hort, Professor 6, 13, 40, 62, 81, 88, 160, 161
hospitals 168
household of faith 46, 47, 165-168
housing 47, 168
Houston 16
Houston, Texas 16
human blood 48
humanity 13, 132
hymn 8, 143, 173
hymns 137
hyper 54, 96, 145
hyper Calvinism 54
hypocrites 50, 51, 172
I forgive myself 158
Iconium 171
idea 12, 77, 81, 124, 133, 139, 140, 156
ideas 19, 76, 81, 113, 119
idolatry 64, 142, 143, 163

idols 34
Immanuel Baptist Church 4, 132, 133
immersion 40, 113, 170
imprisonment 172
in vain 35, 36, 61-63, 66, 102-104, 111, 121, 131, 148, 154, 165
incarnation 5, 94, 95
incipient 140
Index .... vi, 181
Index of Words and Phrases .... vi, 181
individualist 23
Indonesia 19
indwelling 43, 58, 59, 64, 88, 89, 111, 141
Internet 22, 120, 152, 159
interpretation 78, 91
intinction 157
introductory remarks 1
Ironside, Dr. H. A. v
Isaac 20, 25, 68, 70, 71, 91, 114, 115, 119, 120, 122
ISBN i
Israel of God 177
Israel's promises 177
it is written 6, 60, 72-74, 77, 97, 113, 117, 159, 170
I'm Adopted 99
Jack Moorman, Dr. 160
Jaegli, Dr. 119
James 22, 24-26, 34-36, 41, 42, 45, 48, 50, 55, 56, 62, 71-73, 78-81, 106, 112, 126, 137, 144, 151, 154, 155, 160, 162, 172
Jehovah Witnesses 132
Jehovah-Jireh 71
Jeremiah 27, 72
Jeremiah sat alone 27
Jersey, New .... i, v, 22, 27, 101, 116
Jerusalem 1, 9, 18, 20-24, 26, 33-35, 45, 46, 49, 50, 92, 116, 117, 123, 166, 167
Jerusalem Council 33-35, 45
Jesus 1-10, 12, 13, 16-26, 28-31, 34-59, 61-63, 65-73, 75, 76, 78-92, 94-99, 101, 104-107, 110, 111, 114-122, 124-136, 138, 139, 143, 145, 148-150, 153-156, 158, 161, 166, 168, 170-180
Jesus Christ 1-10, 12, 13, 16-25, 28-31, 35-38, 40-59, 61, 63,

Index of Words and Phrases

               65, 66, 68-71, 76, 78-80, 82-86, 89-91, 94-97, 99, 106, 110, 111, 114-119, 121, 122, 124-130, 132, 134, 135, 138, 143, 145, 148-150, 153, 156, 158, 161, 166, 168, 170, 172-180

Jewish religion 34
Joah 47, 48, 167
Job 27, 147
John .... i, 5, 7, 8, 12, 15, 16, 24, 29, 30, 33-35, 38, 40, 41, 45, 48, 53, 54, 56, 58, 61, 65-67, 71, 78, 80, 82-84, 96-98, 106, 107, 111, 114, 116, 117, 122, 124, 128, 129, 132-135, 138, 140, 142, 148, 155, 158, 160, 161, 164
John 6:47 160
John Bunyan's *Pilgrim's Progress* 155
John MacArthur, Dr. 12, 15, 16, 38, 48, 97, 98, 128
John Mark 33, 34
Johnson, President Lyndon B. 144
Joseph Stalin 77
jot 81, 118
joy 59, 124, 131, 146, 147, 149, 154, 157, 160, 164, 167, 180
Judah 27, 69
Judaizers 1, 9, 17, 37, 39, 50, 52, 66, 79, 109, 123, 125, 132, 169
Judgment Seat of Christ 158
judgments 87
justification 25, 26, 54, 127
Kennedy, President John F. 142
Kevin Bauder, Dr. 144
King James 22, 48, 55, 56, 62, 73, 78-81, 106, 137, 144, 151, 160
King James Bible 22, 48, 55, 56, 62, 73, 78-81, 106, 137, 144, 160
Lamb 5, 30, 35, 71, 97, 148
Lamb of God 5, 30, 35
Law of Moses 1, 9, 12, 14, 17, 34, 37, 39, 40, 43, 52, 53, 56, 57, 61-63, 65, 66, 69, 72, 76, 79, 80, 82, 83, 86, 87, 93, 95, 97, 100-102, 104, 106, 109-111, 116, 122, 123, 125-127, 129, 136-138, 141, 159, 169, 174, 176, 178, 180
lay people v
leaven 6, 60, 132, 133, 179
legalism 95, 134
lesbian 91
lesbians 90, 91

levite 138
liberal 30, 31, 107, 118
liberal church 31
liberals 1, 2, 15, 19, 21, 58, 73, 88, 157
liberationists 90
Liberia 47, 167, 180
liberty 37, 38, 94, 123, 125, 136, 137
lieutenant commander 19
lieutenant junior grade 19
lieutenant senior grade 19
lifestyle 132, 142, 176
little bird 4, 5
little foxes 133
live 1, 7, 17, 26, 31, 40, 44, 52, 54, 57-60, 74, 75, 111, 116,
                  124, 128, 136, 137, 145, 146, 150, 160, 172, 176
local church 46-48, 132, 137, 153, 166, 168, 179
loner 27, 157
loners 27
longsuffering 59, 146, 147, 149, 164, 171
Lord Jesus Christ 2, 3, 5-10, 12, 16-25, 28-31, 35-38, 40-47,
                  50-59, 61, 63, 65, 68-71, 76, 78-80, 82-84, 86, 90, 91,
                  94, 95, 97, 110, 111, 114-119, 121, 122, 124, 126-130,
                  132, 134, 135, 138, 143, 145, 148-150, 153, 156, 158,
                  161, 166, 168, 170, 172-180
lordship salvation 12
love 6-8, 26, 45, 54, 58-62, 107, 108, 111, 112, 130, 135-138,
                  146, 154, 164, 167, 170
love of Christ 54, 135
Luther, Martin 143
Lyndon B. Johnson, President 144
Lystra 171, 172, 178
MacArthur, Dr. John 12, 15, 16, 38, 48, 97, 98, 128
magazines 21
magnet 175
major Fundamental Schools 73
map 3
Marie 165
Marine Corps 76
Mark 33, 34, 47, 85, 99, 114, 127, 162, 168, 170, 179
marks 144, 177-179
marriage 26, 34, 76, 91, 142
Martin Luther 143

Index of Words and Phrases

Mary 83
Maryland 22
Masoretic Hebrew Text 73, 81, 160
mass 63, 88
Massachusetts 132
master 16, 39, 41, 88, 106, 179
Matthew 24, 67, 80, 81, 89, 91, 103, 106, 114, 118, 119, 133, 135, 154, 155, 158, 162, 170, 176
meats offered to idols 34
mediator 82-84
mediatrix 83
Mediterranean Sea 34
Meeting 110, 133, 139, 144, 152
message .... v, 11, 17, 36, 41, 42, 73, 81, 109, 112-114, 119, 152, 158, 159
Messiah 21, 116
Messianic Jews 87, 88, 102
Methodist 158, 166, 168
metonym 12, 38, 48, 97
Michigan 16, 88
Michigan Union 88
millennial reign 69, 92, 117
mimeograph 117
Mind of Man 81, 118, 161
ministries 35, 89, 90
ministries of the Holy Spirit 89
Minneapolis, Minnesota 144
miracles 13, 38, 67
missionaries 2, 20, 33, 34, 47, 49, 102, 152, 159, 160, 168
missionary journey 33, 34, 45
missionary journeys 9, 16, 45, 160
Missouri 85
modern versions 6, 55, 161
modernist 13, 30, 88, 118, 157
modernists 1, 2, 15, 19, 40, 49, 58, 73, 88, 107, 157
Mollenkott, Dr. Virginia Ramey 90, 91
money changers 148
Moorman, Dr. Jack 160
Moriah, Mount 25, 70
Mosaic law 37, 57, 88
Moses 1, 9, 12, 14, 17, 19, 34, 37, 39, 40, 43, 52, 53, 56, 57, 61-63, 65, 66, 69, 72, 73, 75, 76, 79, 80, 82, 83, 86, 87,

93, 95, 97, 100-102, 104, 106, 109-111, 113, 116, 117, 122, 123, 125-127, 129, 136-138, 141, 159, 169, 174, 176, 178, 180
Mount Moriah 25, 70
Mount Sinai 115, 116
Mount Zion 24
Mr. R. O. Sanborn 165
Mrs. Waite, Yvonne Sanborn 47, 48
music 9, 145
musician 9
Muslims 30, 119
name names 48
narcotics 14, 117
NASV (New American Standard Version) 81
Naval Chaplain 76, 157
Naval Chaplain Corps 76
Navy 19, 76, 113, 132, 133, 157
Navy Chaplain 113
Nazarite 46
negative prohibitions 151
neighbor 137, 138
neighbour 137
neo evangelicals 15
neo-evangelical 31, 133
neo-evangelicals 73
Nestle-Aland 160
New American Standard Version (NASV) 6, 56, 78, 81, 144, 151, 160
New International Version (NIV) 6, 56, 78, 144, 151, 160
New Jersey .... i, v, 22, 27, 101
New King James Version (NKJV) 56, 78, 144, 151
New York City 11, 121
Newman, Dr. 118
Newton, Massachusetts 132
NIV (New International Version) 14, 56
no respect of persons 41, 42
October 29, 1961 (day of the Newton, Massachusetts riot) 4
of Christ 2, 8-13, 15-17, 29, 38, 40, 42, 48, 50, 53, 54, 57, 63, 64, 66, 69, 92, 96-98, 103, 113, 117, 118, 124, 128, 131, 133, 135, 137, 138, 150, 155, 158, 159, 169-171, 173, 174, 176, 178-180
Okinawa 113
omnipresent 59

Index of Words and Phrases

on me	11, 160
One Bible Only?	118, 144
one silver bar	19
only one speed	28, 110
ordained	22, 26, 36, 82, 120, 139, 160
order blank	vi
order blank pages	vi
orders: 1-800-JOHN 10:9	i
ordinances	12, 52, 87, 89, 125
other	v, 1, 3, 4, 6, 9-12, 14, 15, 17, 22-24, 27, 28, 32-34, 36, 38, 41, 47, 49, 51, 52, 55, 57, 59, 60, 62, 63, 73, 82, 87-89, 92, 93, 95, 99, 100, 113, 116, 117, 125, 132, 138-142, 144-146, 154-157, 160, 161, 163-166, 170
overtaken	153
ox	159, 160
painful flames	121
parachutist	156
Passover	6, 34, 60, 101, 126
Pastor D. A. Waite, Th.D., Ph.D.	i, v
Pastor Joah, St. Solomon	47, 48, 167
Pastor Richard N. Waite	iii
pastors	20-22, 45, 49, 104, 175, 178, 179
Paul	v, 1-4, 8-11, 13-31, 33-45, 48-53, 55-59, 62-64, 66, 67, 73, 75, 76, 78, 84, 90, 93, 94, 101-106, 109-113, 116, 119-123, 125, 126, 130-138, 142, 145, 150, 151, 156, 159-162, 164, 168-180
Paul gloried in the cross	174
Paul's conversion	2
Paul's gospel	30, 35, 36, 41
peace	4, 5, 8, 10, 59, 83, 117, 128, 141, 146, 147, 149, 164, 174, 177, 179
Pennsylvania	22
Pentecostal	44
perfect God	5, 9, 35
perfect Man	5, 9, 35
perfect tense	72, 73, 75, 79, 113, 117, 118
persecute	2, 120, 135, 170
persecuted	2, 18, 28, 66, 120, 121, 134, 135, 170, 171
persecuting	2, 110
persecution	18, 134-136, 169-172, 175
pervert	9, 10
Peter	7, 17, 20, 23, 24, 34, 35, 41-45, 48-53, 57, 60-62, 69, 89,

	97, 125, 131, 137, 155
Pharaohs	164
Philadelphia	22, 70, 101, 118
Philistines	46
phone: 856-854-4452	i
phonograph	117
pianist	28
piano player	28
pie crusts (treaties like)	77
Pilgrim's Progress	155
Pilgrim	155
pillars	45, 46
playboy	142
please	14-16, 51, 100, 104, 108, 116, 133, 137
please men	14, 15
pleasing God	15
poetry	21, 159
poison	132, 133
politician	16
pool	121
poor saints	46, 166, 180
Pope	24, 48, 83, 142
Pope of Rome	48, 142
pork	57, 87
pornographer	39
pornography	39, 40, 116, 117
preach the gospel	22, 36, 104, 159, 160, 168
preached sermons	v
preachers	2, 14, 20, 21, 102, 107, 160
preaching	i, v, 4, 13, 19, 22, 27, 28, 30, 35, 47, 123, 131-133, 159, 160, 167-169, 178, 179
present tense prohibition	125, 161, 164
preservation	73, 75, 80, 81, 117, 118
preservation of the Words	75, 118
preserved	73, 75, 80-82, 113, 114, 117-119
preserved Words	80
President	15, 142, 144, 177
President Kennedy	142
President Lyndon Johnson	144
President of the United States	142
priest	18, 138
principles	27, 55, 134, 167

Index of Words and Phrases

printing	159
printing of books	159
prison	16, 18, 28
Professor Hort	40
prohibition	125, 151, 161, 164, 177
promise	21, 68, 73, 76, 79-82, 84, 85, 91, 92, 100, 114-116, 119, 120, 122, 125, 136, 165
promises	69, 70, 73, 77, 78, 80-83, 85, 88, 91, 97, 114, 115, 118, 165, 177
promotion	19
prophet	11, 27, 137
prostitution	40, 59
publisher's data	vi
pyramids	163
R. O. Sanborn	165
rabbi	83
radio	v, 16, 22, 47, 49, 56, 62, 88, 91, 97, 98, 118, 120, 123, 137, 152, 159, 168, 177
Radio Bible Class	137
radio broadcasts	22, 62
Radio Shack	56
read the Bible	59
reap	66, 161-165
rebellion	29
rebuke	48, 49, 51
red meat	57
redeemed	6, 16, 44, 59, 60, 74, 75, 88, 91, 97-99, 102, 174, 177
Redeemer	5, 16, 96, 97, 150, 155
regenerated	5, 26, 59, 68, 91, 175
repentance	36
resurrection	29, 35, 38, 58, 79, 91, 123
Revelation	17, 23, 35, 67, 117, 175
Revelator	80
re-define	113
Richard N. Waite	iii
righteous indignation	143
riot	4, 131
risen	95, 149
Robert B. Thieme	15
Robert Schuller	13, 48, 156
Roman Catholic	22, 24, 63, 83, 88, 118, 179

Roman Catholic mass 63
Roman imprisonment 172
Roman prison 16
Romans 6, 13, 17, 25, 26, 29, 30, 36, 41, 46, 60, 64-66, 74,
                    85, 86, 92, 94, 98-101, 107, 110, 126-130, 133-136,
                    139, 149, 150, 166, 170, 173, 176, 177
Romans 1:16 13
Russia 77
Sabbath 6, 75, 87, 126
sacrifices 34, 52, 125, 126, 143
saints 22, 29, 46, 83, 132, 166-168, 180
salvation 4, 5, 8, 9, 11-13, 15, 22, 29, 30, 36, 38, 54, 63, 64,
                    66, 71, 88, 98, 103, 113-116, 120, 121, 126, 127, 129,
                    131, 137, 144, 147, 148, 166, 168-170, 177
Salvation Army 166, 168
salvation by works 13
Samaritan 138
Samson 45, 46
Sanborn (various) .... iii, 27, 165
sanctified 1, 9, 24, 76, 80, 100, 107, 109, 123, 128, 145, 180
Sarah 25, 68, 114-116, 122
SARX 115, 140
sat alone 27
Satan 41, 43, 53, 75, 95, 150, 154, 169
Satan's bondage 40, 125
Saul 18, 26, 51, 174
Saul or Paul 174
saved .... v, 1, 5, 7-15, 17, 18, 20-26, 28-31, 34-36, 38, 40-43, 48,
                50-54, 56-59, 63, 64, 66, 68, 69, 71, 72, 74-76, 79, 84,
                87, 88, 90, 91, 94-96, 100, 102, 103, 108-113, 119, 120,
                122, 123, 128-130, 135, 137, 139-141, 145, 149, 150,
                158, 167, 168, 170, 176, 180
Saviour 5, 9, 14, 20, 28, 30, 31, 39, 41, 51, 53, 64, 69, 85, 89,
                    94, 96-98, 100, 102, 110, 125, 143, 150, 155, 158, 174,
                    175, 177
Schnaiter, Dr. Samuel (Professor at Bob Jones University) 118, 119
schoolmaster 86-88, 94, 128
Schuller, Dr. Robert 13, 48, 156
seated 58, 149, 179
second missionary journey 33, 45
Seed .... v, 68, 70, 71, 76, 78, 82, 85, 91-93, 100, 115, 119, 122,
                                                                    161, 163

Index of Words and Phrases

self-contained 157
seminary 15-17, 22, 23, 65, 73, 80, 118, 124, 131, 137, 140, 144
senior chaplain 157
senior chaplains 19
separated 20, 50
separation 50
separatist 48, 133
September 11, 2001 (terrorist attacks) 11, 121
series of books v
sermons . . . . iii, v, 22
seven ministries 89
seven ministries of the Holy Spirit 89
seventeen 84, 142, 150, 153
seventeen sins 150, 153
seventeen specific sins 142
Seventh Day Adventists 87
Seventh Day Baptists 87
sex 90, 125, 142
sex education 142
shed blood 12, 44, 174
shipwrecked 16
short wave 22, 152
shroud 163
sign gifts 44, 67
Silas 33, 34
sin of the world 5, 30, 35, 71
sin question 5
Sinai 83, 115, 116
Sinai desert 115
sinless perfection 54
sinners 6, 9, 14, 20, 22, 29, 31, 39, 42, 53, 55, 59, 60, 109, 127, 176, 180
six thousand six hundred and fifty-three examples 56
sixteen-point type 105
slave 16, 39, 44, 45, 75, 96, 100, 101, 114, 137
slavery 16, 39, 95, 100, 117, 122, 125
social gospel 2, 168
Son question 5
Song of Solomon 133
South Carolina 22
South Jersey 116

Southern Methodist University 158
sowing 161, 162, 164
sowing and reaping 161, 162, 164
sowing to the flesh 164
speaking in tongues 90
speech teacher 158
Spirit of God 24, 27, 43-46, 59, 64-68, 78, 88, 116, 130, 139-141, 143, 145-153, 170, 180
St. Solomon Joah, Pastor (in Liberia, West Africa) 47
stand fast 94, 123-125, 136
Stephen 18, 174
Stewart Custer, Dr. 119
stoned 18, 171, 172, 174, 178
stoned to death 174, 178
stop it... 133, 151
strangled 34
strife 139, 142-144, 163
Substitute.. 6, 35, 60, 158
Sunday .... v, 43, 87, 143, 144, 159
swim 121, 168
swimming 54, 168
swimming pools 168
Syria 23, 26, 49
table of contents vi
taken away 6, 129
tape recordings v
Tarsus 26, 109
team-player 157
teeter-totter 141
temperance 59, 149, 164
temple 43, 44, 58, 64, 111, 140, 148, 150, 160
temptation 104, 134, 154, 155
tempted 103, 153-156
Tenth Presbyterian Church (of Philadelphia) 137
tentmaker 159
Textus Receptus Greek Text 73, 81, 106, 160
THANATOS 97
The faith 25, 26, 28, 29, 38, 42, 47, 53, 54, 58, 59, 66, 70, 86, 123, 124, 128, 150, 166, 177
Theological Heresies of Westcott and Hort 40
theology 58, 124
Thieme, Pastor Robert B. 15, 16

Index of Words and Phrases

thought	15, 19, 21, 33, 53, 55, 76, 81, 85, 108, 109, 112, 116, 124, 133, 163, 174
thoughts	v, 57, 73, 81, 113, 114, 119
three divisions	87
three hundred and fifty-six	81, 161
three-year seminary	17, 23
Thurman Wisdom, Dr.	119
tittle	81, 118
Titus	7, 33-35, 37, 60, 97, 110, 144
tobacco	40
tongues	44, 67, 90
transfiguration	24
transpose	9
Trinity	2, 4, 59, 95
trouble	9, 10, 47, 56, 75, 96, 101, 120, 124, 134, 136, 138, 139, 153, 172, 177
TRS 80 (Radio Shack computer)	56
true humanity	13
Turkey	1, 3, 18, 63, 94, 125, 138
two errors	1, 9, 24, 76
two silver bars	19
two thousand eight hundred and eighty-six	81
two thousand examples	56
U. S. Naval Reserve Commission	19
unbeliever	13, 157, 158
United Bible Society	160
United Methodist Church	166
universal brotherhood	88
universal Fatherhood	88
universalism	13, 38, 98
unsaved	2, 26, 32, 37, 74, 94, 139, 141, 145, 158
U-haul trailer	163
vain	35-37, 61-63, 66, 97, 102-104, 111, 121, 131, 148, 151, 154, 165
versions	6, 22, 29, 55, 62, 78, 118, 140, 142, 151, 160, 161
video	v, 110, 119
virgin	13, 95, 96
Virginia Mollenkott, Dr.	90, 91
virgin-born	13
Waite (various)	i, iii, v, 47, 48, 157
walk	7, 26, 27, 36, 49, 52, 53, 60, 65-67, 71, 84, 120, 129, 131, 139, 140, 146, 150-153, 156, 176, 177, 180

walk in the Spirit 66, 129, 139, 140, 146, 150, 152
walking 26, 27, 42, 52, 59, 82, 107, 140, 151, 153, 155
Wallace, Dr. Dan 80, 118
Walvoord, Dr. John F. 15, 16, 124
want to 2, 10, 14, 15, 17, 18, 21, 26, 27, 33, 35-37, 39, 40, 44,
    48, 54, 56, 57, 62, 75, 78, 79, 83, 87, 101, 102, 104,
    109, 113-115, 126, 129, 131-133, 136-138, 141, 143,
    150, 157, 166, 172, 175, 176
Washington 16
water baptism 40, 89, 113, 170
Wealthy Street Baptist Church 16
website: www.BibleForToday.org i
weeping prophet 27
Weiss, Dr. Harold 158
West Africa 47, 48, 167, 180
Westcott, Bishop 6, 13, 40, 62, 81, 88, 160, 161
Westcott and Hort 6, 13, 40, 62, 81, 88, 160, 161
Which Bible? 16
whip 148
Wisdom, Dr. Thurman 98, 119
witchcraft 142, 143, 163
Women, Men, and the Bible 91
women's liberationists 90
Word 1, 2, 4, 6-12, 15-19, 27, 29-31, 33, 35-40, 48, 50-55, 60,
    61, 67-69, 71, 72, 74, 77-80, 82, 83, 85, 86, 91, 95, 97,
    99, 100, 102-107, 109, 110, 113-115, 117, 119, 124,
    125, 129-138, 141-145, 148, 151, 153, 154, 156, 159,
    160, 163, 165, 168, 169, 172, 175, 179, 180
Word of God 8, 11, 15, 19, 27, 40, 48, 107, 110, 124, 130,
    137, 141, 143, 144, 159, 168, 169
Words .... v, vi, 1, 2, 6, 9, 14, 17, 20, 22, 23, 27, 28, 31, 36, 37,
    42, 55, 58, 59, 63, 65, 70, 72, 73, 75, 78, 80-82, 86, 97,
    107, 108, 111-114, 117-119, 147, 156, 160, 161, 165,
    181
Words of God .... v, 20, 22, 23, 27, 36, 73, 75, 78, 107, 160, 161
works 4, 7, 10, 12-14, 20, 25, 26, 36, 44, 48, 52-54, 57, 59, 60,
    64-68, 71, 72, 74, 86, 95, 97, 100, 109-113, 115, 116,
    119, 120, 122, 125, 126, 128-130, 136, 138-140, 142,
    144, 145, 150, 151, 156, 160, 163, 176, 179, 180
works of the flesh 59, 65, 66, 115, 119, 142, 144, 145, 150,
    151, 163
World Trade Towers (New York City) 121

Index of Words and Phrases

worldlings	176
writer	2, 25
www.BibleForToday.org (Website)	i, 22
YMCA	168
Young Men's Christian Association	168
Yvonne Sanborn Waite	iii
zeal	19, 110, 143
zealous	7, 18-20, 60, 97, 109-111, 123
Zion	24

About the Author

The author of this book, Dr. D. A. Waite, received a B.A. (Bachelor of Arts) in classical Greek and Latin from the University of Michigan in 1948, a Th.M. (Master of Theology), with high honors, in New Testament Greek Literature and Exegesis from Dallas Theological Seminary in 1952, an M.A. (Master of Arts) in Speech from Southern Methodist University in 1953, a Th.D. (Doctor of Theology), with honors, in Bible Exposition from Dallas Theological Seminary in 1955, and a Ph.D. in Speech from Purdue University in 1961. He holds both New Jersey and Pennsylvania teacher certificates in Greek and Language Arts.

He has been a teacher in the areas of Greek, Hebrew, Bible, Speech, and English for over thirty-five years in ten schools, including one junior high, one senior high, three Bible institutes, two colleges, two universities, and one seminary. He served his country as a Navy Chaplain for five years on active duty; pastored two churches; was Chairman and Director of the Radio and Audio-Film Commission of the American Council of Christian Churches; since 1971, has been Founder, President, and Director of THE BIBLE FOR TODAY; since 1978, has been President of the DEAN BURGON SOCIETY; has produced over 700 other studies, books, cassettes, or VCR's on various topics; and is heard on both a five-minute daily and thirty-minute weekly radio program IN DEFENSE OF TRADITIONAL BIBLE TEXTS, presently on about 25 stations. Dr. and Mrs. Waite have been married since 1948; they have four sons, one daughter, and, at present, eight grandchildren. Since October 4, 1998, he founded and has been the Pastor of the Bible For Today Baptist Church in Collingswood, New Jersey. His sermons are heard both on radio and the Internet over "www.BibleForToday.org/audio_sermons.htm"

Order Blank (p. 1)

Name:_____

Address:_____

City & State:_____Zip:_____

Credit Card #:_____Expires:_____

[ ] Send *Galatians--Verse By Verse* by Pastor D. A. Waite ($13+$4 S&H) hardback, 216 pages.
[ ] Send *First Peter--Verse By Verse* by Pastor D. A. Waite ($11+$4 S&H) hardback, 176 pages.
[ ] Send *Fundamentalist MIS-INFORMATION on Bible Versions* by Dr. Waite ($7+$3 S&H) perfect bound, 136 pages
[ ] Send *Central Seminary Refuted on Bible Versions* by Dr. Waite ($10+$3 S&H) A perfect bound book, 184 pages
[ ] Send *Fundamentalist Distortions on Bible Versions* by Dr. Waite ($6+$3 S&H) A perfect bound book, 80 pages
[ ] Send *Burgon's Warnings on Revision* by DAW ($7+$3 S&H) A perfect bound book, 120 pages in length.
[ ] Send *The Case for the King James Bible* by DAW ($7 +$3 S&H) A perfect bound book, 112 pages in length.
[ ] Send *Foes of the King James Bible Refuted* by DAW ($10 +$4 S&H) A perfect bound book, 164 pages in length.
[ ] Send *The Revision Revised* by Dean Burgon ($25 + $4 S&H) A hardback book, 640 pages in length.
[ ] Send *The Last 12 Verses of Mark* by Dean Burgon ($15+$4 S&H) A perfect bound paperback book 400 pages.
[ ] Send *The Traditional Text* hardback by Burgon ($16 + $4 S&H) A hardback book, 384 pages in length.
[ ] Send *Summary of Traditional Text* by Dr. Waite ($3 +$2)
[ ] Send *Summary of Causes of Corruption*, DAW ($3+$2)
[ ] Send *Causes of Corruption* hardback by Burgon ($15 + $4 S&H) A hardback book, 360 pages in length.

Send or Call Orders to:
THE BIBLE FOR TODAY
900 Park Ave., Collingswood, NJ 08108
Phone: 856-854-4452; FAX:--2464; Orders: 1-800 JOHN 10:9
E-Mail Orders: BFT@BibleForToday.org; Credit Cards O K

Order Blank (p. 2)

Name:_____

Address:_____

City & State:_____Zip:_____

Credit Card#:_____Expires:_____

Other Materials on the KJB & T.R.

[ ] Send *Inspiration and Interpretation*, Dean Burgon ($25+$4 S&H) A hardback book, 610 pages in length.
[ ] Send *Summary of Inspiration* by Dr. Waite ($3 + $2 S&H)
[ ]Send *Contemporary Eng. Version Exposed*, DAW ($3+$2)
[ ] Send *Holes in the Holman Christian Standard Bible* by Dr. Waite ($3+$2 S&H) A printed booklet, 40 pages
[ ] Send *Westcott & Hort's Greek Text & Theory Refuted by Burgon's Revision Revised--Summarized* by Dr. D. A. Waite ($7.00 + $3 S&H), 120 pages, perfect bound.

[ ] Send *Defending the King James Bible* by Dr. Waite $13+$4 S&H) A hardback book, indexed with study questions.

[ ] Send *Guide to Textual Criticism* by Edward Miller ($7+$4)
[ ] Send *Westcott's Denial of Resurrection*, Dr. Waite ($4+$3)
[ ] Send *Four Reasons for Defending KJB* by DAW ($3+$3)
[ ] Send *Vindicating Mark 16:9-20* by Dr. Waite ($3+$3 S&H)
[ ] Send *Dean Burgon's Confidence in KJB* by DAW ($3+$3)

[ ] Send *Readability of A.V. (KJB)* by D. A. Waite, Jr. ($6 +$3)
[ ] Send *NIV Inclusive Language Exposed* by DAW ($4+$3)

[ ] Send *26 Hours of KJB Seminar* (4 videos) by DAW ($50.00)
[ ] Send *Defined King James Bible* lg.prt. leather ($40+$6)
[ ] Send the "DBS Articles of Faith & Organization" (N.C.)
[ ] Send Brochure #1: "1000 Titles Defending KJB/TR"(N.C.)

Send or Call Orders to:
THE BIBLE FOR TODAY
900 Park Ave., Collingswood, NJ 08108
Phone: 856-854-4452; FAX:--2464; Orders: 1-800 JOHN 10:9
E-Mail Orders: BFT@BibleForToday.org; Credit Cards OK

Order Blank (p. 3)

Name:_____

Address:_____

City & State:_____ Zip:_____

Credit Card#:_____ Expires:_____

More Materials on the KJB &T.R.

[ ] Send *Heresies of Westcott & Hort* by Dr. Waite ($6+$3)

[ ] Send *Scrtvener's Greek New Testament Underlying the King James Bible*, hardback, $14+$4 S&H

[ ] Send Scrivener's **Annotated** Greek New Testament by Dr. Frederick Scrivener,$35+$5 S&H HB;$45+$5 S&H Leath.

[ ] Send *Why Not the King James Bible?--An Answer to James White's KJVO Book* by Dr. K. D. DiVietro, $10+$4 S&H

[ ] Send *Forever Settled--Bible Do*cuments & History Survey by Dr. Jack Moorman, $20+$4 S&H. Hardback book.

[ ] Send *Early Church Fathers & the A.V.--A Demonstration* by Dr. Jack Moorman, $6 + $4 S&H.

[ ] Send *When the KJB Departs from the So-Called "Majority Text"* by Dr. Jack Moorman, $16 + $4 S&H

[ ] Send *Missing in Modern Bibles--Nestle-Aland & NIV Errors* by Dr. Jack Moorman, $8 + $4 S&H

[ ] Send *The Doctrinal Heart of the Bible--Removed from Modern Versions* by Dr. Jack Moorman, VCR, $15 +$4 S&H

[ ] Send *Modern Bibles--The Dark* Secret by Dr. Jack Moorman, $4 + $2 S&H

[ ] Send *Early Manuscripts and the A.V.--A Closer Look*, by Dr. Jack Moorman, $15 + $4 S&H

Send or Call Orders to:
THE BIBLE FOR TODAY
900 Park Ave., Collingswood, NJ 08108
Phone: 856-854-4452; FAX:--2464; Orders: 1-800 JOHN 10:9
E-Mail Orders: BFT@BibleForToday.org; Credit Cards OK

The Defined
King James Bible

UNCOMMON WORDS DEFINED ACCURATELY

I. Deluxe Genuine Leather

✦Large Print--Black or Burgundy✦

1 for $40.00+$6 S&H

✦Case of 12 for✦

$30.00 each+$30 S&H

✦Medium Print--Black or Burgundy✦

1 for $35.00+$4 S&H

✦Case of 12 for✦

$25.00 each+$24 S&H

II. Deluxe Hardback Editions

1 for $20.00+$6 S&H (Large)

✦Case of 12 for✦

$15.00 each+$30 S&H (Large)

1 for $15.00+$4 S&H (Medium)

✦Case of 12 for✦

$10.00 each+$24 S&H (Medium)

Order Phone: 1-800-JOHN 10:9

www.ingramcontent.com/pod-product-compliance
Lightning Source LLC
Chambersburg PA
CBHW062208080426
42734CB00010B/1840